THE ACCOUNTANTS MILLIONAIRES' CLUB

THE ACCOUNTANTS MILLIONAIRES' CLUB

HOW TO BUILD A £1 MILLION PRACTICE WHILE WORKING FEWER HOURS WITH LESS STRESS

HEATHER TOWNSEND

with SIAN KELLY, PAUL MILLER,
SHARON POCOCK & GUY ROBINSON

Excedia Group Ltd
International House,
24 Holburn Viaduct,
City of London,
EC1A 2BN,
United Kingdom
Tel: + 44(0)1234 48 0123
www.accountantsmillionaire.club

First published 2018 (print and electronic)

ISBN: 978-0-9932506-7-5 (Print)
978-0-9932506-9-9 (PDF)
978-0-9932506-8-2 (ePub)

Praise for the book

“Let me put it simply. This is not just a truly brilliant book, it's a must-have. It's direct, it's deep and it's full of superb case stories that make it truly human too. Do this: flip to the questionnaire at the front of the book. Answer it honestly. And then read every word that follows. Act on every insight. Your firm will never be the same again."

PAUL DUNN, CO-AUTHOR OF FIRM OF THE FUTURE

“Packed with learnings from a group of the UK's leading Xero practitioners who are harnessing technology to deliver transformational client service. A comprehensive, straight-talking guide built on real world learnings from the industry's most innovative firms."

GARY TURNER, CO-FOUNDER, XERO

“If you are an accountant with big dreams and aspirations, you'll probably want to read this book. If you are hitting a ceiling and you just can't figure out where to start. Pick up this book, read it and go make your personal ambitions a million pound reality."

TRENT MCLAREN, GLOBAL HEAD OF ACCOUNTING AND SALES AT PRACTICE IGNITION

“The Accountants Millionaires' Club is one of the most comprehensive, practical, step-by-step guides to growing an accountancy practice that I have seen. It is truly designed to get smaller practitioners working **on** their practice versus in it, and gives them all the information they need to build their own *£1 million pound* practice. Accountants really struggle with where to start and the steps to building a successful plan for growth and this book overcomes those challenges. Overall, great book."

JENNIFER WARAWA, SAGE EXECUTIVE VICE PRESIDENT - PARTNERS, ACCOUNTANTS & ALLIANCES

"Never before have I read such a comprehensive guide to growing a sustainable Accounting firm. The book is literally jam-packed with practical and proven strategies that work – all backed up with clear examples. There's no hype and hope here – so refreshing."

MARK JENKINS, DIRECTOR, THE GAP 2014 LTD

"Building a million-pound practice was never going to be easy but this book makes it seem achievable. Covering the wide range of skills needed to successfully scale a business/practice, with stories that demonstrate a deep understanding of the challenges accountants face, it focuses on the detailed practical steps needed to turn ambition into action."

ALEX REDMOND, FOUNDER OF ARTISAN ACCOUNTS

"This is a great book! I wish this was published 5 years ago. This could have saved me a lot of reading and work developing a successful firm. It is a manual for ambitious firms and shows how to grow and to survive the digital revolution that the industry is facing at the moment. Highly recommend this book."

DRS. M. SPOELSTRA RA, ACCOUNTANTSKANTOOR SPOELSTRA & SCHERER, WINNER OF THE DUTCH NATIONAL ACCOUNTANCY AWARDS

"Heather's book is a practical and incisive guide for accountants who want to grow a successful, profitable and sustainable practice. Packed full of great case studies from real firms, with detailed examples and checklists too, this will become a much used and much loved industry resource."

RICHARD FRANCIS, FOUNDER OF SPOTLIGHT REPORTING

"Congratulations Heather on another amazing book. Not only does it help accountants get a clear sense of purpose but the Growth Assessment Tool and workbook means you can focus on the must dos, manage progress and make change happen!"

ALEX DAVIS, INTUIT QUICKBOOKS UK

"Great read. Heathers advice is clear and simple with inspirational stories throughout where her clients HAVE taken steps to change their business around, and put in place foundations and processes to build the firm that works for them as opposed to the other way round. A must-have book for all Accountants and Bookkeepers as they grow their business in this ever-changing landscape."

DEBBIE SPOONER, ADVISOR TO CLOUD PRACTICES

"An essential reference for both existing accountancy business owners and those just starting the journey – keep it to hand!"

RICHARD FEAKINS, CO-FOUNDER OF MOORE FEAKINS

"There is something here for every accountancy practice. The book is full of nuggets of wisdom and practical, commercial advice to grow your business."

CAROLINE PLUMB OBE, FOUNDER OF FLUIDLY

"What a great book! Essential code on how to practically leverage the potential of a technology led accountancy practice"

RICHARD SERGEANT, PRINCIPLE POINT

Acknowledgements

Robert Watson has edited all my books. I think he deserves a medal – particularly for untangling this manuscript and helping make it the great book it has become. Thank you Robert!

Thank you to Lisa for proof-reading the book and being a brilliant person to work with.

A big thanks to Caroline Plumb OBE at Fluidly and Mark Jenkins at The Gap 2014 Ltd who have helped the fund the production of the book. Both Fluidly and The Gap are great tools for any accountancy practice wanting to systemise how they deliver services to their clients.

I've been meaning to write this book for nearly 2 years now. If it wasn't for Julie Creffield inspiring me to set a Big, Fat Stupid goal, I'm not sure that this book would have seen the light of day. 46 days to write AND edit a book with a full client load is not something I want to experience again. (Well, not for a little while anyway)

And a final thanks to my 4 muses, Sian, Paul, Sharon and Guy; who have all inspired me to write this book. Your growth stories are what brings this book alive and gives it a beating heart. The day the 4 of us started to work together was a truly lucky day for me.

Contents

Introduction

Aiming to build a one million pound practice might be for financial freedom, status, kudos, creating a retirement nest egg or to win a bet. This book will show you how to reach that level.

Case study: Giselle

Giselle started her practice with the intention of building a business which could work around her family responsibilities. As Giselle embraced modern technology, fixed fee billing, cloud accounting and a client-centric way of working, her firm grew rapidly and in 24 months the firm had 100 clients with a £150k of gross recurring fees (GRF). But then her growth began to slow down. She struggled to hire in the right members of staff and she couldn't get out of firefighting mode. There were just too many clients screaming out for her time and attention.

It was at this point that Giselle thought enough is enough. She couldn't go on working this way. The first thing she set about changing was moving out of firefighting mode. This was crucifying her ability to run her practice and still be present for her family. So, she put up her firm's fees by 30% and sold £20,000 of fees which represented her 40 smallest clients. These 40 clients took up over 60% of her time. After she had done this exercise, her GRF was £160k, but for only 60 clients. This gave Giselle the breathing space to take a day out of the business every week to really think what she wanted to do with her practice.

On one of her morning walks, Giselle decided that she would grow a one million pound practice, with the aim of achieving this within the next 5–8 years. Not only that, but she would only spend one day a week running the practice. To maximise the capital value of her practice, it needed to be able to run without her being present. Her practice would bring her financial freedom and become her future pension fund.

Giselle first did a SWOT on her firm. She identified that she was still struggling with getting her staff to perform to the level required, her staffing costs were too high, and the clients she was winning were often the low fee, low recovery, highly needy clients. After she had done a SWOT on her firm she set aside time with her team to create the Growth Vision for her firm. She and her team turned her Growth Vision into a 3-year Growth Plan to lift the firm from £160k to £500k.

Over the next 90 days, the whole firm focused on their first One Big Focus. (See Chapter 3) This was to increase the practice's capacity by a third through improving the efficiency of how they worked. Every member of her three-person team had Growth Tasks to help the firm get more efficient. They did this by putting in place a practice management system so that they could properly plan their workflow and capacity requirements. Then at each weekly 'Rhythm' team meeting (see Chapter 3), they process mapped one of their workflows to identify ways to automate it and make it more efficient.

Giselle never had a shortage of Leads; her Clients were brilliant at recommending her firm. However, Giselle recognised that if she was going to create a one million pound practice within 5–8 years she needed to be able to attract and win the right sort of client. So, she approached a marketing agency to help her do this. The first thing the agency suggested she did was a Client Portfolio Analysis to find out the right type of client for her firm to target.

From the Client Portfolio Analysis she identified that her most profitable and enjoyable clients were creatives. She worked with the agency to break her niche down into the type of creatives she wanted to attract: web designers, marketing agencies, interior designers but not freelancers or one-man bands. The agency designed a funky new logo for her firm, new business cards and a bright, cheerful and engaging website.

Giselle interviewed five of her creative clients and identified what they wanted from their accountant. Based on this research, she put together two compliance packages for creatives: *Time Saver* and *Cash Flow Maximiser*. Alongside those two packages, Giselle had a number of advisory services that her clients could take. Examples included business planning, cash flow forecasting, business coaching and profit improvement sessions. In Giselle's 3-year Growth Plan she wanted to win one new client every week, with an average client fee of £3,000. If Giselle was to work fewer hours the firm's marketing needed to be able to run without her. This is why she then invested £2,000 a month in outsourcing the firm's blog and social media marketing presence on LinkedIn, Instagram and Facebook. She and her team ran bi-monthly client seminars on how to use cloud technology to run their creative businesses more effectively. With the capacity the team had freed up by increasing their efficiency by a third, Giselle was able to train her team to deliver the firm's advisory services to their client base.

It took about three months for the new marketing plan to kick in, but Giselle soon found that she was generating about eight good qualified Leads a month, and she would normally convert six of these into Clients. This meant her practice doubled in size in a year. To cope with the growth, Giselle modelled the capacity requirements of her firm going forward. This helped her identify when was the right time to recruit in a new member of the team.

In the end, Giselle took four years to grow a 15-employee, one million pound practice, with a 45% net profit margin. And yes, she is only working one day a week in her practice. She credits the rapid growth to her and her team's unrelenting focus on their 3-year Growth Plan.

Why is it so hard to grow a one million pound practice?

Growing your accounting practice normally means long hours, high levels of stress and balancing your personal income requirements with keeping enough cash in the business to invest in growth. In effect, you often create a job for yourself with no guarantee of a pay cheque at the end of the month. The irony is you probably started your own practice because you didn't want to be tied to a corporate job, and wanted the freedom of being your own boss. This book will show you how to get your practice to run smoothly and profitably without you having to be there most of the time.

Once you have mastered the art of winning clients the early days of growing an accounting practice are relatively easy. However, the troubles start when a firm needs to employ staff. The hardest stage of growing an accountancy firm is from £150k to £500k turnover. This is because the firm's owner enters the Work In/Work On Trap (see Chapter 4 for more detail). The owner keeps getting dragged back into the business, so the practice's growth stalls. Chapters 6–8 will show you how your role will change and the resources you need around you to avoid the intense frustration of the Work in/Work on Trap.

Many growing firms are run too leanly, both in terms of spare capacity and cash flow. As a result, small issues often turn into full-blown crises, requiring the owner's time to sort out. Chapter 9 will show you what workflows you need and what systems to invest in to cut out the majority of small issues or mistakes, thus increasing the efficiency and effectiveness of the operation.

In the early days of their accountancy practice many accountants are happy to take on any client with a pulse and a tax return. As a result, they often build themselves client portfolios with price sensitive, low fee, needy and low recovery type clients. Or as they are often called *legacy clients*. These legacy clients often act as a barrier to a firm's growth as they suck up too much of the firm's time for scant reward. Part 3 of this book will show you how to attract in exactly the right type of clients to fuel your firm's growth.

As you read this book you will hear case studies from other accountancy firms and snippets from Sian, Paul, Sharon and Guy's growth stories; how they went about growing a one million pound practice. What worked, what didn't work. And how they overcame the very obstacles that you may be grappling with in your firm.

About Sian's practice Inform Accounting

Inform Accounting, at the time of writing, is a £500k practice based in Sutton Coldfield, with 14 members of staff. Many of Sian's staff are apprentices who, as the firm grows, will grow into account manager roles for the firm. Just as Sian can't resist a great bargain on a coat or pair of new shoes, she can't resist hiring more members of staff. But as her firm grows and her staff mature, she predicts that her ratio of turnover to staff will reduce the nearer she gets to being a one million pound practice. Sian built her practice with the ambition of scaling it from day one. But it also had to allow her to pick up her three children from the school gate. Don't ask her to do a year end set of accounts, as she never has. She came from industry and has always had staff to help with the day-to-day compliance tasks. Over the next few years her practice is predicted to grow by £100–150k each year. And if you ever have the privilege of meeting Sian, you know she will make this happen.

About Paul's practice Cornish Accounting

Cornish Accounting, at the time of writing, is a £450k rural based family practice in Bodmin, Cornwall with 10 members of staff, including Paul's wife, son and daughter. Just as Sian can't resist a new pair of shoes from her shoe-making client, Paul can't resist trying out every new piece of software or training course for accountants. Although he promises us he is much better than he was. After many years of static growth, Paul is now motivated to grow a one million pound practice to provide a decent business for his son to take over in the next 5–10 years. Given that Paul is never happier than when he is out winning work or being with his Clients, his practice is predicted to grow by £100–150k a year, with a significant portion of this growth coming from local/national pubs and restaurant businesses and advisory services. Paul is a real action taker and likes nothing better than getting stuck into a One Big Focus. (See Chapter 3)

About Sharon's practice Kinder Pocock

Sharon has often been described as a pioneer and leading thinker for small accountancy firms. There are not many accountancy awards for innovative or client-centred firms that she has not won or been highly commended. She likes nothing better than automating, integrating and connecting up systems to make her Clients' businesses more efficient. And on top of that she's also one of the nicest accountants you will ever meet. It's only now her boys are older that she is actively working on growing her firm. Her Hereford-based, 4-person practice turns over £210k, and will grow slowly for the next year or so as she gets a stable team around her, but then accelerate after that.

About Guy's practice Xebra Accounting

Guy's always been a deep thinker. His vision has always been to deliver a real-time accounting service to his Clients. Now that technology has pretty much caught up with his vision, he is a very happy man. At the time of writing his Southampton-based practice has grown by 40% each year for the last two years. He intends to maintain that growth and become a one million pound practice in 2020. Underpinning this bold ambition are detailed 3-year Growth Plans, well-documented systems and processes, and an energy to show what is really possible when you deliver a truly proactive and real-time accounting service to your clients.

Who is this book for?

This book has been written for owners of small accountancy practices who would like to grow a one million pound practice with a net profit margin of 40+%, whilst still paying themselves a commercial salary. Most of the guidance in this book is still applicable to bigger size practices who want to grow or increase their profitability.

The book has been written for sole practitioners. If you are in a multi-partner practice it is recommended that every partner reads a copy of the book, then all the partners work together to *all agree* on a Growth Vision and 3-year Growth Plan for the practice.

This book teaches you how to scale up your practice, with a net profit margin of 40+%, while working fewer hours with less stress. This isn't a book which will give you lots of heavy-going theory. Nor is it a thinly valued sales brochure or style-over-substance kind of book. It's a book which is chock full of practical suggestions which will inspire you to take action and achieve your goal of becoming a one million pound practice.

Along the way you'll discover exactly how:

- Guy goes out and wins clients with an average minimum fee of £6k.
- Paul, from his base in rural Cornwall, is able to attract hospitality clients from all over the UK who take both compliance and advisory services.
- Sharon increased her net profitability by 119% and boosted her monthly fees via direct debit by 60%. All as a result of implementing a fee increase for 90% of her clients.
- Sian is able to sign up most of her clients via the firm's website and on the basis of a phone call rather than a face-to-face meeting.
- Guy doesn't need to worry about cash flow as he has ALL his clients on the cloud who pay him in monthly instalments via direct debit.
- Sian now has a practice which grows by £100k a year and runs reliably without her; allowing her to take most of the school holidays off to be with her children.
- Paul outsourced his firm's social media marketing and in doing so doubled his monthly Leads. All for the cost of £120 a month.

- Sharon was able to save 4-8 hours when onboarding new clients via an investment in standardising and automating their new client onboarding process.
- Sian has found and grown her own high performing team of cloud-savvy account managers.

How to use this book

This book can be used in two different ways. It can be read from cover to cover. Or you can use the Growth Self-Assessment Tool to see which areas you need to prioritise to grow a one million pound practice. If this book is going to help you build a one million pound practice don't ignore the exercises or questions it poses. Be brave, make a positive commitment now to your firm by making the time to answer the questions, and complete the action points and exercises in each chapter.

In each chapter, you will see the symbol. This is where any traditional or conventional wisdom, which you may agree with, about growing an accountancy firm will be challenged.

Throughout the chapters are exercises for you to do to put into practice which you have just learnt.

The book is split into 3 Parts, supported by a Workbook which you can download from http://www.accountantsmillionaire.club.

The Workbook

For you to get the most out of this book and take action, there is a free accompanying Workbook containing a series of exercises that have been fully road-tested with clients. The exercises will help you get to grips with the ideas and frameworks contained in this book.

The symbol is used throughout the book to show you where there is a matching exercise. To get the Workbook and the full pack of companion material head over to http://www.accountantsmillionaire.club.

And finally …

You don't need to complete this journey alone. Come and join us as a member of the Accountants Millionaires' Club. We'd love to be by your side helping you grow your very own one million pound practice.

Heather Townsend
heather@heathertownsend.co.uk

Sian Kelly
Sian.kelly@informaccounting.co.uk

Paul Miller
paul@cornishaccounting.com

Sharon Pocock
Sharon@kinderpocock.co.uk

Guy Robinson
guy@xebraaccounting.co.uk

The Growth Self-Assessment Tool

Before you go any further in this book, download your copy of the Growth Self-Assessment Tool and fill it out. Your results from the tool will help you form the basis of your 3-year Growth Plan and prioritise which chapters you need to read first.

The Growth Self-Assessment Tool is available to download from http://www.accountantsmillionaire.club.

For each of the statements in the table rate yourself between 1 and 5. After you have finished rating yourself, prioritise reading the chapters where you have scored the lowest.

Poor/Rarely = 1	Your score (1-5)	Excellent/Always = 5	Go to Chapter
Getting to the starting gate			
I am firefighting nearly all of the time and just don't get good quality time to stop and think – unless I am on holiday. Even if I am on holiday I regularly find myself checking back in with my staff to make sure that everything is being done as requested. I am struggling to keep on top of the day job, let alone have time to work on my practice to grow it.	1 2 3 4 5	I have high quality thinking and reflection time built into my daily, weekly and monthly schedule. This thinking time gives me the headspace I need to be truly in control of my practice and grow my practice to my timescales. I typically have eight hours or more a week set aside to grow my practice.	Chapter 1
I find that I typically work very long hours and I am almost always working at weekends. I find it very hard to delegate to my team, and often just do it myself as it will be quicker.	1 2 3 4 5	My team know exactly their roles and responsibilities and I delegate regularly to them. They are always hungry to take work off my hands. I am not tempted to hold onto work and trust them implicitly to get on with whatever I give them.	
I haven't taken the time to consider why I want to grow a one million pound practice. I'm not sure what needs to change with my practice in order to grow it.	1 2 3 4 5	There is a real passion, genuine excitement and total unity from me and my team on why we want to grow a one million pound practice. I have utmost clarity on the strengths, weaknesses, opportunities and threats for my practice.	Chapter 2
We either don't have a Growth Vision or a 3-year Growth Plan, or my Growth Vision and 3-year Growth Plans are not supported or backed by my staff. No-one is really focused on growing the practice. My staff and I normally just get the day job done and don't worry about any future Growth Plans.	1 2 3 4 5	I have built a Growth Vision and 3-year Growth Plan for my practice which excites and motivates me and my staff. My staff are more than supportive of our 3-year Growth Plan, they are actively driving it with me. Everyone in our practice can tell you about the Growth Vision for our practice. There are visual reminders around the office about our Growth Vision and our 3-year Growth Plans.	Chapter 3
The day job always takes priority over growing the firm. Staff are more concerned with getting their normal work done rather than working on growing the business. The responsibility and burden for growing the business always falls to me.	1 2 3 4 5	Time is set aside daily, weekly, monthly, quarterly and annually to review and progress our firm's 3-year Growth Plans. Every quarter we set 90-day plans for the whole firm to focus on one thing we want to change. Each member of staff relishes the chance to do something different from the day job. They all know exactly what they are tasked to do to help the firm grow.	

Building a firm foundation for growth			
The growth of my practice keeps stalling as I am constantly pulled back into the practice to fight fires, deal with crises or deal with client work that my staff can't or won't do. Clients often bring in their records late and we will often work silly hours to get their work done before the deadline.	1 2 3 4 5	I have carved out enough time to work on my practice, as per my 3-year Growth Plan, to keep the growth of my practice consistent and steady. I can completely rely on my staff to cope with most problems without needing to involve me. I have mapped out when I will hand over my responsibilities as I grow. Our clients have been trained to get their information to us well in advance in their deadlines.	Chapter 4
My practice regularly over-trades and runs at over 100% of capacity. We always have a backlog of client work and there are never enough hands to get all the work done. At peak periods my staff and I work really long hours which can leave us burnt out.	1 2 3 4 5	My practice normally runs at 80% capacity and we have enough resource to cope efficiently with all the peaks and troughs in our firm's workload. Our days of firefighting are a very distant memory.	
If we have done a Client Portfolio Analysis for our firm it was a long time ago. If we do review our clients it rarely, if ever, results in any action from me or my staff. We are very reluctant to disengage from clients.	1 2 3 4 5	Every six months we do a complete Client Portfolio Analysis and identify recommendations to increase the profitability and turnover of our practice. These recommendations are always enthusiastically implemented within three months of doing the analysis. We are prepared if necessary to disengage from clients who are no longer a good fit for our practice.	Chapter 5
We don't have the time to keep our firm's management accounts up-to-date and don't monitor our KPIs. In fact, we struggle to produce high quality up-to-date KPIs to identify how well the practice is running.	1 2 3 4 5	Every month the top team in our practice looks at our KPIs and management accounts. We put together an action plan for any areas of the business which are becoming unprofitable. Our staff are always keen to get stuck into the action plan.	
When my salary as the owner of the firm is taken out of the firm's figures, the firm breaks even or makes a loss. We don't know where we are losing money in the practice or have the time to work out where our profit leaks are. Staff often do stuff for clients where we should be charging them.	1 2 3 4 5	The net profitability of our firm runs at over 40%. Every piece of client work has a budget of time allocated to it. We root cause every piece of work which goes over budget, and put in place an action plan to correct any problems. Staff are absolutely clear and confident about what is included in a client's service level, and what services they should charge a client for.	

It has been over 12 months since our clients had a fee increase. Our client fees are inconsistent and I am the only one in the practice who can quote for fees. We know we need to put some client fees up, but haven't yet prioritised this.	1 2 3 4 5	Every year we implement an annual fee increase for our clients. Our clients expect this increase and don't quibble about it as they routinely tell us about the value we bring to them and their business. All of my staff know how to quote the right fees for a client and I am not expected to be involved in setting fees for clients. We use a quoting tool to make sure that our clients get a consistent, honest, transparent but profitable fee for their workload.	Chapter 5
We still bill by time after the job has been completed. Our WIP and debtor days are very high – well over 100 days. We have problems with bad debts and don't ask our clients to pay via direct debit and monthly instalments. Billing for non-standard ad hoc work often gets forgotten. If I don't badger clients to get their records in on time my cash flow will suffer.	1 2 3 4 5	We offer fixed fee billing to all our clients. All our clients pay in monthly instalments via direct debit. Any extra pieces of work outside of our normal client packages are billed and collected within a month of finishing the work.	
I often worry about how I am going to pay the wages at the end of the month. I am living hand-to-mouth with my cash flow and often forgo paying myself in order for the business to survive.	1 2 3 4 5	We ruthlessly monitor our cash flow every week and always ensure we have enough access to cash to fuel our 3-year Growth Plans. I can sleep very easy at night as I always know I have enough cash in the bank. Our debtors and WIP is practically zero and we rarely have problems with bad debt.	
Our firm's job descriptions are out of date and I have given little or no thought to how my firm's structure will evolve as we grow. My staff don't know how their roles will change over time. There is little or no time allocated to staff development beyond what is required for CPD purposes.	1 2 3 4 5	I know exactly how my firm's structure will change as the firm grows. I have job descriptions for each role and can show my staff members how their role will develop and change as the firm grows. I use a firm-wide development plan to help my staff develop as the firm grows. I have an awesome mix of staff who want to develop and advance their career as the firm grows, but also staff who are very content doing what they are doing.	Chapter 6

We struggle to recruit in new members of staff and almost always need to use the services of a recruiter to find new staff. We often have long gaps between people leaving and their replacement being hired.	1 2 3 4 5	We are always on the look-out for potential good members of staff. We find that nearly all of our new hires approach us rather than us having to use the services of a recruitment consultant. Our firm is seen as a great place to work and to develop a career as an accountant.	Chapter 6
We often make bad recruitment decisions. Either our staff leave within 18 months or we get stuck with poor performers who we struggle to performance manage. And that's if we have the time and inclination to performance manage them. When they join us staff are expected to sink or swim. Very little training beyond how to use our firm's systems is given to new starters.	1 2 3 4 5	We have virtually no turnover of new members of staff as our staff are always shouting about how great a firm we are. We have a new staff onboarding process in place which helps them quickly get our firm culture and start performing to the level we need them. Every new member of staff has their own personalised development plan and is allocated a buddy or mentor to help them settle in.	
No plan exists to identify and intentionally develop the talent within my firm. Development for my firm happens on a haphazard basis, often based on who shouts loudest.	1 2 3 4 5	A plan to identify and intentionally develop emerging managers and leaders is carefully monitored by myself. Each member of my team has a personal development plan to help them perform and develop in the short, medium and long term. The people managers in my practice and I regularly sit down with each of our team members to talk about their performance and development.	Chapter 7
If difficult conversations happen at all, they rarely go well. Feedback is rarely given and staff are afraid to give honest feedback to senior members of the firm.	1 2 3 4 5	The firm has developed a culture where timely feedback (both positive and negative) is given to all staff. Critical feedback is always given sensitively and in private. Difficult conversations with staff and clients – particularly about billing matters – happen promptly and successfully.	
No capacity or resource plan exists for the firm. The firm is often very short-staffed in peak periods and gets caught out by staff being away on study leave or holiday. Holiday requests are normally granted without checking whether the firm can afford for staff to be away at that time.	1 2 3 4 5	The firm has a rolling 12-month capacity and resource plan which is religiously reviewed monthly. Study leave and staff holidays are included in the plan. New staff members are hired 3 months before they are needed and the firm has the available cash reserves to fund the hire. The firm very rarely operates over 100% capacity.	Chapter 8

Staff tend to work in their own silos doing things their own way. Ways of working, if recorded, are out of date and rarely followed. The firm does not measure its efficiency and finds that its wages are over 40% of the total firm revenue. The firm has very manual ways of working and has not invested in technology to automate its processes. I rarely take more than a few days away from the firm as it would fall to pieces if I wasn't there.	1 2 3 4 5	All the workflows in our firm are systemised and staff always adhere to the firm's ways of working. Every system and firm process is reviewed at least once a year to make sure the firm is still utilising best practice and working efficiently. Wherever possible manual entry has been eliminated from our processes and technology has automated how we do things. The firm has a KPI which is monitored monthly to check that it is working effectively. I can happily and properly take 2 weeks off and forget about the firm, AND still have a healthy firm to come back to. Wages and outsourcing costs are less than 30% of the firm's total revenue.	Chapter 9
Leads are not tracked or qualified. The firm often forgets about leads and fails to follow up with leads who have gone quiet. Members of the firm don't know how to spot an opportunity with an existing client. The firm is often caught out by lots of clients suddenly converting and not having the capacity to deal with the new influx of client work.	1 2 3 4 5	Every enquiry the firm receives is tracked and qualified before being progressed. The firm has identified each stage of its sales pipeline and knows the conversion rate for each stage of the sales pipeline. The sales pipeline is reviewed at least weekly and staff members given action points to progress leads in the sales pipeline. The firm calculates a weighted sales forecast in order to drive its capacity plans. Leads which have gone quiet are regularly followed up. All staff members excel at spotting opportunities with existing clients.	Chapter 10
We tend to act as order takers with our clients and see which of our firm's services they want to buy. We rarely spend time in sales meetings finding out about their goals, aspirations, challenges or world. Clients rarely buy anything more than compliance services. We find that clients often want us to reduce our prices. We often find that our sales meetings with leads are a waste of time as the leads are either not ready to buy or are not a good fit for our firm.	1 2 3 4 5	We rarely waste time on business development meetings with leads which are going nowhere. Clients are clamouring to buy more than the bare minimum from the firm and we find it easy to upsell clients to buy advisory services from the firm. We spend over half of any of our sales meetings really understanding the clients' world and their challenges. All of our staff have been trained to be curious with clients and find out what our clients are trying to achieve with their business. Clients rarely ask us for a discount or to reduce our prices as they understand the value they get from working with us.	Chapter 11

Scaling up your practice			
We have not considered the benefits of growing organically or by buying an accountancy practice.	1 2 3 4 5	We have identified whether we will grow organically or by buying another practice. If we have decided to buy an accountancy practice we know when we want to buy it and what it will help the practice do.	Chapter 12
It is very difficult to distinguish between my firm and local competitors. I have not taken the time to truly develop a niche for the firm, and are more concerned with how to make my firm as attractive as possible to as many clients as possible.	1 2 3 4 5	My firm is well known for a niche market, and our profile in that niche is so strong that we attract 'pre-sold' high quality clients to our firm. If you did a Google search for our firm you would instantly get what sectors we specialise in and how we help our clients. Clients never quibble about paying a premium fee for our firm's services.	Chapter 13
If we have a marketing plan at all it is poorly researched and very generic.	1 2 3 4 5	Our firm's marketing plan is all geared towards the needs of our Client Personas. Our Client Personas match exactly the types of clients we thrive on working with. We have carefully researched our niche market and know the journey our prospects take in order to become a client.	Chapter 13
Our firm's services are still sold on a service-by-service basis. If we have packaged up our firm's services we call them bronze, silver, gold.	1 2 3 4 5	We have built 2–4 packages for our compliance and recurring services. These services are meticulously tailored to the requirements of our niche market, including a name for each package which means something to clients. Clients find it clear what they are buying and able to self-select which service package is right for them.	Chapter 14
Even though we tell our clients about the advisory services we offer they rarely seem interested in buying them.	1 2 3 4 5	We find it easy to sign up clients to buy our advisory services which we sell as a solution to their problem. Very often new clients will buy our advisory services on top of our normal compliance packages. We don't find it hard to get our clients to buy our firm's advisory services.	Chapter 14

I do not have a marketing plan to produce a predictable number of leads, improve conversion rates, increase the average revenue per transaction and increase the transactions per client. The results of spending on marketing and advertising are unmeasured and unmanaged. Any revenue growth is largely down to luck.	1 2 3 4 5	I have an aggressive, measurable marketing plan to produce a predictable number of leads, improve conversion rates, increase the average revenue per transaction, and increase the transactions per client so profits increase significantly. Results of the marketing plan are being measured and improved on a weekly basis.	Chapter 15
Key account management for our clients is rarely done at all. There are no relationship plans in place for key clients. Clients are rarely, if at all, categorised.	1 2 3 4 5	All clients have been categorised, and service levels delivered based on the client category. Key accounts have been identified and each key account has a proactive key account plan and relationship plan, and the plans are helping us gain a greater slice of the client's business. Client portfolio analysis is proactively completed.	Chapter 16
Client service standards and processes, if in place, are not automatically followed.	1 2 3 4 5	My staff are obsessed about delivering extraordinary client service. Our client proposition is carefully tailored to each client, and there are processes and systems in place to make sure we deliver and truly 'wow' each client. I can rely on our clients to generate over 60% of all our qualified Leads each month.	
The firm and staff really don't have a social media presence. If my staff or I do have a social media account these are rarely updated and not focused on delivering valuable content to our clients. There is very little understanding within the firm about how to use social media to drive new business for the firm.	1 2 3 4 5	My staff and I really stand out on social media, particularly in regards to our niche market. All the staff members maintain up-to-date and engaging social media accounts which help to amplify the reach of our firm's social media presence. The firm has both accounts for staff and a business page on LinkedIn and other social media platforms where our clients congregate. Everyone in the firm understands how their efforts on social media add up into the firm growing its profile and attracting new clients.	Chapter 17

The firm does not have a content plan and very rarely produces any content.	1 2 3 4 5	The firm has a Content Plan which is used to regularly produce and share content to help the firm's ideal client progress through their buying journey. The content is produced on schedule and is seen by the firm's ideal clients, introducers and existing clients. The content the firm produces helps the firm generate the right amount of leads, reduces the time for clients to buy and increases the firm's client conversion rate.	Chapter 17
I, and others in my firm, have not built up a network of introducers who regularly refer the right type of work into the firm.	1 2 3 4 5	My staff, who are targeted to win new client work, and I maintain regular communication with a close network of introducers who regularly refer and recommend us to our ideal clients. Each introducer has a Relationship Lead within the firm, which is not always me. We are equally proactive at helping them achieve their business and career aims. We have a formal plan to keep us in touch with our best introducers. We use both face-to-face and online tools to help keep us top-of-mind with our network of introducers.	Chapter 18
The firm either doesn't use events to win clients, or struggles to generate any new client work from its events. If we do run an event we often have to cancel due to low attendance.	1 2 3 4 5	The firm uses events to win new client work. Events are costed and run in a way so that they generate at least a 10 times return on our marketing investment. The firm's events are normally always fully booked. The firm has built up a targeted mailing list to easily encourage people to attend our events.	Chapter 19

Getting to the starting gate

Growing a one million pound practice all starts with you, your firm's owner. With this in mind, part 1 is all about the things you need to do *before* you can start to grow your practice.

It starts with showing you how to free up your time in order to have the time to grow your practice. Then how to create a Growth Vision and 3-year Growth Plan.

Don't be tempted to skip these 3 chapters of the book. They are fundamental to the rest of the book. The diligence in which you do the exercises in this part of the book will underpin how successful you will be growing a one million pound practice.

1

How to find the time to grow your practice

Topics covered in this chapter:

- What is headspace and why you need it to grow your practice
- 6 sensible ways of creating the time you need to grow your practice
- How to delegate effectively

The whole aim of Chapter 1 is to allow you to eliminate enough work from your desk in order to free up one whole day a week, every week. Sounds challenging? But that's the magnitude of the change you need, and from Chapter 2 to the end of the book it is assumed that you have eight hours a week to design and implement your Growth Plan.

What is headspace and why you need it to grow your practice

Having headspace is essential if you want to grow a one million pound practice. For the purposes of this book, it is not about meditating or being mindful. It is about giving your mind the freedom to think, pause, reflect or go where it needs to go. This means getting the brain away from the day-to-day distractions of life as an accountancy firm owner (emails, calls and discussions with clients or staff) and also your responsibilities outside of work (issues around family, home, shopping, cooking, housework, bills). Giving yourself the permission to have headspace is like giving your brain a new office with a whiteboard, on which to design a new practice and plan for its implementation. When you down tools and go on holiday you normally give yourself precious headspace time. This is why you almost always come back from a holiday brimming full of ideas for your practice. It's also why taking the time to have a long shower is a great way to generate ideas.

It is really important that as you read this book you have the headspace to consider the different and sometimes radical approaches it will ask you to adopt, as you grow your practice. The more time you have for headspace, the more chance you have to do deep, quality thinking. The ideas in this book can't wait until you go on holiday in order to be implemented on your return. That's why it's essential that you don't just free up time to do stuff, but also to have essential headspace time.

Just as planning a three-month holiday to ten countries would require a lot of detailed planning, your pursuit of a million pound practice requires much thinking and consideration of multiple options. You will be using your eight hours of headspace to do strategic work. For some people, they can think at the gym, doing an individual sport, walking, cooking or listening to music. This is fine, however you must keep a notebook and pen, or phone handy to record your ideas as you go. Once back in the office, turn vague ideas into actions you can take which will support your growth trajectory.

Headspace has more benefits than just giving you the time and space to identify how to grow your practice. It will reduce your stress levels and put you back in control of your practice.

What stops us from having daily headspace time?

The norm for society is to be busy. Life now happens at a million miles an hour and people are bombarded by 24/7 information which comes at them from the moment they open their eyes. Whether it is the newsfeed of their social media platforms or the rolling 24/7 news, the email which is available to them on their smartphones, it is becoming harder and harder to switch off from the hustle and bustle of daily life.

It's not just the pace at which people now live their lives. The most common mode for a small accountancy firm owner is firefighting. Firefighting is the enemy of high quality headspace. If business as usual for you in your practice means forever putting out fires, then you need to change how you are operating. Growing your practice will come after you have spent clear time planning for that growth.

Why not just find the time for headspace?

When you are swamped with client work, which is all urgent, the last thing you want to hear is *just make the time* or *try to work smarter.* After all, if it was that easy you would have already made the time. As you read through this book you will realise that your role as a practice owner is going to change over time. You are going to get more and more time to do the stuff you love. However, to get to the good stuff you will need to become comfortable with changing how you work and how your practice works. Finding the time for headspace is just the first change you will need to implement on your way to becoming a one million pound practice.

Case study:
Sharon's Growth Story

I was finding that from the moment I set foot in my office, I was constantly inundated with client and staff queries. I, and the team, were constantly firefighting, and I was feeling out of control. Instead of getting my work done at the office, I would then take it home and work late in the evenings and at the weekends. This way of working was ramping up my stress levels and making me ill. My family was getting fed up with me. I had no quality headspace time. Everyone always wanted a piece of me. Something had to change. I started to work at home on a Monday to focus on marketing and strategy. This helped me to feel more in control and plan my time better, so that I stopped working in the evenings and at weekends.

To stop the constant queries and get back in control I instigated a weekly Rhythm Team Meeting (See Chapter 3) and a Daily Operational Huddle. The weekly team meeting helped us to focus on what needed to get done that week. The short, sharp 5–10 minute Daily Operational Huddle with my team, eliminated all the staff queries and made sure they had everything they needed from me to get their work done.

Case study: Guy's Growth Story

I have always considered myself one of the profession's deep thinkers. I find it very difficult to get the time to properly think and reflect on a day-to-day basis. There are always so many interruptions, distractions and client work that needs to be done. However, walking our two Saint Bernard dogs every day gives me that much needed bit of sanity and headspace. I was finding that this dose of headspace was good, but not enough. This is why I asked my co-authors to form a monthly mastermind group with me. Every quarter I take a day out of the business. We meet the evening before our mastermind day in a location central to us all. I find that relaxing, talking and working with my fellow co-authors – who I trust implicitly – inspires me, but gives me that much needed headspace time to truly work on my plans to grow the business.

The day itself is also headspace, involving five heads. Each of us gets constructive feedback on our Growth Plans from the other four members. Almost always one of us has seen another practice already doing these types of improvements, so the sharing of experiences adds real richness to our Growth Plans.

As the founder of your firm, there are no rules to say you have to work the longest hours, or work the hardest in your firm, or even work full time hours.

Case study: Paul's Growth Story

I've trained my team to know that if the red light is on my phone they should only interrupt me if the office is burning down. This means that I can always get some decent headspace time during the working day if needed.

How to find an extra 8 hours a week

Firstly, stop kidding yourself that this will happen when you get through the current busy period. When was your last real quiet period? Or enough of a quiet period to do more than take a break and recharge your batteries? That's the problem; when you subscribe to the illusion of tomorrow, you never quite manage to take the first step and get started.

Don't be tempted to cut the target down from eight hours. The more you think big, the more it encourages your brain to think laterally and differently; potentially to consider some great solutions which you would have never considered if you were only trying to find an extra three hours a week.

The best way to find an extra eight hours a week, is start as you mean to go on. Start right now by booking yourself an hour out of your hectic schedule. Switch off your phone and your computer, get out of your office and go for a walk. As you are walking start to play around with the idea of giving yourself 8 hours a week to focus on growing your practice. What is stopping this from happening? What would have to change for this to happen? Is your firm under-resourced? Do you need to delegate more? Do you have the right people doing the right stuff?

Case study: Raj

Raj and his father were partners. No other staff and no office. They were working full-time and profits had plateaued. Raj had a vision to be a virtual accountancy firm. So he set up an ambitious Growth Plan.

He outsourced half of his Year End Accounts work, releasing himself for eight hours. In that headspace he decided to outsource all of his Year End Accounts and VAT returns and gave himself another free day. He used his freed-up time to dedicate to marketing his practice and automating his processes. At the end of the following quarter the practice had twelve new clients and £36k extra revenue.

Based on that success, Raj wrote into his Growth Plan to replicate what he had done for the following three quarters.

Identify and fix your personal productivity gaps

The reality is that everyone has got their own bad habits which limit their productivity. This could be the simple stuff to fix such as relegate social media to your lunch time and commute to work. Or it could be the harder stuff to fix such as overcoming your personal reluctance to delegate some of your workload downwards. See later on in this chapter for more tips around delegation.

📖 Personal Productivity Gaps

Ditch your unprofitable clients

When was the last time you took a long, hard look at your client portfolio? If it's like many accountancy firms, it was probably over a year ago. Things change and before you know it a client may not be profitable any more. By regularly doing a client portfolio analysis, i.e. twice a year, you can identify where your firm is losing money on clients. Then every week, exit 1–2 clients until you have the headspace time you need.

📖 Client Portfolio Analysis

Outsource your compliance work

There is no rule to say that someone directly employed within your practice needs to complete your clients' compliance work. You could subcontract to a local self-employed accountant or bookkeeper, or outsource your work to a specialist accounts outsourcing firm. Some outsourcing firms, such as Global Infosys, work on a pay-as-you-go basis so you can turn them off or on when you need them, rather than being tied into a fixed-term contract. You may find by investing to reduce the backlog of client work you release your time sufficiently to focus on moving your practice forward. See Chapter 8 for how to start outsourcing your compliance work.

Case study: Simon

Just before the start of the busiest period of the year, Simon's practice lost half its accounts team. Simon calculated that every remaining member of the accounts team would need to complete 2 sets of Year End Accounts every day for 3 months if the practice was going to meet all their clients' deadlines. Clearly not possible. So, Simon outsourced his Year End Accounts backlog to a specialist accounts outsourcing company. The quality of the work which came back was so good that within 6 months, Simon was outsourcing 80% of all his Year End Accounts work. The decision to outsource proved to be a turning point in the growth of his practice. It gave him and his practice the headspace and capacity to grow and add in higher value advisory work. His profitability doubled within 3 months of starting to outsource. His good staff members stayed and grew with the practice. The staff members who he didn't want to keep all voted with their feet and found new roles within 3 months of the practice starting to outsource.

Hire in more staff

If a client wanted to grow but couldn't afford to hire in a new member of staff, what would you advise them to do? Take on funding to fuel their growth? Or see if they could recruit someone into a part-time role? It's time to take your own advice and hire in more staff to give you the headspace and capacity to grow your firm.

Case study: Sharon's Growth Story

I was struggling to get everything done. I'd already outsourced some of the firm's day-to-day compliance work to an outsourcing firm. My time was being sucked up in project managing the outsourcer and staff, client queries and producing management reports for our best clients. Unfortunately I didn't have the cash reserves or turnover to justify hiring in a full-time member of staff. Nor did I need another trainee. So I hired in a part-time qualified accountant. My new team member was delighted to join a local growing progressive accountancy firm who believed in flexible working. I managed to free up my time, but also gain a valuable member of the team at a cost I could afford.

Does your practice give you freedom to work when you want in a way you want? Or have you just built yourself a job?

Audit how you spend your time

It's very easy to mistake being busy for progress. The firms which successfully grow to be a one million pound practice have cracked the challenge of getting the right people to do the right things. When it comes to getting the right people to do the right things, it starts with you, the firm owner. A great way of doing this is to do an audit of your time using the Red/Black/Blue Model.

Case study: Light Bulbs

The owner of a £700k turnover practice did an audit of where he spent his time. He realised that he still had too many responsibilities, including being the person in the practice who bought and replaced the dead lightbulbs. So he delegated the job to his practice manager who then contacted the office cleaning contractors. The office cleaners not only took over the job of replacing the dead lightbulbs, but also checked the smoke alarms. Because of their buying power, each bulb was half the price of the local DIY store. A further benefit was no employee had to climb on chairs to change the bulbs. As a result, the practice owner gained valuable headspace and the practice manager found a better way of sorting out the dead lightbulbs.

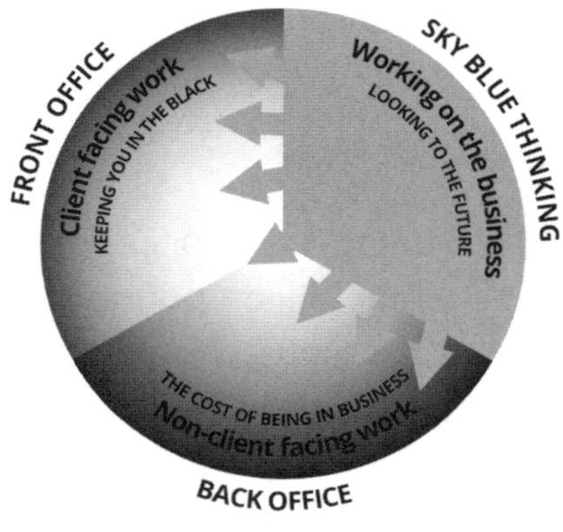

Diagram 1.0: Red/Black/Blue model

To use the Red/Black/Blue model to audit how you spend your time firstly make a note over a 2-week period of exactly *what* you are doing and *how long* you are spending on an activity. Then for each activity code it red, black or blue and add up how much time you are spending on each Red/Black/Blue activity.

Red work: This is your non-client facing work (i.e. your back-office stuff) and the stuff that you just have to do (i.e. the cost of being in business, such as your expenses and performance reviews with staff). Very often your management responsibilities fall into this area.

Black work: This is your client-facing work, such as client work, account management and networking.

Blue work: This is your strategic *blue sky* thinking time. It's all the things you do to invest in the future for your firm. For example, business planning for your firm or attending a conference to get an insight into the future. Very often your leadership responsibilities fall into here.

Your aim is to increase the time you spend on Blue work, and ditch, delegate or do differently the Black and Red work.

Once you have finished the analysis on how you are spending your time, then be honest with yourself and identify what you shouldn't be doing and take action to change it. After all, growing a one million pound practice all starts with you freeing up your 8 hours of time a week.

Red/Black/Blue Model

> “If it can be delegated, it must be. Never work on something that someone less experienced than you can do – your career will be on hold and you'll become more and more obsolete with each passing day.
>
> *DAVID MAISTER*

Delegate effectively

If you can delegate effectively, then you will be well on your way to freeing up 8 hours a week to work on growing your practice. The reality is that poor, ineffective or a lack of delegation from owners of accountancy firms is often their biggest time drain. It's fair to say that delegation isn't something that comes to an accountant in practice naturally. When you are hard-wired to want to do the best job as possible for a client, the last thing you want to do is let the quality of work slip by letting someone else complete the work. However, this mindset is exactly the mindset that you will need to change if you want to grow a one million pound practice and work fewer hours.

If you don't feel that the people you delegate to are competent, then it is your responsibility to develop them so that they *are* competent. Or to be very blunt, manage them out of the practice so you can replace them with competent people. After all, you get the team you deserve.

Here are four ways of minimising risks when delegating:

Identify the risks

When delegating a responsibility for the first time – or if the stakes have risen considerably – do an analysis of where the risks are. That way, you can put in place an action plan and a structure to minimise the risks.

Monitor the risks

When you know where the high risks are, you are then in a position to monitor those areas. For example, if you delegate the management of a budget and cost centre, until the budget holder is completely up-to-speed, you will want regular updates on the spend going through this account.

Use management by exception

After you have agreed a plan of action with the person you are delegating the responsibility to, agree when you will have a progress update or what to do if a problem occurs. This way you will be involved if anything deviates from the ideal. You can then help to develop contingency plans as necessary.

Build in controls

There are several controls that you can build into a project or responsibility. For example, spend or budget limit, project milestones and key performance indicators. Have the person that you delegate to provide regular feedback and reports on progress-to-date, and agree this when you give them the work.

Summary

To begin your journey to the one million pound level, you need to clear at least eight hours out of your working week by exiting weak clients and offloading non-strategic tasks to others in your business or to outsiders. Use the tools in this chapter to achieve this free headspace within four weeks, then you can proceed to the next chapter.

Action points

- Download your *Accountants Millionaires' Club Workbook* and complete the exercises Personal Productivity Gaps, Client Portfolio Analysis, Red/Black/Blue Model. Look at the results of your exercises and write an action plan to create eight hours to focus on plans to grow your practice.

- Write down a list of your responsibilities in your practice. Now go through each responsibility and ask yourself, *Should I be doing that?* If not, should it be delegated, ditched, delayed or done differently? Then take your list to someone not involved in your practice and see what they suggest you should be doing differently in order to free up your time.
- Schedule a 4-hour workshop with up to five key people in your practice. Go through a list of all your clients and agree which are the 20% you are going to ditch. Then the following day, revisit the Ditch List, confirm it, then design an Action Plan and timeframe for proceeding. Also assign people to the task. Be clear with your people that this is to free up one whole working day each week to advance the practice and create the space to take on new, fresh clients.

2

How to make sure that you sustainably grow your practice

Topics covered in this chapter:

- The Growing Pains Model
- What ingredients are needed to sustainably grow your practice

In the last chapter, you were invited to carve out headspace – valuable thinking time – to start the transition to grow your firm. Given that this transition could mean a total transformation of your firm it is important that you get your team on board with your Growth Vision. In this chapter, you will identify your current situation, particular your firm's stage of growth, and identify the compelling reasons to grow your practice. This will then start the process to get your team onboard with your Growth Vision.

Current situation

You've picked up this book because you have a Growth Vision to be a one million pound practice. It's now time to identify the true extent of your current situation, in order to understand what needs to change to fulfil your Growth Vision.

Two tools often used to fully understand a firm's current situation are a SWOT analysis and a STEEPLED Analysis.

If your firm's Business Model is still heavily based on solely delivering compliance and tax planning services to your clients, it is now out of date.

SWOT and STEEPLED Analysis

A SWOT Analysis looks at the internal and external elements of your firm. SWOT stands for Strengths, Weaknesses, Opportunities and Threats. Groups or individuals can carry out a SWOT Analysis. A SWOT Analysis normally gives you a great mandate for change in your practice.

The exercises use the known information about the firm and the landscape in which it operates to:

- Identify the *strengths* of the firm. These are positive things about your firm, which help you perform as intended or better than expected. Typically, these strengths are completely under the firm's control.
- Identify the *weaknesses* of the firm. These are the opposite of strengths, but still within the firm's control. These weaknesses are stopping the firm from performing at the desired level, delay progress or give your competitors an advantage over you.
- Spot the *opportunities* that may arise or already exist. These tend to be positive external forces or factors beyond the firm's control.
- Pinpoint the *threats* the firm is facing now or in the future. Threats are the opposite of opportunities. They are external forces or factors, which jeopardise the firm from achieving its intended goals and performance.

If you haven't yet moved to a paperless office, why not? There is no reason now to ask your staff to print off emails or documents to put in a paper-based client file.

A STEEPLED Analysis is very similar to a SWOT analysis. In a STEEPLED Analysis you identify the external driving forces that could materially impact your firm. Your STEEPLED Analysis is a great way to expand on the Opportunities and Threats you identified in your SWOT Analysis.

STEEPLED stands for:

Social, Technology, Ethical, Environmental, Political, Legal/Regulatory, Economy, Demographics

📖 SWOT Analysis

📖 STEEPLED Analysis

The scalable firm of the future

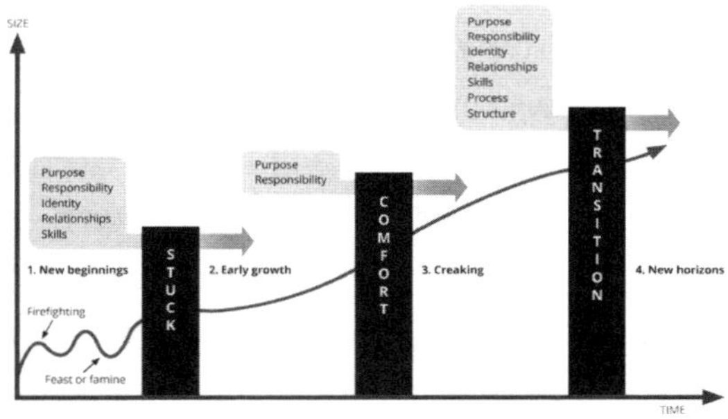

Diagram 2.0: The Excedia Growing Pains Model

Typically any firm is in one of the 5 stages of growth, as shown in the Growing Pains Model. The Growing Pains Model can be used to analyse what needs to change to move you from whatever stage you are in to the next stage of growth.

Stage 1: New Beginnings

This stage is characterised by rollercoastering emotions, firefighting and very often 'feast or famine'. There is often an absence of established systems, process or infrastructure to drive the growth. It can seem like it is always one step forward and two steps back. As growth increases it comes to the first of the Brick Walls, the Stuck Brick Wall. When your practice is in this stage, you will often hear people say they are stuck. The only way to get through the Stuck

Brick Wall is to invest time and resource on defining your purpose (*Why are we doing this?*), responsibilities (*Who is responsible for what?*), investing in your identity (*What will we be known for?*), the relationships you surround yourself with and the skills people need to get to the next stage of growth.

Stage 2: Early Growth

The Early Growth stage starts when a business exits the Stuck Brick Wall. This stage starts with calmness and confidence. Typically plans will now have been made and these are being implemented. Steady and sustainable growth (the early green shoots of growth) starts to happen. This growth continues until you hit the second brick wall, the Comfort Brick Wall. You may even hear people say that we've grown to a point where we are now comfortable, but not where we need to get to. Not every business will hit the Comfort Brick Wall. Many will sail through this. This is where growth slows because you've grown enough to stop feeling the pain that propelled you forward. The only way to get through this brick wall is to refocus on your purpose (*Why are you doing this?*) and responsibilities (*Who needs to do What by When?*).

Stage 3: Creaking

The previously steady and sustainable growth starts to level off in this stage. Typically, this is because one essential element of the business model or operation is now running at capacity and cannot be scaled up any further. For example, this could be the point where the owner of the firm realises that the structure that got them to this point, will not take them to the next point of their growth. At the end of this stage, businesses experience the third brick wall, the Transition Brick Wall. After a period of high emotion, the business starts to internally reflect on what it wants and needs going forward. This could take the form of a complete rethink of the business model. Similar to the Stuck Brick Wall, the only way through this brick wall is to focus and invest time and energy on defining your purpose, responsibilities, investing in your identity, relationships and skills. To get through the Transition Brick Wall also takes an investment in processes and structure. As a result of the internal focus and soul-searching which goes on in the Transition Brick Wall, the business typically takes a decision about its future growth: whether to plateau and eventually decline or grow further.

Stage 4: New Horizons

The business now steadily grows.

📖 Growing Pains Model

What ingredients are needed to sustainably grow your practice?

Running numbers through a spreadsheet to create a business plan is a comparatively easy job for an accountant. It's the finding and developing the right people, coupled with getting them to work the way you want them to, which is the difficult part of growth. A good way to view your plan to scale up to a one million pound practice is as a long-term change project. After all, it's pretty much guaranteed that as your firm grows it will totally transform itself. The 'people' side of this long-term change project has 5 features.

Your accounting firm is a business. It should be able to pay you a commercial salary AND still make a 40+% net profit margin.

Create a Growth Vision which excites your staff

In order to become a one million pound practice you need to have clarity about the intended future state, and with much more detail than just a statement to 'become a one million pound practice'. Without clarity and agreement about the future state there will be confusion and inertia.

A great Growth Vision will:

- Declare your intention, that you want to become a one million pound practice
- Be visual, so that people can see how the future will look and know what it will feel like to be part of the growing firm.
- Be exciting and positive
- Be simple to understand and be easy for people to talk about.

Allow people to let go

Beware that when change happens, people have to let go of the old methods which might have been tried and tested over many years. Staff will have a feeling of loss, and some might grieve for a while. People, particularly accountants, get comfort from the status quo. They know where they are in the world and how they fit in. Your Growth Vision will challenge that status quo. This means that your role is to identify, often on an individual level, what people might perceive they will lose as a result of your Growth Vision. Then allow your staff the time to let go of the old ways of doing things.

Shared need and urgency

If your Stakeholders – staff and clients – can't or don't want to see the need to change to grow to be a one million pound practice, this can put the brakes on growth. You see this happening time and time again when an accountancy firm owner comes back from a conference with a whole set of great ideas which he or she wants to implement. Despite a huge amount of enthusiasm and good intentions the ideas are never sustainably implemented because Stakeholders, consciously or sub-consciously, derail the changes. Derailment can happen in many ways:

- Staff don't have time to do anything more than the day job
- Staff don't have the budget or can't find the budget to invest in growth
- Staff refuse to change to the new way of working
- Clients may vote with their feet and find another accountant.

Great ways of ensuring that Stakeholders are on board with your Growth Plans is to do some stakeholder mapping. Who is impacted by the growth of the practice and how supportive do they need to be for the growth to happen? To help increase the momentum for growth and the inevitable changes, it will be useful to identify the short- and long-term gains if your people change, compared with the short- and long-term discomfort you will all experience if the firm doesn't grow. Intense short-term discomfort is normally the easiest way to get a mandate for growth. Sometimes you may need to create the pain to help your staff and clients move forward.

📖 Stakeholder Analysis

Available resources

Growing a firm takes ambition, time and money. You've got the ambition and now made the time. But a lack of cash can really stifle a firm's growth. These are some examples of how cash can be directed towards the things that are probably listed in your Growth Plan:

- To pay for a new firm website to stimulate lead generation
- To buy-in staff ahead of when you need them
- To pay an external supplier to do something that you do now to release your time; for instance, doing social media for your firm

- To pay for a new office when you grow out of your current office space or decide to stop working from home
- To invest in new technology for the firm.

Skills

Whether it is getting to grips with a new online accounting system or learning other different methods, growing your practice will mean your staff will learn new skills. Sometimes firms don't realise this, or there isn't enough support given to the staff to implement and embed their skills. If staff are not given the time and resources to learn and utilise the skills needed to grow the practice, then it can cause large levels of anxiety and tension. These are common scenarios where this happens:

- *For us to implement our new strategy the managers need to step up and lead*
- *To hit our new forecast for gross recurring fees, we need our managers to be able to spot opportunities with their clients for additional work*
- *We are going to train the staff to be able to handle new business enquiries which come via the phone*
- *It is just a slightly different way of doing things, the staff should adapt very quickly*

Case study: Sian's Growth Story

I wanted my practice to run without me. But I quickly realised that I would need to develop a new breed of accountant if my firm was able to routinely offer more than just compliance or tax type of services; e.g. management accounts, helping clients get their businesses into the cloud, business planning and business coaching. I had structured my firm right from the outset so that I would never have to do a client's Year End Accounts, tax return or bookkeeping. However, it was my clients wanting my commercial acumen, the benefit of my years of experience in industry, which was stopping me growing. Stuff that I couldn't easily get my current members of staff to do. After all, the ability to put together a set of accounts does not help you advise clients on how to run a business.

I hired in school leavers and embarked on an ambitious training programme to get them to be both cloud accounting experts and also develop their commercial acumen. After they were competent with bookkeeping, I then got them doing management accounts rather than Year End Accounts. I needed them at an early stage in their career to really understand how a business ticks and grows. After all, the future of accountancy is not doing Year End Accounts, it's helping clients achieve their personal and business goals.

Take some time to consider what skills you and your staff will need to develop if you are going to achieve your Growth Vision.

📖 What skills are needed for the future exercise

Growth Plan

Given the many demands on your time, you need a Growth Plan in order to focus both you and your staff on the day job, but also on what needs to be done to grow the firm. In the next chapter, you will put together the Growth Vision for your firm as well as your Growth Plan.

Summary

You need a strong personal *Why* and an exciting Growth Vision to grow your practice, otherwise it won't grow. After all, if you are not clear on why you should grow your practice, what hope do you have in convincing others to make the change with you? It's important to gain the hearts and minds of your Stakeholders and go forward with the Growth Vision.

Action points

- Using your *Accountants Millionaires' Club Workbook* complete a SWOT and STEEPLED analysis of your practice. From that work, identify what are the driving forces to grow your practice. Then identify the key changes your practice will need to make to be profitable and sustainable in the future.
- Talk with other accountancy firm owners on how they are adapting to the digitisation of the profession, the move to real time accountancy and how technology is changing how accountancy is done.
- Using the Growing Pains Model, identify where you and your firm are on the model. What do you need to stop, start, change or continue in order to move your firm to the next phase of growth?
- Do a Stakeholder Analysis for your firm. Who are the real influencers you need on side in order to grow your practice?

3

How to create a shared Growth Vision and Growth Plan

Topics covered in this chapter:

- How to create a Growth Vision
- How to create the 3-year Growth Plan for your firm
- How to get your staff engaged and supportive

By buying this book you have stated your intention to grow a one million pound practice. It's one thing to know you want your practice to grow significantly, it's another thing entirely to make the growth happen in an easy, orderly and planned way. As always with these things, the devil is in the detail. Your staff, if they are to willingly support you to make the changes, will need the detail about what the future looks like. This chapter takes you through step-by-step to create an exciting Growth Vision and 3-year Growth Plan that staff want to achieve.

If you are reading this book as part of a multi-partner practice, you will need to get your other partners fully committed to your Growth Vision. If you cannot gain that commitment, there is no point continuing in the book. To be blunt, imagine three admirals standing on a ship's bridge, and the general direction is to take the ship to the Greek islands, just as they have done for many years. Suddenly one announces that the Caribbean is a better place to go. Unless the other two actively commit to the changed destination, you know the ship will steer into the Mediterranean.

How to create a Growth Vision

Without a doubt, most of you reading this book will be motivated to grow a one million pound practice to enjoy the personal financial benefits. However, that outcome is personal and it will never motivate Stakeholders to help you. So, by all means talk about that vision at home, however for the workplace the vision is only ever about growing the business.

Do you have a constant quest to improve how your practice runs? This constant quest will separate your firm from the rest of the pack.

Case study: Greg

Greg worked in a firm which had a management buyout. The two new owners of the practice presented to the staff their vision to grow a one million pound practice. This centred fairly heavily on the new owner's aspirations for their future lifestyle, including buying sports cars to race. Despite their enthusiasm, neither the staff nor the clients could get motivated by what was clearly an outcome quite remote from the day-to-day business.

You will have personal reasons for wanting to achieve the magic million pounds level. It might be lifestyle, or a retirement nest egg, the challenge or just ego. But be clear that your *personal reasons are private* and strongly motivating for you alone. However the focus of this book is to grow your practice and have your staff actively helping you with that growth.

Now that you have clarity on your personal agenda, it's time to park it. The rest of this chapter and book is focused on helping you create for your practice a Growth Vision.

Your Growth Vision can be internally or externally focused. Or a mixture of both. But the best Growth Visions encompass the *What's in It for Your Stakeholders* – your staff and clients. Here are some examples of Growth Visions:

We are going to grow the practice in a profitable and sustainable way, so that we reach, within 10 years, a turnover of one million pounds at a net profitability level of 40%, servicing 300 clients with 20 members of staff. ***[INTERNALLY FOCUSED]***

Within 5 years our firm will grow to be a one million pound practice and the leading local independent accountancy firm, but known nationally for its innovative practices and ways in which we wow our clients. ***[EXTERNALLY FOCUSED]***

Delivering excellence in client service will be the cornerstone of how we grow within 5 years to be a 3-office one million pound practice. ***[EXTERNALLY FOCUSED]***

A compelling Growth Vision has to be drawn up with your staff and clients' needs in mind. After all, you won't be able to achieve your vision without the active help and support of them all. The more externally focused your vision, the more compelling it will be to others around you.

Nothing ever good came from staying in your comfort zone.

Key ingredients of a compelling Growth Vision

Clear

The best visions are succinct and unambiguous to your Stakeholders. You and your Stakeholders should be able to easily visualise what the future state looks like. If you can't take a picture or video clip of the future state, then you probably need to go back to the drawing board.

Time bound

The most compelling visions have a timeline attached to them, otherwise they are just dreams. Timelines create a sense of urgency and momentum.

Measurable

Your Growth Vision needs to have indicators which measure progress. This is an important motivator for staff.

Boundaries

As part of the Growth Vision it is important to clarify what is exactly in scope for the firm and what is out of scope. If you fail to identify these boundaries then you may find that your staff start working on the wrong things. After all, when firms start chasing *any* growth, this is often when problems happen in a firm.

Case study: Paul's Growth Story

I'd tinkered with the idea of growing my practice in the past. In fact, I'd even hired a business coach to take me through a growth accelerator programme. If I'm honest, there wasn't any book or programme about growing your accountancy firm that I hadn't read or attended. In the end, my firm's growth had plateaued at £350k turnover. On reflection, I knew what had to be done but I let my staff influence too many of my critical decisions. I was engaging my people, but too much so.

Family has always been very important to me. My wife, son and daughter all work in the practice. I realised that I wanted to be in a position in ten years to handover or sell my practice. That would give my wife, children and grandchildren a stable financial future. My Growth Vision is firstly about building a one million pound practice with a 40+% net profit margin, with me working significantly less than the 50–80 hours a week I do now. As part of this Growth Vision, I don't want to be responsible for the day-to-day running of the practice. I don't even want to do the normal role of an accountant. I want to play to my strengths and my 30+ years of being a business owner, and use my business coaching skills to work with my clients to help them grow their business. I want to have the time to indulge with my wife our passion for travelling. Our practice has always been a family-orientated rural Bodmin-based practice. I don't see that changing. And, I know our staff value the fact that we look after them.

Case study: Sian's Growth Story

After my children were born I didn't want to ditch my career, but knew I couldn't work the hours I used to in my industry role. This was why I started up my own practice Inform Accounting. I don't see myself being an accountancy firm owner forever. I see my firm as a means to an end. My firm has already been built in a way which allows me to only work school hours and take most of the school holidays off with the family. My Growth Vision entails me growing the firm so I can maximise its capital value. In other words as it grows, it will be able to run without me.

The best way to make sure that everyone shares in the Growth Vision to become a one million pound practice is to spend time – and more time than most people think is needed – on fleshing out the details of what the future state actually looks and feels like. Not everyone in your current firm will want the firm to grow. And that's to be expected, especially among the longer-serving staff.

📖 Growth Vision Exercise

How to create a 3-year Growth Plan for your firm

You have a Growth Vision to become a one million pound practice. Great. It's now time to convert the intention into a plan to make this happen. The reason why you use a 3-year timescale is not because everyone should be able to grow a one million pound practice in 3 years. It's because the pace of change is so fast, trying to project more than 3 years ahead is a waste of time.

Create the 3-year Growth Plan by following these steps:

Step 1: Begin with the Growth Vision you have created in the Workbook exercise.

Step 2: With your senior people, brainstorm fertile areas to work on, which will take the practice forward to achieve the Growth Vision. The results of the self-assessment in this book will form the basis of many of the areas that your firm will need to work upon. They should include getting increased efficiencies from current methods, work that could be outsourced, old methods which can be ceased altogether, expansion of existing work to new clients, and basically anything which will contribute to growth. When you are doing this work, reference any existing business plans you have for the practice. As you build your Growth Plan these plans will become obsolete and superseded.

For example, when Ewan put together his Growth Vision he identified the following areas that the firm needed to work on:

- *Decreasing the firm's salaries as a percentage of turnover from 43% to 30% by increasing the firm's turnover and improving the efficiency of the firm's Deliver It processes. (See Chapter 9)*
- *Helping his son, Joe, start to win his own portfolio of clients.*
- *Releasing himself from planning the workflow for the firm*
- *Increasing the firm's average client fee by getting more clients to take advisory services*

Step 3: After you have brainstormed as a group, identify core Themes for your Growth Plan. These Growth Plan Themes will be broad in nature, but there should be general consensus that these Themes will be the best to work on and will be the quickest and most effective way of sustainably and profitably growing your practice. These Themes could include items such as growing your existing client accounts, upskilling your people so your firm can offer more than compliance type services to clients, increasing the profitability of the firm, reducing the employee turnover rate and so on.

Ewan took the areas for improvement and identified 3 core Themes for his firm's Growth Plan

- *Increase the firm's efficiency*
- *Develop staff members to step up*
- *Sell advisory services to existing clients*

Step 4: Break each Theme down into Growth Actions so that there is a degree of specificity and no ambiguity.

Some of Ewan's Growth Actions to sell advisory services to existing clients consisted of:

- *Running a monthly client seminar to help them buy into business coaching from the firm.*
- *Doing a Client Portfolio Analysis of existing clients to see who would be likely to want or need advisory services from the firm.*
- *Researching what elements were needed in the firm's business coaching package*

Step 5: Look at your KPIs, and identify the Numbers Which Matter. These are the KPIs which if your practice really focused on achieving them, will demonstrate the progress of your practice against its Growth Plan. Collate all the information for how your practice is performing right now for the Numbers Which Matter. Arrange them into logical business areas, in a table form.

Ewan identified the following Numbers Which Matter for his firm to see how well they were progressing at selling advisory services to existing clients:

- *% of existing clients taking advisory services from the firm*

- *monthly revenue for advisory services*
- *number of attendees at monthly client seminar*
- *number of Leads generated from the monthly client seminar*

Step 6: Set out the target of each of the Numbers Which Matter, year by year, for the 3-year term of the Growth Plan. At this point, intelligent estimates will be fine.

	Now	Year 1	Year 2	Year 3
% of existing clients taking advisory services from the firm	7%	20%	30%	40%
Monthly revenue for advisory services	£2,540	£10,000	£25,000	£40,000
Number of attendees at monthly client seminar	0	10 per seminar	15 per seminar	15 per seminar
Number of Leads generated from the monthly client seminar	0	3 per seminar	5 per seminar	7 per seminar

Table 3.0: Extract from Ewan's table of Numbers Which Matter

Step 7: Cross-check that the reaching of all targets will result in the achievement of the 3-year Growth Plan. If not, return to the second step.

Of course, the detail of your Growth Actions still needs to be fleshed out, as follows:

Step 8: It is quite likely that a further breakdown into Growth Tasks will be necessary. You need clarity around the What, How, Who and When, plus how these will impact the Numbers Which Matter. Again, table format is suggested.

Ewan took his Growth Actions to sell more advisory services and broke these down into smaller Growth Tasks. He identified who in his firm was responsible for the Growth Tasks.

What	How	Who	When	N-W-M
Run a monthly client seminar to sell business coaching	Plan dates for seminar in firm calendar	PM	Jan	No. of attendees at monthly client seminar
	Prepare list of clients to invite to each monthly seminar	PM	Jan	No. of leads generated from the monthly client seminar
	Order catering for each seminar	RM	Week before event	
	Practice presentation for seminar	AM	Week before event	No. of leads generated from the monthly client seminar

Table 3.1: Extract from Ewan's Growth Actions.

Step 9: Obviously there needs to be consideration to balance the magnitude of each Growth Task, against the timeframe required, and then identify what further resources are necessary: people, special training, money.

At this point, you have a full work list for the next three years. This will be overwhelming to you and your staff. Here is a way to give structure to them, and also create a sense of urgency.

Step 10: Identify a One Big Focus for the Quarter, where you nominate a Theme for that Quarter. This Theme is one of the Themes you identified as part of the process to build your 3-year Growth Plan.

After Ewan put together his 3-year Growth Plan he decided the first Theme to work on for the firm as a One Big Focus was to sell advisory services to existing clients.

Step 11: Your people then choose Growth Tasks which collectively will address that Theme, so the practice sees a determined focus on that topic. Having a One Big Focus stops your practice suffering from initiative overload.

Ewan involved his team in brainstorming how each person within the firm could contribute to achieving the One Big Focus. Here are a few of the Growth Tasks his team agreed to do as a result of the brainstorm. One of his team agreed to look at their client list to see if they could run some sector specific client seminars. The client managers agreed to outsource more Year End Accounts work to free them up to call each of their clients quarterly to find out how things were going.

Finally, the Growth Tasks can create a flurry of activity in the practice, which is exciting, but you do need to have indicators set so that progress through real results can be monitored:

Step 11: Each Growth Task needs one or more Numbers Which Matter, and it is recommended that each responsible person does this in collaboration with you. The Numbers Which Matter need to be easy to measure, and be able to represent progress for their Growth Task.

To keep track of progress against the Growth Tasks, Ewan identified a Numbers Which Matter for each Growth Task. His Numbers Which Matter included:

- *Number of clients called each quarter by account manager*
- *Attendance at each monthly client seminar*

Step 12: Numbers Which Matter are reported weekly in a visual form, such as a 'dashboard'. Of particular importance is that progress is easy to see. For example, shown in a colour-coded form. Green means this Growth Task is on track for completion; Amber means that progress has dropped a bit low and so an intervention by a team member is required. Red indicates that the completion date is not going to be met, which of course means that major corrective action is needed, which will involve you the owner of the firm.

The type of 3-year Growth Plan being developed by you will stimulate change and momentum for growth in your practice. Your role is to keep that momentum going, even during busy periods for the firm. Your day job now includes monitoring the progress of the firm against its Growth Tasks. As a result, you will need to plan time into your diary to attend meetings where people are reporting their Numbers Which Matter. These are called Rhythm Meetings, since they tick over with regularity. The agendas are basically the same, and while the firm is progressing well with its Growth Actions, and the indicators are Green, the meetings are short.

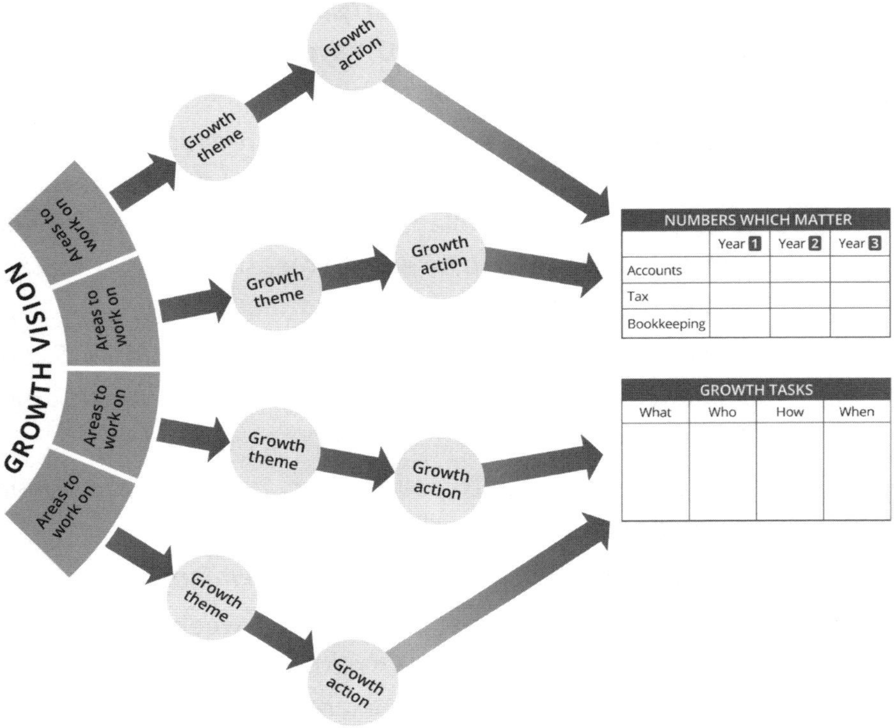

Diagram 3.2: 3-year Growth Plan

Rhythm Meeting Agenda

The purpose of a Rhythm Meeting is always to check progress against the firm's Growth Actions. Rhythm Meetings are short and focused. They may be extended if Reds are being reported.

The typical agenda for a Rhythm Meeting:

- Celebrate any key achievements
- List of actions which are Green and, therefore, no need to discuss.
- List of actions which are Amber and agree quick inter ventions to get these back on track

- List of actions which are Red which will result in deep discussion and identification of corrective actions required. You will have involvement here and you will need to add follow-through into your diary.

Sequence of Rhythm Meetings

The reporting of progress and the taking of corrective action (when required) is essential if you are going to achieve your 3-year Growth Plan. The monthly and weekly rhythm of meetings does that. There will also be less frequent meetings which aim to set things up for the subsequent Quarter. This is the overall suite of meetings:

Rhythm Meeting Title	Meeting Focus	Who	Length
Annual Leadership	Review 3-year Growth Plan and set One Big Focus for the coming quarter	Leadership Team	4–8 hours
Annual Staff	Identify and allocate Growth Tasks to achieve the One Big Focus.	Leadership Team plus all staff	4–8 hours
Quarterly Leadership	Review progress against Growth Plan and set the next One Big Focus	Leadership Team	2–4 hours
Quarterly Staff	Identify and allocate Growth Tasks to achieve the One Big Focus.	Leadership Team plus all staff	2–4 hours
Monthly Leadership	Review progress on One Big Focus	Leadership Team	1–2 hours
Weekly Team	Review progress on Growth Tasks	Team members and managers (as appropriate)	1 hour
Daily Operational Huddle	Daily work issues	Discrete operational teams	10 minutes

Table 3.3: Sequence of Rhythm Meetings

📖 3-year Growth Plan

How to get your staff engaged and supportive

Everyone has a different reaction to change. Some people love it and will actively try and bring about change. Other people will spend a huge amount of energy avoiding change to try and preserve the status quo. People's reactions can be influenced by how they are feeling that day, how the change impacts them and how they normally react to change. As mentioned in the previous chapter, your staff will need the opportunity to grieve for how things were, before they can move onto embrace the exciting future you have planned for the firm. Although everyone reacts differently to change, most people go through something called the Emotional Cycle of Change, as identified by Elizabeth Kübler-Ross. Your role with your staff, in order to get them engaged and supportive, is to help them through their own Emotional Cycle of Change.

People going through change typically pass through five recognisable stages and these stages are not always undertaken in a linear fashion. Whilst the stages cannot be avoided, it is not untypical for people to suppress their true feelings when they go through change. This suppression leads to anxiety, and in turn stress. Your role is to help your staff (and clients) through the cycle.

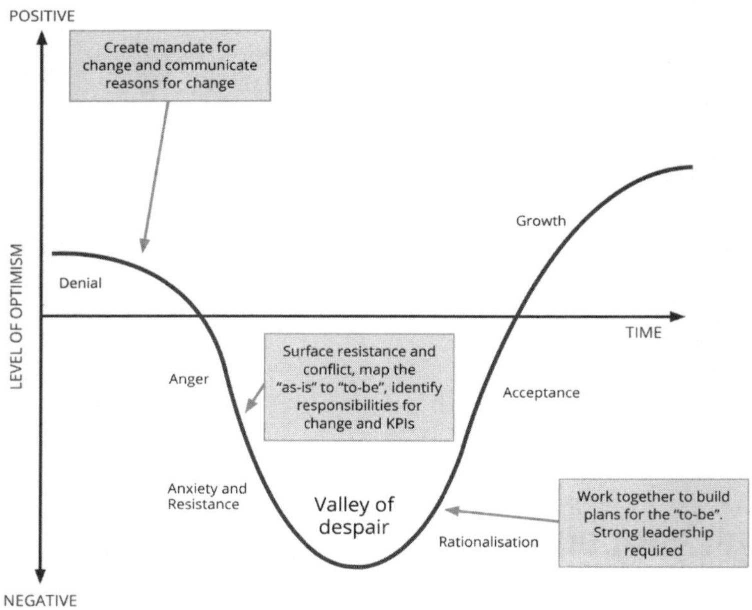

Diagram 3.4: Emotional Cycle of Change

Denial

In this stage people don't yet, or don't want to, realise the full impact, whether positive or negative, the change will have on them. To help people in this stage you need to regularly communicate to them. People need to hear time and time again, what the actual change is and the effects it may have. It is important that you communicate as much as you can tell at this stage. If you don't communicate, people will *fill in the blanks* for themselves and then you've lost control.

Anger

When people fully get what is going to happen to them, and if this perceived to be negative, it is not unusual for them to get angry. Whilst it is tempting to want to cover up or suppress this anger from surfacing, it is important to let people vent their feelings. When anger is allowed to surface and be appropriately handled, it leads onto the next stage.

Rationalisation

When denial and anger have passed, people normally want to make sense of what is happening to them. They will try and make what is happening to them make sense with their own perspective on the situation and take on life. This rationalisation will make perfect sense to the individual but not necessarily anyone else.

Acceptance

This stage may occur very quickly. People who have made it to this stage will start thinking about the future state. This is a good time to work with people to identify new ways of working and behaviours needed for the future.

Advance

In this stage people will be positive about the future state. It is only when people have transitioned into the growth phase can you expect them to be fully supportive and engaged with your plans.

Why do some people resist change?

Despite what you may tell your staff often they will see your plan to grow the firm as a threat. As a result, they will try and preserve and protect what they see is important to them. However, because we are often dealing with the murky and non-rational sub-conscious mind, logic often goes out of the window. You may tell your team until you are blue in the face that, for example, the new piece of technology will make their working lives better in the long term, but their interpretation of a situation will always sway them regardless of what the facts actually are. Their understanding and thoughts on the matter will normally always be incomplete or inaccurate. After all, they don't have all the specifics in the way that you have. Their own explanation and 'story of what is going on' will always be taken more seriously than the realities of the situation.

How to 'unstick' your staff who are resisting your Growth Plans

There comes a time when you realise that despite all your verbal or written logical and well-reasoned arguments, the message is not hitting home. Your staff are just not buying into your Growth Vision for the firm. In this situation, you have probably got a really stuck core of people. Further verbal or written persuasion is not going to work. In fact, it will probably make them even more entrenched as they start to see your influencing tactics as more of a threat, nagging or you being manipulative.

With an entrenched core it can be tempting to give up on your plans to grow. Instead of giving up, you need to try some alternative routes to influencing this stuck core.

A good way of helping unstick people is to use stories to move people forward. A well-told story can get the most entrenched and cynical accountant to put aside their cynicism. The reason that well-told stories work is that people get involved in the story and stop playing the critic.

The best influential stories will have a beginning, middle and end. They will be vivid and fire up people's emotions and imagination. Ideally your staff should identify with the main character or situation and realise that what is happening, could happen to them. Make sure that your stories are infused with optimism. That is, show how there is a way to avoid the horrible or negative stuff happening to them.

Your staff leaving may be the best thing that could happen to you

When the staff who are resisting your 3-year Growth Plan leave, it can often give the firm that much needed shot in the arm to get on and make stuff happen with fresh recruits. It can be exhausting dealing with staff who just don't or won't accept that the practice needs to change or grow.

Case study: Guy's Growth Story

I'd come back from the mastermind group with the rest of my co-authors, excited and buzzing about the future. In my head, it seemed like a really sensible low risk way of progressing the practice. I – and my team – just needed to knuckle down and make it happen. The next day I just couldn't wait to take them through the plans I had in my head. All was going so well I thought … Until my Number 2, you know the member of staff who you delegate to the most, resigned. She decided to move to another local practice which seemed like a safer, less risky option.

I met with her and did some deep reflection, asking her what I could have done to keep her on side. She said that my Growth Plans seemed like very risky, and it would have made all the difference if she could have seen some concrete ways of how the firm was going to get there. Or how other similar firms had got there. That hit hard, because I *did* have all of that information, I just failed to see that my people needed it. Communication was where I really fell down. I then realised I needed to spend far more time in the future talking to my staff about my Growth Vision and Growth Plans.

Summary

You need to draw up a Growth Vision and share it with your Stakeholders, particularly your staff. Then create your 3-year Growth Plan, the Growth Actions and your Growth Tasks. Monitoring of progress is essential if you want to achieve your Growth Vision.

Action points

- Create a Growth Vision for your practice.
- Think about a time when you went through a period of change which was forced on you by external circumstances. How did your mood and emotions change over time? What personally helped you get through the period of change?

- Use the results of the previous chapter's exercise to identify your Stakeholders, to decide on what you need to do to get the Stakeholders to champion and support your Growth Vision to become a one million pound practice.
- With the senior people in your practice create a 3-year Growth Plan for your practice. Identify the core Themes for the Growth Plan and expand each Theme into Growth Actions. Then identify your Numbers Which Matter.
- Identify a One Big Focus for the next Quarter in your business. Set up a meeting with all your staff where you talk them through the reasons for the One Big Focus. Split your staff up into their normal teams to identify Growth Tasks in order to achieve the One Big Focus.
- Create a Numbers Which Matter dashboard which your staff update and report on weekly.
- Implement the Rhythm Meetings in your firm to review progress against the One Big Focus and the firm's 3-year Growth Plan.

PART II

Building a firm foundation for growth

Just as you are advised to not build a house on a foundation of sand, it's the same with your practice. It is so much easier to grow a practice when it is built on a firm foundation. That means in reality:

- The practice is profitable; i.e. net profits are over 40%
- There is enough cash in the bank to pay the suppliers and wages for at least 3 months
- The right people are doing the right things
- The firm's Leadership Team are making decisions which are right for the short and long term – particularly when it comes to resourcing

- The practice has efficient internal processes which are scalable
- The practice has invested in cloud-based technology, both internally and for clients

All too often accountancy firm owners don't build a firm foundation and move straight into scaling their practice. They then wonder why scaling their practice is so tough! Your problems with your firm don't go away when you scale up. They just magnify or multiply the bigger you get. It's like trying to drive a car with the handbrake on. Yes, you can move forward, but it's hard work. This part of the book looks at how to build a firm foundation:

- How to get the right amount of resources; e.g. cash, time and people in your practice
- How to avoid one of the major brakes on growth, the dreaded Work In/Work On Trap
- How to deliver higher yield services such as advisory
- How to maximise the performance of your firm, in order to provide a firm foundation for growth.

4

How to avoid the Work In/Work On Trap

Topics covered in the chapter:

- What is the Work In/Work On Trap?
- How to stop yourself falling into the Work In/Work On Trap
- Different ways to fund your growth

When firms hit the Transition Brick Wall, they often enter a painful part of their journey, where their growth is brought to a shuddering halt by the Work In/Work On Trap. In this chapter, we analyse why this trap occurs, what this trap is and how you can get you and your firm out of the trap in order to get you through the Transition Brick Wall.

The Work In/Work On Trap: What is it?

The simplest definition of the trap is where you, the firm owner, gets sucked back into working *in* the business rather than working *on* the business. Going back to the Red/Black/Blue model, (see Chapter 1) this is where Red and Black activities severely limit your time and attention in order to focus on Blue activities, i.e. the type of activities which will help you grow your firm in the long term. The net result of this is that your practice growth gets stuck. You either get yourself out of the Work In/Work On Trap or you decide to opt for Controlled Decline rather than New Horizons. (As per the Excedia Growing Pains Model) You will know if your practice is in this trap because it will be characterised by a period of intense frustration; often punctuated by minor crises which blow up to become major crises. It will feel as if for every step forward you then have to take three steps back. The good news is that if you avoid the trap you probably limit the pain and frustration which is associated with the Transition Brick Wall.

The problem with being a very small firm, i.e. under £500k turnover, is just when you think you have exited the Transition Brick Wall, and are full steam ahead to the merry land of fast growth, something unexpected will happen which will throw you off course. Before you know it, you'll be back in the Work In/Work On Trap.

Case study: Seema

Seema had grown her practice to £200k. She had two members of staff and the practice was growing by about £8k a month. All was going very well. However, as the firm got to £270k, Seema found that her time was being taken up almost solely with servicing the firm's client work. Reviewing 80 sets of Year End Accounts, creating 20 sets of monthly management accounts and answering the clients' ad hoc queries left no time for Seema to focus on Blue type activities.

Her two members of staff were struggling to complete all the clients' bookkeeping and Year End Accounts work AND get the 2-4 monthly new clients onboarded on time. It all came to a head one day, when a juicy new client worth over £10k a year to the practice decided not to join the practice due to the time to properly onboard them. When Seema sat down with her members of staff to find out what was the problem she also realised the practice had a large backlog of Year End Accounts to process. She could see that her two members of staff were working really hard, but were just overloaded. With the firm heading towards a seasonal peak in workload, something had to change. Seema realised that if she was going to stop the current crisis from reoccurring and nip any impending problems in the bud, she was going to have to do things differently. She needed to get out of the Work In/Work on Trap. The first thing Seema did was take the tough decision to exit 10 poor quality clients. These were clients – if she was honest – that they were losing money on. This gave Seema some breathing space and time to do Blue-type activities. Seema set about automating their new client onboarding process to free up capacity in her team. She was determined they were never going to lose a client again due to poor new client onboarding!

Unfortunately, two months later her client administrator dropped a bombshell and handed in her resignation. Even though Seema found a replacement fairly quickly, she was still without a client administrator for 4 weeks. Seema and her team member had to take over her client administrator's roles and responsibilities. Once again, Seema had no time for Blue-type activities and so was back in the Work in/Work On Trap. Until their new client administrator was up-to-speed, Seema had to put a stop to winning any new clients. They just didn't have the capacity as a firm to deal with the work on their desks, let alone add in more clients to the firm.

Seema learnt from these experiences and realised if she was going to protect her time to do Blue-type activities, she needed more resource in their practice. Seema decided not to go down the outsourcing route. Instead she chose to implement a drastic 25% increase in fees. Yes, she lost 5% of her clients. But in the process, she freed up enough of her time and built her cash reserves so she could afford to hire in two more members of staff. With her two new members of staff contributing well to the practice she was finally able to escape the Work In/Work On Trap.

Why does it take so long for small growing accountancy firms to scale up?

If you think about how a small accountancy practice scales it normally starts with one person, the founder, being the firm. They do everything for this firm; marketing, client work, requesting information from clients etc. Of course, with an accountancy practice it's very difficult to scale beyond an annual turnover of £60k without adding in extra resource (unless you are an interim contractor or specialist tax advisor). As the firm grows the firm owner is having to take difficult decisions about what responsibilities and tasks they are *not* going to do and either delegate, outsource, do differently or ditch these tasks or responsibilities. Couple that with the fact that small accountancy firm owners are not normally held up as role models of delegation, and you can see why it's so easy for a firm to fall into the Work In/Work On Trap. See Table 4.0 for how the responsibilities of a firm owner will change as they grow from being a 1-person firm to a 3-person firm.

Given the fact that a practice needs to be pretty substantial, i.e. over £500k, before the owner can truly delegate all their client responsibilities, the owner is always going to make a conscious choice about how chargeable they can be, i.e. how much of the time will they allocate to Black-type activities not Blue-type activities (see Chapter 1 for more about the Red/Black/Blue Model). More so in the early days of the practice, but the more chargeable they are, typically, the more profitable the practice is. However, the more chargeable they are, the less time they can allocate to growing their practice.

It's not just about how much time the owner is spending being chargeable in the business. Very often a small growing firm is just being run too leanly. This could be that the firm is running at over-capacity or running low on cash, or normally both. When a firm is

1 Person Firm	2 Person Firm		3 Person Firm		
Firm Owner	Firm Owner	Client Administrator	Firm Owner	Client Administrator	Junior member of staff
Responsibilities	Responsibilities	Responsibilities	Responsibilities	Responsibilities	Year end accounts prep
Strategy	Strategy	Chasing clients for records	Strategy	Chasing clients for records	Bookkeeping
Sales and marketing	Sales and marketing	Payroll	Sales and marketing	Payroll	VAT returns
Year End Accounts prep and review	Year End Accounts prep and review	Filing clients' returns'	Year End Accounts review	Filing clients' returns'	Personal tax returns
Tax returns (VAT, Corporation Tax, Personal Tax)	Tax returns (VAT, Corporation Tax, Personal Tax)	Diary Management	Corporation Tax Returns	Diary Management	-
Tax Planning	Tax Planning	-	Tax Planning	-	-
Chasing clients for records	Planning the workflow	-	Planning the workflow	-	-
Planning the workflow	Bookkeeping	-	Management Accounts	-	-
Bookkeeping	Management Accounts	-	-	-	-
Management Accounts	-	-	-	-	-
Filing clients' returns'	-	-	-	-	-
Payroll	-	-	-	-	-
Diary Management	-	-	-	-	-

Table 4.0: How the responsibilities of a firm owner changes as it grows into a 3-person firm

being run too leanly it doesn't have the resilience to navigate any bumps in the road. So, what should be minor dramas become major crises, and the owner finds themselves working long hours again and working *in* the business again. Then despite their best intentions, the growth of the practice stutters and stalls.

You advise your clients to seek funding to finance their business's growth. So why don't you take your own advice?

How to prevent your firm from falling into the Work In/Work On Trap.

If you are implementing your 3-year Growth Plan this will put you into a good position to avoid falling into the Work In/Work On Trap. With some well-made Growth Plans and some mindset changes it is possible to quickly get out of the Work In/Work On Trap.

Grow your cash reserves

Cash isn't the whole answer, but when you can pay for extra resources it does make it easier to avoid being sucked back into working *in* the business.

Here are methods you can use to increase your cash reserves:

- Put in place a price increase (See Chapter 5)
- Exit from unprofitable client accounts
- Take on external funding, e.g. bank loan or overdraft facility (see later in this chapter)

Whilst some of these options may seem unpalatable for you right now, many firms are not charging enough. This means they can easily and quickly increase their cash reserves by implementing a fee increase and charging new clients more. Every time we've helped a firm increase their fee levels for both new and existing clients they have been pleasantly surprised just how few clients they have lost. Very often it is the clients you *want* to lose that are the ones which will go if you implement a fee increase.

Case study: Sharon's Growth Story

I was well and truly in the Work In/Work On Trap. I knew I needed to find the time to pause and put together a decent 3-year Growth Plan. But there was always just another thing to do. And normally always something very urgent for a client. I just didn't have any time to do Blue-type activities. Looking back with the benefit of hindsight I was probably at rock bottom. My business and personal bank accounts were dangerously low and I was working a 70+ hour week. I sat down with my coach and poured my heart out to her. She gave me some tough love and together we put together a plan to start to free up more of my time so I could do a proper 3-year Growth Plan. Together we realised that if I put up my fees this would be a quick way to get some much-needed cash in the business. I could then use this extra cash to give me the breathing space to outsource some of my compliance work.

Our strategy for the fee increase was also to bring all of our clients in line with how we wanted to work. No more clients resisting coming onto our preferred accounting package or not paying monthly by direct debit. Within 12 months of instigating the fee increase, our cash flow had radically increased and our WIP reduced to virtually zero. No more waiting around for clients to bring in their records before we could get paid. Our gross profit increased by 28% and our net profit by 119%.

Putting our fees up was the first step in our growth to become a one million pound practice. The fee increase gave me the breathing space to put in place my 3-year Growth Plan. Not only that, I had the headspace to plan how I was going to spend my time and get the firm out of the Work In/Work On Trap.

Identify what responsibilities and tasks you can delegate or stop doing

The plants, or more accurately the daily watering of the plants, became the tipping point for Sharon. She realised she didn't need to water the plants, and could stop worrying about who was going to water the office plants, if she wasn't going to be in the office. After all, any one of her team could water the plants. And it wasn't just the plants. It was also keeping their client meeting room tidy and always set up for the next meeting. So, she added to her firm's Client Administrator role the front of house responsibilities for the practice. Of course, this included keeping the client meeting room tidy and watering the plants! It may not be the plants for you, but take a look at what are doing. Then decide on what can be delegated, done differently, delayed or ditched. (See Chapter 1 for tips on how to delegate effectively.) For example:

- What can be automated to remove any elements of manual entry?
- What can be automated to reduce the amount of chasing clients to get their records in?
- What client facing tasks can you delegate to others in your practice?
- What marketing, IT or HR-related activities, e.g. looking after your website, can you outsource?

Red/Black/Blue Model Exercise

Stop the crises

When firms are growing but under £500k in turnover, they often struggle with lots of mini and major crises. This is normally a sign that your firm is well and truly in the Work in/Work On Trap. These crises almost always blow up to be much bigger than they really need to be. As a result, you get pulled back into the business.

Crises happen for many reasons. Often these are due to poor forward planning, team members having slightly different ways of working, making mistakes or stuff keeps slipping through the cracks due to poor practice management procedures. To stop these regular crises, you need to systemise what you do and have one way of working. (See Chapter 10 for more about systemising your practice)

Using the Rhythm Meetings (see Chapter 3), in particular the daily Operational Huddle and the weekly Team Meeting, can help you stay in control and take the steps to stop a problem becoming a crisis. In addition, measuring the Numbers Which Matter and watching the Dashboard (see Chapter 3) your people can easily spot a trend occurring and head off a crisis before it becomes a crisis.

No more Mr (or Ms) Nice Guy

There is a reason Heather now spends pretty much all of her working time with accountants. They are genuinely nice people. (Give yourself a pat on the back if you are an accountant reading this!) However, this niceness combined with a desire to please, and a fear of difficult conversations, often means being too accommodating with poor performance from staff, and bending over backwards because of disorganised clients. If you are a UK-based accountant how many times have you worked far too many hours in November or January, because your clients have been disorganised with their record keeping? How many times have you had to stay late because a staff member has let you down or done a poor job? Keep being too accommodating to clients or allowing staff to get away with poor performance, and you find yourself being pulled back into the business again to get the work out the door.

Too many accountancy firm owners allow their staff to get away with mediocre performance at best for fear of rocking the boat. If you are serious about growing a one million pound practice you need staff around you who are going to help you get there. This means getting serious with your existing staff. Either coach them to develop the skills or performance you need, or counsel them out of the business.

Exit from your low fee, low recovery and needy clients.

As mentioned in Chapter 1, there is an easy way to quickly free up your time or capacity in your practice. Disengage from the clients who are unprofitable. You could even increase your cash reserves by selling these clients onto another firm for a fee.

Different ways to fund your growth

As mentioned earlier, most owners get pulled into the Work In/Work On Trap due to not enough having enough cash, time or people. One of the ways to get out of the Trap is to increase your cash reserves. To do this most accountants self-fund their growth, particularly in the early days of their practice. This could be by foregoing their own income from the practice or putting in their own capital to fund the firm's growth. Whilst there is nothing wrong per se about self-funding your growth, unless you have access to decent amounts of capital, it can make it harder to quickly scale or get the right resource in place. You would routinely expect your clients to access funding to fuel the growth of their business, so why not for your own practice? Firms will sometimes access funding to help plug a temporary gap in their working capital.

Common sources of funding for a firm, both for growth (and working capital)

Capital introduced by the owners or partners of the firm: Typically, this happens at the start-up of a firm or when a new partner is admitted to the partnership.

Bank loans: These are normally paid back over the long term and used to fund capital items (e.g. IT equipment, moving premises) and to ensure that there is sufficient working capital to keep the firm going.

Long-term overdrafts: Overdrafts are typically used to smooth cash flow fluctuations in the business, such as unpaid bills. The interest charged on a long-term overdraft is normally significantly higher than a bank loan.

Retained profits: Only part of the firm profits is paid to the owners of the firm. The remaining profits are retained and used to meet the costs of maintaining and growing the firm.

Invoice factoring: This is where a factoring company will give you instantly, normally, 80% of the value of your invoice, minus any financing fee. It is typically used for long-term project work where you can only bill on completion of the project.

Alternative financing: There are many different types of financing routes now available to accountancy practices. These include online lenders such as IWOCA, who specialise in short-term working capital loans. IWOCA will give you access to a line of credit in minutes. Or you could crowdfund your funding requirements, in return for a slice of equity, via a crowdfunding investors site such as Crowdcube.

As with any investment decision it is always wise to take independent advice before entering into an agreement with a lender or selling any equity in your firm.

Summary

The Work In/Work On Trap is a common growing pain experienced by small accountancy practices at the Transition Brick Wall. It is where the owner is prevented from spending time on growing the business. Normally because they are spending too much time, whether temporarily or permanently, on Red or Black-type activities.

To avoid the trap:

- Increase your firm's cash reserves and consider accessing external funding.
- Free up your time and firm capacity by exiting your unprofitable clients.
- Use the Rhythm Meetings to keep the focus on both the day job AND your 3-year Growth Plan.
- Measure and monitor your Numbers Which Matter and take prompt and corrective action to stop a problem becoming a full-blown crisis.
- Don't put up with poor performance from your staff. Either coach them to perform, at the level you need, or help them to gracefully exit.
- If clients are late with their information, build in a fee penalty or put their work to the back of the queue.

Action Points

- Draw up a possible future structure chart for your one million pound practice. Then draw up the key stages your firm structure will go through to get there. At each stage work out what your responsibilities will be. Check back to your personal agenda and Growth Vision; does this all align? Then write down what responsibilities you will allocate to others and at what stage of your practice growth this will happen.
- Do a cash flow forecast for your practice. Ask yourself whether you have enough cash to pay your ongoing bills but also fund your 3-year Growth Plan. If the answer is no, consider ways in which you can increase your cash reserves.
- Do a fee benchmarking exercise with other accountancy firm owners. If your fees are low compared to your peers, prioritise a fee increase with your clients.
- Implement the Rhythm Meetings, particular the daily Operational Huddles and the weekly Team Meeting. Use these meetings to keep an eye on the Numbers Which Matter Dashboard to stop any problems developing into a crisis.
- Do the Red/Black/Blue Model exercise in the workbook. To help you free up your time identify which of your responsibilities could be done differently, ditched, delayed or delegated.
- Investigate outsourcing some of your responsibilities or the firm's functions, e.g. marketing, year-end accounts to free up your time. Talk to other firm owners who have outsourced some of their responsibilities. What did they learn? What can you put in place to avoid their mistakes?

5

How to increase your firm's cash flow and profitability

Topics covered in the chapter:

- How to do a Client Portfolio Analysis to improve your firm's profitability
- How to exit from clients you no longer want to service
- How to implement a fee increase
- How to move to monthly billing via Direct Debit and systemise your billing for ad hoc pieces of work

It seems a little strange to be writing a chapter in a book for accountants about how to increase cash flow and profitability. If you are reading this chapter and can answer yes to the next 3 statements then feel free to skip reading this chapter:

- Our net profitability after tax is over 40%
- We bill our clients by Direct Debit monthly and our WIP is practically zero
- We have enough cash in the bank to fund the next 3 months of growth and pay all our bills, including wages

As you may have already guessed, this chapter will show how other accountants have got their practice on a firm financial footing in order to grow.

How to do a Client Portfolio Analysis to improve your firm's profitability

A Client Portfolio Analysis is where you look at exactly what each client has spent with you year by year for the last 5 years. The best way to do this is produce a spreadsheet with this data on. (See Diagram 5.0)

At the Accountants Millionaires Club website, http://www.accountantsmillionaire.club there is a free template to help you do a Client Portfolio Analysis.

	Sector	Structure of business	Lifecycle	Size	Services	Relationship Lead	Location	Potential to refer	Source
Client A	Creative	Partnership	Mature	Medium	"Done for you" + Bookkeeping	Simon	North London	High	Client G
Client B	Charity	Charity	Mature	Small	Value	Kiran	North London	Low	Bank A
Client C	Creative	Ltd	Mature	Medium	"Done for you" + Bookkeeping	Simon	North London	Medium	Client G
Client D	Contractor	Sole Trader	Mature	Small	Personal Tax Return	Simon	North London	Low	Friend
Client E	Creative	Ltd	Mature	Medium	"Done for you" + Bookkeeping	Simon	North London	High	Client G
Client F	IT	Ltd	Growth	Medium	"Done for you" + Bookkeeping + Management accounts	Kiran	West London	High	Bank A

Diagram 5.0: Example Client Portfolio Analysis

Step 1: Produce a spreadsheet of all your clients and what they have spent with you by year for the last 5 years.

Step 2: Identify the different types of clients, e.g. by sector, structure of business, stage of business lifecycle, source of business etc. See Table 5.1 for ideas of ways you could segment your data.

Step 3: Identify which Client takes which service from the firm and record this on your spreadsheet.

Step 4: If not done already, identify on the spreadsheet who is the Relationship Lead for each Client.

Segment	Examples
Sector	Food Retail (Baker, Grocer, Butcher), E-commerce only, Café/Restaurant, Service-based retail (hairdresser, dry cleaners, etc.), Product-based retail (book store, toy store, etc.)
Structure of business	Sole trader, Partnership, LLP, Ltd, Social Enterprise, Not for profit, Charity
Business lifecycle stage	Not trading yet, start up, growth, mature, decline, dormant
Size	Big, medium, small
Services they take from us	Year End Accounts, Tax returns, VAT, Bookkeeping, Companies House Filing, Management Accounts, Virtual Finance Director, Business Planning, Tax Planning
Relationship Lead	Simon, Heather, Kiran, Joy
Location	Flitwick, Ampthill, Maulden, Bedford, Luton, Milton Keynes, Northampton, Silsoe, Barton-le-Clay
Potential to refer us	High, medium, low
Source	Existing client referral, bank manager referral, referral, website, word-of-mouth

Table 5.1: Ways in which an accountancy firm who specialises in retail businesses could segment their data in a Client Portfolio Analysis

Step 5: Add to your spreadsheet, if you have the figures, the profitability for each Client per year.

Step 6: Identify a way of grading each Client which has meaning for you and your firm. Your grading will be closely aligned to your 3-year Growth Plan.

Grade each Client A to D where:

A Important Client either because they are strategically important, pay a high fee or regularly give us client referrals, or something else which is relevant to your 3-year Growth Plan

B Potential to become an important Client

C A small, but profitable Client who is unlikely to grow

D Unprofitable, tough to work with or poor at paying fees

Step 7: Interrogate your data. In particular, ask these questions of the data:

- How much do you earn from your top Clients on average per year?
- How much are your repeat, loyal Clients worth to you in total?
- Are there any trends for the most profitable Clients, biggest Clients or least profitable Clients?
- Which Clients are unprofitable or barely profitable?
- Which Clients could probably take on more services from us?

Case study: Paul's Growth Story

When I looked at my Management Accounts I could see that something wasn't quite adding up. Our turnover was healthy, but our profitability was very poor. Something wasn't right! My team were all complaining that they were very busy, but on my numbers, I could see that we should have capacity to service another £50-100k without a problem. So, I reinstated timesheets in our practice to see how the team was spending their Clients and on what Clients. Our timesheet records were only used internally, not to bill from.

After 3 months I decided to do a Client Portfolio Analysis and looked at our timesheets. When I looked at our Bookkeeping Clients I could see that we had a large section of Clients where our workload had grown substantially, but our fees had stayed static. In one instant, we were losing over £10k on just one Client's bookkeeping work. Yes, it took time to do the Client Portfolio Analysis, but the level of insight I got – particularly on Clients where we were losing money – was amazing. Not only did it flag up where fees needed to go up for clients, but also that there was a process or systems problem in the Bookkeeping team. We should have picked up the unprofitable clients much earlier than we did. But as they say, hindsight is a wonderful thing.

I then allocated to my Head of Bookkeeping a Growth Task to put together a plan to increase the Bookkeeping fees for our unprofitable Bookkeeping Clients, but also sort out our internal processes to increase our efficiency at processing Bookkeeping work. Within 3 months our Bookkeeping function was profitable again.

Step 8: Put together an action plan to rectify the problems you have identified or exploit the opportunities you have identified.

📖 Client Portfolio Analysis Exercise

The results of your Client Portfolio Analysis must form the basis of a One Big Focus for your firm. For example, if you identified in your Client Portfolio Analysis that a large proportion of your Clients were not profitable enough, your One Big Focus for the next quarter would be to make these Clients more profitable. This could be via selectively disengaging from some of the Clients, putting in place a fee increase or operational improvements.

Case study: Kiran

When Kiran did a Client Portfolio Analysis for his firm he discovered that 50% of his firm were creatives, e.g. marketing agencies, website designers, and 25% were professional service firms. The remaining 25% were a hotchpotch of local businesses and sole traders, e.g. trades people, small cafes and retailers, contractors. Kiran calculated that these local businesses and sole traders probably took up 60% of the capacity of the firm. Most of these clients were only just breaking even.

Kiran took the decision to focus his firm's efforts on providing a highly tailored service for his creative businesses. His One Big Focus for the quarter was to move his firm to be a specialist in creative businesses and professional services. He sold off his non-creative or non-professional services clients to a local accountant for a 30% cut of the first year's fees. With his team, they identified new specialist services they could offer to their creative businesses. By selling on 25% of his firm's client portfolio, Kiran freed up his time to focus on his 3-year Growth Plans. His net profitability increased by 30%. A year after ditching 25% of his client portfolio, Kiran's practice had grown by 40%.

If your firm's wages + software subscription costs are more than 33% of your firm's turnover, you have a problem with inefficiency or your fees are too low.

How to exit from clients you no longer want to work with

Your Client Portfolio Analysis is likely to identify clients which no longer fit with your firm and its future strategy. This could be for many reasons; e.g.

- Their profitability is low.
- They refuse to work the way you want them to; e.g. adopt your firm's preferred accounting package or pay monthly via Direct Debit.
- They are the low fee and/or low recovery clients.
- They are potentially legacy clients who now no longer fit with the type of clients you want to be working with.

Many firms have a core of low fee, low recovery or needy clients who have been with them for a long time. They are often referred to as legacy clients. These are often the clients you took on when you were desperate for any client. Just as long as they had a pulse and a tax return! The benefits of exiting clients, whether legacy or not, are many:

- It frees up your firm's capacity to work with the more profitable clients that you and your staff love working with.
- It gives your firm capacity to win the type of clients you really want to work with.
- It gives the staff a huge morale boost. After all, no-one likes working with difficult clients.
- It can free up your time to work more *on* the business rather than *in* the business.

Use timesheets not for billing but to monitor capacity and analyse each job for profitability.

Case study: Sharon's Growth Story

From the very early days of my practice I've taken on charity clients. Many of my charity clients supported causes which were very important to me. After doing a Client Portfolio Analysis I realised that our small portfolio of charity clients didn't fit with how our firm now worked. Dare I say it, these Clients really needed the services of a traditional accountant.

It was a huge wrench for me to even consider disengaging with any of my Clients. I really do care passionately about all of them. Our strategy of wowing our clients is something that we as a firm really try to live and breathe. I asked my team about our charity clients. They confirmed to me that they were lovely people to work with, but they always took far longer to process than their fee merited. I hated doing it, but in the end, I took the hard decision to give these clients away to another local accountant who I knew would give them a more appropriate service.

Before you disengage with a client you want to consider whether you will recommend another accountant to them *or* sell their business to another accountant. When you sell a book of business to another accountant you will typically take a percentage of their first year's fees.

Case study: Paul's Growth Story

My team often joke with me that I've not only built up one accountancy practice in Bodmin, Cornwall, but also the other two local accountancy firms. I've always been very hot on only taking on the right type of clients. With our potential new client questionnaire, we probably pre-qualify out over 60% of all the new client leads we receive. If a client lead isn't right for us, we will normally sell them onto one of the other local accountancy firms!

Before I decided to grow the firm to become a one million pound practice we had a rule that we would only service a maximum number of 200 clients. But one of my skills is winning work. So, for every new client we took on, we needed to disengage from a client. Every six months, the team and I would do a new Client Portfolio Analysis to identify which of our clients was no longer a good fit for the firm. Similar to the new client leads we pre-qualified out, we would sell onto a local accountant any clients we disengaged with.

No one likes to feel rejected and it never makes good business sense to treat a soon-to-be former client badly. Use these tips to successfully exit a client:

- Have their books and accounts completely up-to-date before having the conversation about exiting them.
- Don't leave them without an accountant. Either sell their business to another accountant or make introductions to accountants who are a good fit for their business.
- Don't exit them via email. It's poor form. Show an amount of respect and ring the clients or better, see them face to face.
- It's not going to be a particular easy conversation, but putting it off just makes the conversation harder.

How to implement a fee increase

The quickest way to increase cash flow and profitability is to implement a fee increase for clients. That's why, normally one of the first One Big Focus for your firm will be a fee increase. As mentioned in Chapter 4, everything becomes that little bit easier when your cash flow is healthy. Use our simple profitability calculator at http://www.accountantsmillionaire.club to model the impact on your profitability of putting up your fees. The most successful accountancy practices are the ones where they have trained their clients to expect an annual increase.

Case study:
Suzy

Suzy started her practice with the vision of delivering exceptionally high client service to her clients. She wanted to be a true trusted advisor. But, as her practice grew organically she was left with lots of little clients who just didn't need more than help with basic compliance stuff. She decided as part of her Growth Plan to have a One Big Focus to drastically increase her available capacity by doubling her clients' fees and disengage with half of her clients. After completing her fee increase, her turnover largely stayed the same but her profitability went up by 200%. She finally had the time to be the trusted advisor to her clients.

Case study: Paul's Growth Story

I was always taught that clients need to expect that their fees will go up each year by a small percentage. When we have initial discussions with potential new clients we tell them that our fees will go up every year. There are normally no exceptions to this rule. Given that our clients are expecting an annual fee increase, and we pride ourselves on the service we give our clients, we rarely get any push back from clients.

Decide on what to charge

Before you decide to put your fees up, whether for a handful of clients or your whole client base, you need to decide on what to charge. As your practice grows and evolves, so will your cost base. For example, a sole practitioner with no staff members working from a home office will have a significantly lower cost base than a sole practitioner with 5 staff members and an office. This means that as your practice grows, both in terms of staff numbers and software subscriptions, you need to review your fee structure. Ideally you want to review your fee structure every 12 months. If you've not put up your fees in over 12 months, you are probably leaving money on the table.

Many accountancy firms will base their fee rate on local competitors and similar-sized practices. Whilst benchmarking your fees is a valuable exercise to do, this exercise shouldn't dictate how much you can charge. You have no idea exactly what makes up a local competitor's service offering. Are their clients getting a *stripped down, no frills, all extras are paid for* kind of service, or are they getting for that fee a luxury kind of service where everything is bundled in.

Fees stated on a website can never give you the full insight as to exactly what is or isn't included in a firm's service to their clients.

Once you have decided what to charge, it's important that you build a quoting tool for your practice. This could be either buying one of the quoting tools on the market or by creating your own quoting tool in a spreadsheet application.

Case study: Sharon's Growth Story

I'd lost my confidence when it came to quoting fees. In fact, I'd become my own worst enemy. I'd say a price to a potential new client and then before I'd even finished the sentence I'd be offering them a discount. I'm now very ashamed to admit it, I would even undercut the prices I had on my website. Worst still, I had trained my clients that if they asked for a discount, they would get it.

As a result, my fee levels were all over the place. Most of them were based on my business model when I used to be a one person practice working from my home office. There was no consistency and my staff didn't know what to quote clients. So, I became the only one in the practice who could quote fees for a new client. This became unsustainable as our practice started to grow.

To help me, and the rest of the team, be able to quote a price, and know it was a fair price and profitable for us, I created my own simple quoting tool from a Google Sheet. When a new client asked for a quote I would calculate it in front of them using my quoting tool. It literally took me minutes to calculate this quote. It also gave me the confidence that I was quoting the right level. The clients could see how their fee was made up, and so stopped pushing back and seeing what I could do to lower my prices.

It wasn't just the quoting tool that made the difference. It was how I acted in a new business meeting. I shifted my mindset to stop taking on any new client just to win a new client. It needed to be a good 2-way fit. After I had suggested a fee to a client I trained my brain to stop and pause. In fact, on my notepad for new business meetings I always make a note to STOP TALKING after I state a proposed fee for a client.

Identify who needs their fees to be put up

Once you have decided on your new fee levels, go back to your Client Portfolio Analysis and identify who needs to have a fee increase. Use your quoting tool to identify what their fees need to be. It is always easier to implement an ad hoc fee increase at the end of a client's financial year. Once you've identified who needs a fee increase, put together an action plan for when you will have the fee increase conversation with each client.

Case study: Sharon's Growth Story

I was dreading having fee increase conversations with clients. I hate confrontation and will normally go out of my way to avoid these types of conversations. However, the first part of my Growth Plan involved implementing a fee increase for over 90% of our clients. I'd also bundled into the fee increase conversation the requirement for clients to adapt to our ways of working, e.g. move to Xero and go onto monthly billing by Direct Debit. Because I really struggle with difficult conversations I didn't want to tell clients that if they didn't use Xero we couldn't act for them. So, I decided that any client who didn't move to Xero or go onto monthly billing by Direct Debit their fees would double.

I was worried that clients would take offence at a fee increase or just wouldn't accept it. Or would agree to the fee increase but not going onto Xero or monthly billing. Or worst still, decide to find another accountant.

I started having fee increase conversations with the easy clients. These were either our really unprofitable clients, or the clients that the team and I didn't mind losing. I discovered as I had the fee increase conversations that:

- The more fee increase conversations you have the easier it gets.
- Faced with the threat of a huge hike in fees, clients are far more likely to move onto monthly billing via direct debit and your accounting package of choice. Even if in the past they have been adamant that they won't work this way!
- Don't make the fee increase optional. You need to stand firm. Your price is your price.
- Anticipate their objections and have a prepared answer for these. It then makes it so much easier to deal with resolve any resistance from clients.
- Get someone, like a coach, to keep you accountable to having these fee increase conversations.

As a result of my fee increase conversations with clients, our monthly fees via Direct Debit went up by 60% and our net profitability by 119%. We only lost 3 clients in the process.

Start using your quoting tool with your new fee structure for all new client enquiries

Negotiating a fee increase is never easy. This is why it is essential to get your new clients in at the right rate. In your fee conversations with new clients it's particularly important not to train your new clients into thinking that there is a deal to be done. This needs to be avoided at all costs. Accountants often train their clients to think that there is always a deal to be done by, for example, giving a new client a first-year discount when they ask what can be done to lower your fees, or underquoting the fees stated on your website. At the end of the day, if you train a client from the outset that there is a *deal* to be done or a *discount* to have, this is the mindset the client is likely to have throughout your relationship. Whilst there is no guarantee that they will become a difficult client, it is then always going to be tough to get this client onto a profitable fee basis. After all, it's hard to negotiate fees up from a low starting point.

Preparing for your fee increase conversations

Asking a client for a fee increase is one of the hardest conversations that any accountant will need to do. It's amazing how many accountants will try and wriggle out of fee increase conversations or procrastinate so that the call is never made. Clients can avoid emails about fee increases, so the best way to implement a fee rise is to phone or have a face-to-face meeting with each of your clients to let them know about the fee increase.

Before you start to have your fee increase conversations take a moment to analyse why you've delayed these fee increase conversations in the past. It can be for a multitude of reasons, such as:

- Not confident to have the difficult conversation with a client.
- Worried the client will react badly to the conversation.

- Concerned that too many clients will leave as a result of fees being put up.
- Not sure what to say if the client pushes back when the fee increase is proposed.

Every accountant who has put their fees up is always worried at the outset that they will lose too many clients. Without exception, the reality is that they have lost at most a handful of clients, but gained a significant increase in their net profitability.

Before you start to have the fee increase conversations do the following:

- Create an action plan of who is going to speak with each client affected.
- For everyone who will be having the fee increase conver sations brainstorm with them the typical objections and how to respond to these.
- Pick clients who you don't mind losing as your first few conversations.
- After you have implemented a few fee increases take stock. If necessary, make adjustments to how you are presenting the reasons for the fee increase to clients.

How to move to monthly billing via Direct Debit

Traditionally accountants used to bill clients based on how much time they spent on their financial affairs, and after they had finished the work. This way of working normally leads to high WIP and lockup. If you bill in this way you are often held to ransom by your clients as you can't start (or finish) their work until they have brought in their records for you. This way of billing also leads to a lumpy cash flow.

More and more small accountancy practices now bill their clients monthly via Direct Debit. It has many benefits for both the accountant and the client. The client knows in advance what they will be paying for their compliance work. They also get to preserve their cash flow by spreading their payments over the year. The accountant gets paid regardless of when the clients bring in their records, and can reduce their WIP and lockup to virtually zero.

Case study: Sian's Growth Story

Having started my practice from scratch, I was determined to set it up in a way which didn't cause me problems in the future. Having seen so many firm owners get really stressed about whether they would be able to pay the wages at the end of the month, I never wanted to get into this position.

As a result, our way of working is that all our clients pay their fees monthly by Direct Debit. There are no exceptions. We just wouldn't take a client on if they won't pay their bill this way. We use integrate GoCardless with Xero. This means that when we raise an invoice it is automatically taken out by Direct Debit and additionally automatically reconciled.

My business model is such that my recurring monthly payments by Direct Debit always are enough to cover the wages and normal monthly costs. This means that I am never worrying towards the end of the month about whether I will have enough money in the bank to pay my wages.

Case study: Guy's Growth Story

When I was a partner for BDO and Moore Stephens, a lumpy cash flow didn't really impact me personally. After all, we had so many clients there was always enough cash coming in and a decent overdraft facility with the bank. After a year or so of starting my practice I realised that I couldn't survive with a lumpy cash flow. I was running myself into the ground cajoling clients to bring their records in so I could bill them for the work. This was why I decided to originally start to bill my clients by instalments on a monthly basis. It made sound financial sense. I, rather than my clients, needed to be in control of when I billed them.

After a few months of billing my clients via monthly instalments. I realised something else. It fundamentally changed our relationships with our clients. As we billed them monthly, they had an expectation they would hear from us monthly. Rather than as we had done previously, at key points in the year, when we wanted them to bring their records in.

As a result of changing how we billed we got much closer to our clients. Pretty much becoming, as I had always wanted to, a true trusted advisor to them.

Case study: Kai

As part of Kai's Growth Plan to improve the efficiency of the practice he needed to move his clients from a time-based, pay as you go basis, to fixed fee billing paid by monthly instalments via Direct Debit for on-going compliance work. He completed a Client Portfolio Analysis to understand what his fixed fees for compliance work should be in order to achieve a 70% gross profitability for his practice. He then took these figures and created a quoting tool and put each of his clients through the quoting tool. This gave him every client's new proposed fee.

When he had done this he then then decided how he would move people to paying monthly. At the start of a client's new financial year he moved them to paying a fixed fee by monthly instalments via Direct Debit. However, to take account of the work that they needed to do after the client's year end, the client only started to pay their monthly instalments three months into their financial year.

It took Kai just over a year to move everyone over to fixed fee billing paid in monthly instalments. His turnover increased by 30% and his net profitability by 70%. He was able to reassign the firm's own bookkeeper and credit controller to work on client work as his WIP reduced to zero, and all his monthly recurring invoices were reconciled automatically in Xero.

Tips to move your clients to billing monthly via Direct Debit:

- Aim to move your clients to monthly billing at the start of their new financial year. Otherwise it can get really complicated accounting for what they have paid for and what they need going forward.
- If a new client joins you part way through their financial year, start their monthly billing from the start of their new financial year. Then bill them on an ad hoc basis for any outstanding work from their current financial year.

- Heavily penalise clients with higher fees if they refuse to move to monthly billing via Direct Debit or disengage from the client.
- Use a software solution such as GoCardless with Directli, to automate the collection of your invoices via Direct Debit on the day they are due. Directli will even automatically mark your invoices as paid and reconcile them for you.
- With new clients, give them a provisional monthly fee for 3 months. At the end of the 3-month period review their fee level and adjust up or down as necessary.
- Introduce monthly billing via Direct Debit in combination with a fee increase. You can then incentivise clients to move to Direct Debit and monthly billing by offering them two different fee levels. With the lower fee level being the one they would get if they moved to payments via Direct Debit and monthly billing.

When you have moved your clients onto monthly billing via Direct Debit you will need to have a process to capture ad hoc work for the client. It is essential that your staff know what is included in the client's monthly fees, so they know when to charge for anything on top of this. A tool such as Practice Ignition will allow you to quickly send the client a proposal for an ad hoc piece of work. Then when the client signs the engagement letter, Practice Ignition will automatically send the invoice and take payment.

Summary

The quickest and easier way to increase your firm's cash flow and profitability is to implement a fee increase for your clients. Do a Client Portfolio Analysis to help you identify the unprofitable clients. Your analysis is a great source of insight to enable you to:

- Upsell relevant additional services to your clients
- Identify who are your most profitable clients
- Have clarity on your firm's sector specialisms.

Moving your clients onto monthly billing via Direct Debit will have a transformational impact on your firm's cash flow. No more waiting for clients to bring their records in before you can get paid.

Action plan

- Do a Client Portfolio Analysis for your firm. Identify who are your most profitable clients and which clients are unprofitable.
- Interrogate your analysis to identify opportunities to sell more services to clients.
- Create your own or buy a quoting tool for your practice to enable everyone in your practice to quote a consistent fee to a prospect or existing client.
- With the results of your Client Portfolio Analysis, implement a fee increase for your unprofitable clients or disengage from these clients.
- If you are not already billing every client monthly via Direct Debit, then create a plan to move all your clients onto monthly billing via Direct Debit at the start of the next financial year.

6

How to build the right team around you

Topics covered in the chapter:

- How to map your future structure to support the growth of your firm
- How to attract the right team members to your firm
- How to retain and develop your best people

Following your 3-year Growth Plan will be easier if you have the right team in place. Not only that, your practice will be a great place to work in. Getting the right team around you is probably the hardest part of growth to crack. Not only is there currently a profession-wide shortage of accountants, there is also a need for a new breed of technology-savvy accountant. This chapter talks about how your structure will change as you grow and how to ensure you are able to attract, develop and retain your best people.

The future accountancy firm structure

The genie is well and truly out of the bottle. Cloud and digital accounting is here to stay. *If your 3-year Growth Plan didn't say this, then write it in now. Your practice is going to be in the cloud within 12 months and all your clients within the 18 months.* The move to real-time accounting is only being accelerated as tax collecting bodies around the world (e.g. HMRC in the UK) exploit the technology now available. This means that the accountancy firm of the future is going to look very different to the structure of the traditional accountancy firm. As compliance work becomes more and more commoditised, the firms that do well will be the ones who are structured to help their clients:

- Automate their financial data flows so that the client and they can see on a real-time basis what is happening at the client's business.
- Achieve their business and personal goals, through the adoption of advisory services delivered via an account management role rather than the traditional accountant role.

The firms which invest NOW in delivering a real-time cloud-based accounting service to their clients will be the firms which experience rapid growth over the next few years.

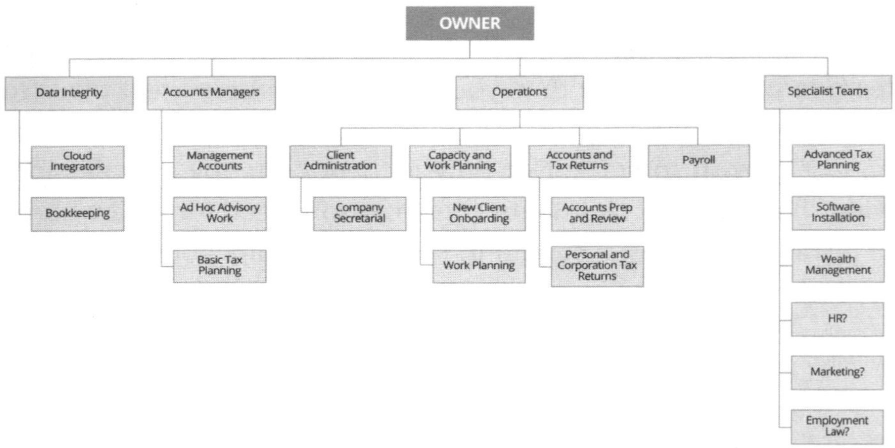

Diagram 6.0: Firm of the future structure

This means that for the accountant, new roles will emerge. In actual fact, the forward-thinking progressive accountancy firms already have these roles in place. E.g.

- The bookkeeper role will become far less about inputting in numbers, but making sure the numbers, regardless of their source, that flow into the accounts are correct.
- There will be a new Cloud Specialist role, which is less about accountancy and more about helping clients automate

their data flows, have real time visibility of their numbers and get their various systems to talk to each other.

There is a huge demand in the UK market for Cloud Specialists. This role is focused on helping clients get onto the cloud and automating their financial data flows.

If you want to scale your practice you need to stop giving yourself organisational hobbies, such as business development or delivering advisory services to your clients. Your role should be to lead the practice not BE the practice.

Case study: Mike

In 2016 Mike's firm, a UK-based Accountancy Firm with a £1.2m turnover, decided to make good its stated intention to go paperless. To do this they went through all their client files to see what stuff they needed to keep digitally and what could be ditched. They rejigged their workflow from clients and to the outsourcing companies they used in order to keep all their records digitally. Within 3 months, they were a completely paperless practice.

Once they had done this they ditched their filing cabinets. To celebrate going paperless they refurbished their office. 3 months after the filing cabinets left the building, the staff moved into their newly refurbished light and spacious office.

There has always been an account manager role in most accountancy firms. This is the person who is the first port of call for a client, and ensures that they get the service they require. This role will change drastically over the next few years, and the types of people needed for this role will also change. See Table 6.1 for how the role will change.

The types of skills your staff will need to gain include:

- Working in the cloud, in particular how to help their clients automate the flow of their financial data.
- Management accounting, i.e. how to help the client look forward with their business rather than reporting on the past.
- Commercial acumen.
- Advisory skills, in particular coaching and facilitation.

Some of these skills can be learnt on the job, e.g. working in the cloud. Whereas others such as coaching and facilitation are best served by attending a workshop or course.

	Past	Now
Role purpose	Keep them legal with their compliance requirements and save them tax	Help their clients achieve their personal and business goals
Skills required	Accountancy qualification, good with numbers, detail orientated	Good with people, excellent communication skills, commercial acumen, project management
Typical responsibilities	• Prepare and review Year End Accounts as well as tax returns.	• Project manage the client's requirements to achieve their personal and business goals.
	• Lead a team of junior staff who help prepare the compliance work for the client.	• Grow their existing client accounts
	• Liaise with Payroll team and specialist tax team when required	• Liaise carefully with the firm's specialist teams and operational hub where necessary.
Size of client portfolio	Large – up to 150 clients	Small to medium – up to 50 clients

Table 6.1: How the account manager role will change

You can't deliver a truly proactive service to your clients without having real-time access to accurate and up-to-date client records. Is it time to offer bookkeeping to your clients?

Case study: Sian's Growth Story

I've always treated my practice as a business first and foremost. It has to make money, both now and the future. When I put together my 3-year Growth Plan I needed to work out how to find my future account managers, i.e. the people who would become my clients' first port of contact. Given that qualified staff were both expensive but also in short supply, I decided to grow my own account managers. Additionally, by taking school leavers instead of qualified or part-qualified accountants, I wouldn't have to get them to unlearn the traditional accountancy way of doing things.

Hiring school leavers is always a gamble. At the tender age of 18 you never quite know who is going to become a brilliant accountant, and who may not be suited to the career. So, my hiring criteria focused primarily on looking for the right attitude. Typically, a desire to help and be people orientated, whilst being detail focused.

The accountancy institutes are still training up accountants in the old ways of working. I needed to fast track my new recruits so they were digitally and IT savvy, but could still navigate around a set of management accounts. So, I built an in-house training programme for them which focused as much on increasing their commercial acumen as well as their accountancy knowledge. For example, the ability to produce management accounts and interpret them is prioritised before learning to produce a set of Year End Accounts.

Your structure will evolve as your firm grows. What works for you now will definitely not be an appropriate way of working in the future. It's important that when you are making hiring decisions you are aware of your future structure so a short-term decision doesn't compromise your long-term plans. See Diagram 6.2 for how a typical firm's structure changes as it grows from one person into a one million pound practice.

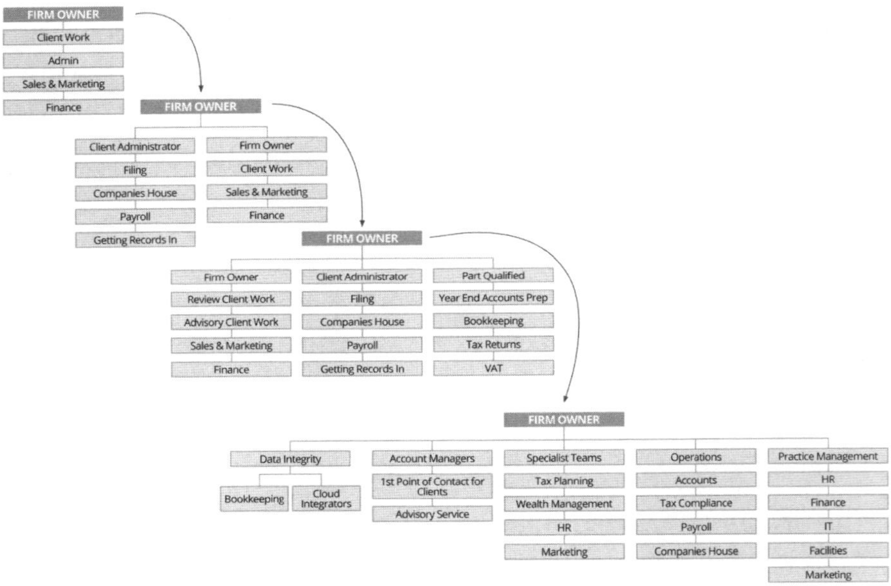

Diagram 6.2: How the accountancy firm structure changes as it grows

Are you the best person to be running your firm? Or would a CEO or COO do a far better job and let you get on with doing what you love? Just because you are the founder of your firm doesn't mean to say you need to run your firm.

Let's look at the common way that most accountancy firm's structure evolves as they grow. Most accountancy firms start with one person being the firm; the founder. This person does everything for the firm and normally works from their home office. They have responsibility for:

- Account management
- All of the work involved in servicing their clients' compliance requirements; e.g. requesting records, completing and filing tax returns, running the payrolls
- Sales and marketing
- Planning the workflow
- Helping clients get their financial affairs onto the cloud
- Management accounts and reporting when requested by their clients
- All the admin of running an accountancy practice

As the firm grows the owner of the firm needs to bring in more people to take on these responsibilities. In addition, as the firm grows the owner's responsibilities will increase to include additional responsibilities, which will also need to be delegated or outsourced to a team member including:

- Practice management, e.g. HR, IT, the firm's own finances
- Operations management, e.g. resource planning, capacity planning

The best way to map your future structure is to do a brainstorm of exactly what tasks each individual member of your firm, including you, does now. Put each task onto a post-it note. Once you have exhausted the brainstorm look at your post-it notes. Cluster your post-it notes into tasks which naturally fit together. Then challenge yourself whether these tasks naturally fit under an existing team member's responsibilities or a new role for the firm. If you have decided to fit the tasks under an existing team member's role, consider their available capacity. Have they got the capacity to do all the tasks and not become a bottleneck in the firm's workflows? If they haven't got the capacity could automating a process or doing a process differently free up their capacity? If not, then reconsider your decision not to create a new role. Do a check on the tasks you have allocated to yourself. Which of these would be better done by someone else if you are going to be freed up to grow the firm? If necessary, go back and recluster the tasks to free up more of your time.

You will now have a list of roles and tasks that each role is responsible for. It's time to decide on reporting lines in your firm, i.e. who reports into whom. The best way to do this is make sure that no one person has more than 6 people to manage and to also consider how much of your time you want to be managing people.

If you want to grow your firm and deliver advisory services to your clients, you can't be the only person who can deliver the advisory services.

Map future structure

Case study: Rose

Rose had built up her own practice when her children were growing up. Now her children were teenagers and thinking about heading off to university, it no longer suited Rose to be tied to her practice.

Rose had built her practice on the principle that it needed to be able to run without her. In fact, 6 months before she sold the firm she had dropped her hours down to 1 day a week to give her the time to compete in a 100km ultra marathon.

Her practice was valued significantly higher than a similar sized practice as Rose had been able to prove to the buyer that the practice pretty much ran itself.

How to attract the right team members to your firm

Small accountancy firm owners often complain that their biggest barrier to growth is finding and keeping the right staff. This is probably the biggest challenge facing the industry as a whole. The reality of the current accountancy job market is there is a severe shortage of accountants wanting to make a career in practice. This is a hangover from the 2008-2013 global recession, where the large firms severely curtailed their graduate recruitment and many accountants left practice to go into industry, or left the accountancy profession altogether.

> “You can't outspend the giants, but you can out-think, out-teach, and out-help them.
>
> *BRIAN HALLIGAN, CEO OF HUBSPOT*

When you are a small accountancy firm it often seems like you can't compete with the bigger firms who have the muscle to pay the larger salaries. However, when you as a firm play to your strengths, you not only have the opportunity to attract in good staff, but to keep and grow them. Here are ways in which other small accountancy firms attract and keep good staff.

When hiring new members of staff look for staff who get your *why*. If they don't get your *why*, they will be a poor fit for your firm, but may flourish elsewhere.

Grow a strong local profile

Being small, you need to think creatively about how to grow your local profile in order to attract high quality staff to your firm.

- Local newsletters: In every town or village there are local newsletters regularly going out to just the sort of people you want to attract. It normally costs a fraction to place a job advert in the newsletter compared to your local newspaper. Newsletters are sent out regularly by parish and town councils, schools, sports clubs, churches and other faith organisations.
- Enter accountancy and local awards: Winning or even being shortlisted for an award is an excellent way to grow a local profile. The local awards will almost definitely attract a decent amount of local and free PR. It's also easy to get featured in your local press if you or your firm win a national award. People like to join what they perceive to be a successful businesses. Your award is a great way of demonstrating that your firm is a successful business.
- Have a branded car: It's quite cheap to have a magnetic sign made up for your car. If you drive to work or use your car locally, it's a great way to let people know you are hiring.

Be authentic and unstuffy

The more traditional practices often have a rule that staff are not allowed to listen to music via their headphones while they work (seriously!). Given how much distraction there is in the typical accountancy office, listening to music via headphones while you work can be great way to focus and increase your productivity. Nurture an office environment where you ditch rules for rule's sake; e.g. "You must wear a suit and tie into the office", and creating a great environment to work in, is a good way to attract in young and switched-on staff.

Look at your employee handbook and challenge every rule on how staff need to behave when employed by you. If the rule doesn't help create an inclusive environment where staff are able to perform to the highest level of their ability and create a great experience for clients, change it.

Introduce flexible working

If you can run your practice without relying on employees who want to work full-time during normal office hours, you will attract a broader talent pool to your firm. There is a huge talent pool of people who for many different reasons, don't want to work normal office hours, 5 days a week from the office. Very often part-time or flexible workers have an incredibly strong work ethic and are very loyal. After all, finding an interesting and challenging part-time role is never easy.

Given the advances in technology, can you play to your strengths and build up a workforce who want to put their work hours around their other responsibilities in life? Could you offer part-time working, early starts, late finishes or the ability to work from home some of the week? Very often the top 100 firms struggle to give their staff this flexibility. Small firms really can compete with the larger firms by offering their staff flexible working and non-standard working hours.

Today's clients do not expect their accountant to be at the end of the phone 5 days a week from 9:00 – 17:00. In fact your firm's clients may prefer to speak to their accountant outside of the normal office hours.

Tailor your staff perks

There are all sorts of ways that you can make your staff benefits that little bit more meaningful. And in a way that many large firms just can't do. For example, can you let your staff bring their dog into work? Can you organise for a personal trainer to run an exercise session over lunch for staff in your firm's meeting room?

Case study: Paul's Growth Story

As an early adopter I understood the power of the cloud very early on. I was one of the first Xero practices in the UK. However, I needed my staff to come on the journey with me. We'd had a good year and I wanted an experience which would help bond my staff together as a team. So, a few years back I took the whole of the practice to Xerocon in Sydney, Australia. It gave us so many shared memories and really helped to bring us together as a team. But more importantly, my staff got to see what the future as a cloud based practice could be really like.

Case study: Sharon's Growth Story

We are a small team and don't have much flexibility when it comes to capacity. The buck really does stop on only a few shoulders! To help thank my team for their hard performance in the week, I buy in lunch on a Friday if the team has hit their targets.

Be proactive with your recruitment

You never know when you are going to need your next new member of staff. If you are always thinking one to two hires ahead of what you need, you can hire early if a good opportunity presents itself. This means doing things like:

- Have a careers section on your website.
- Use LinkedIn to start to build a relationship with potential employees.
- Build connections with the local training colleges.
- Offer internships or work experience to students from your local schools or colleges.

Case study: Olivia

Olivia took over the family firm from her father. The firm was in desperate need of modernising. Her staff were very resistant to change and just wanted to work the way they had done for the last ten years. In her 3-year Growth Plan she paid special attention to the type of staff she wanted in the firm.

As she started to bring in change, she found that the staff who were particularly stuck in their ways started to voluntarily leave the firm. In fact, over a 3-year period she found she had replaced every single member of staff.

Given that cash flow was very tight, she didn't have the money to spend on recruiters. Instead she set about becoming her own recruitment agent. She paid for LinkedIn Premium and identified all the qualified accountants who identified as being within 20 miles of her firm's office. She then proactively contacted every accountant who looked like they could be a good fit for her firm. It was hard work and involved a large amount of conversations which never quite went anywhere. However, she found that as a result of her proactive conversations she was able to hire in great new team members.

For every new member of staff she hired, she had on average 3 decent candidates to choose from. As more and more new and enthusiastic staff members came on board, Olivia found that the culture of the firm rapidly changed for the better.

Make your firm an exciting place to work

Accountancy and exciting are not normally two words that people put together! However, employees are attracted to successful firms with a strong vision and purpose, particularly if they can play an important part in helping to grow a successful firm. Be proud about your growth ambitions and let staff know how they will help the firm achieve its Growth Vision.

Here are some ideas to help make your firm an exciting place to work:

- Change your firm's branding so you ditch the safe grey and navy blue. Add in a bright colour to your firm's brand and include this on the firm's business cards and colour scheme in the office.
- Put up inspiring photographs on the walls which mean something to the people in your firm.
- Ditch dress down Friday in favour of a business casual dress code every day of the week.
- Bring in cake to celebrate employees' birthdays.
- Have a social fund for staff entertainment which the firm contributes to when it hits its financial targets.
- Encourage your staff to form sports teams and participate in local leagues.

Set up a bonus pot to be shared with all staff based on the firm's performance. When your staff can directly share in the firm being more successful, they are more likely to perform to a higher level.

How to retain and develop your new starters

You've bitten the bullet. Double-checked your cash flow and decided you can afford to hire a new team member. However, according to the Wynhurst Group, 22% of staff turnover happens in the first 45 days. According to the Robert Half, a specialist finance recruiter, the top reasons why employees walk out soon after being hired are:

- 32% because of inability to meet the expectations of them.
- 19% because the role did not meet their expectations.
- 18% found they had a poor fit with the corporate culture.
- 10% had an inability to integrate with the team.

Most of the top reasons can be either completely eliminated or drastically reduced with management time and effort both during the recruitment process and the new employees' first 100 days in the role.

Carefully recruit for both attitude and experience.

The top 3 reasons for people not staying for longer than a year can normally be eliminated by a careful but thorough recruitment process. It's not enough to check that your potential new hire can do the job. You need to check to see whether they have the right attitude, values, expectations of their employer and ways of working to fit into your firm.

Often firms don't have clarity about the sort of person they want to hire, and the level of skills they need to possess. When the chips are down, and you are under a huge amount of pressure, say for example in the run up to a busy period, it is all too easy to recruit someone who walks through the door and says they can do the job. The more you compromise on actually who you need in the role, the greater the chance of there being a poor fit between the individual and the firm. Before you start the hiring process, prepare a detailed job description for the vacancy which details:

- Key responsibilities
- What success looks like for the role
- How their role interacts with other roles
- Who they will report into

You can download a free sample job description at the Accountants Millionaires' Club, http://www.accountantsmillionaire.club.

Remember that recruitment is a two-way process. It's not just about you picking a new member of staff. It's also about a potential member of staff deciding if they want to work for your firm. This means your recruitment advert and literature (e.g. job description) needs to sell the benefits of working for your firm. But it also needs to give your potential staff members a window into the culture of your firm. This means being open about the not so glamorous parts of the role, e.g. *We work hard and play hard as a team. Everyone pulls together in the busy periods, even if this does mean some long days and late nights in January.*

In your recruitment process, aim to do the following:

- Have more than one interview. For junior members of the team, do as Sharon does and set them tests to see how they would cope with the demands of the job. Or bring them in for a paid trial day to see how well they fit in with the team.
- Do check their references carefully. If possible aim to have a verbal conversation with their manager from their previous role. When checking references ask questions based on

anything you noticed about the person in the interview, such as: *We couldn't help noticing the strong odour of sweat in the person's clothes. Is he always like that?* Then ask them this question: *If the person returned to your firm, would you reemploy them immediately?* You'll be surprised how many times the referee pauses, takes a deep breath, and then says a quiet, "No".

- Prepare a detailed job specification for the vacancy, including what success looks like for this role. Link the job descriptions to the targets in your 3-year Growth Plan.
- Use an interview plan which probes their proven ability to achieve the objectives of the role *and* their preferred behaviours to get the job done.
- Include other team members within the interview process so you can get their views as to whether they would fit in the team. This could be by having a coffee with the potential member of staff or getting them to sit in during an interview. Listen to these views!

How a potential new member of staff interacts with your receptionist whilst they are waiting to meet you can tell you a lot about them as a person. Do ask the receptionist's opinion.

Set short-term realistic performance targets for the new joiner

There is always a huge amount to take in when you start a new job with a new employer. It's really important that you don't overwhelm your new joiner with too much stuff in their first few weeks. Don't expect your new team member to just *sink or swim*. Yes, being thrown in at the deep end is sometimes the reality of what happens to a new member of staff. But if you need to do this, always make sure that they have the equivalent of a life belt to help them.

In their first week consider giving them daily objectives to achieve. Then spread these out to weekly, then monthly objectives to hit. As a minimum, they will need to understand:

- How their role fits in, in particular how their role contributes to the firm achieving its quarterly One Big Focus.
- How they will know when they are making a difference.
- Some personal short-term objectives to hit or things to achieve to get them up-to-speed quickly.

Have mini-performance reviews during their probationary period

An employees' probationary period is not just a legal nicety. It is a period of time where you can assess their suitability for the role. At defined points in their probationary period, e.g. end of week 1, week 4, week 8 and week 12, sit down with your new employee and have a frank and honest conversation about how they are finding the new role. This is your opportunity to set short-term realistic objectives for them, whilst teasing out and resolving any niggles from both sides.

Build a structured training plan for them

Their training plan needs to include everything that they will need to complete in their first 6 months in the role to be fully performing and integrated within the team and firm culture. For example, this is likely to include:

- Technical training sessions on the firm's software and key processes; e.g. the accounting platform your firm uses
- Meet and greets with the Stakeholders
- 1:2:1s with their line manager

- Mentoring and shadowing sessions
- On-the-job learning.

There is nothing stopping you from starting their training before they officially join. For example, you could send them information to read before they start.

This could include:

- Pen portraits of their team members and Stakeholders.
- Copies of business books that will help them get on in the firm.
- FAQs about the firm and the office they will be working in.
- Their training plan for their first month in the job.

Involve them in the firm's culture

The first few weeks in a new role are probably the most crucial to helping a new joiner get settled in quickly and stop feeling like the new boy/girl. The sooner that someone can feel settled and at home, the quicker they will perform at their best ability. During their first few weeks take the time to demonstrate to them how pleased you are that they joined. After all, the last thing you want is for a new joiner to feel buyer's remorse and leave before they get properly started.

How to retain and develop your existing members of staff on a very limited learning and development budget

Ask any accountant in practice what they want from their employer and their answers will include these things:

- Interesting work and career progression

- Empowerment and control over their work life
- To feel valued, recognised and appreciated

In order for staff to feel they can progress their career within your firm, they need to understand how your firm is going to develop over time and the opportunities that will exist for them. That is why it is essential to not only have developed your 3-year Growth Plan but also widely communicated it to your staff. Your staff need to be able to see how they can develop within your firm as well as the opportunities available for them to develop in to.

In order for staff to feel that they have career progression they need to have the opportunity to develop their skill set. If you don't actively develop your staff or give them the option of developing you will find that your staff leave. But, very often, there isn't the money available to fund lots of training for your staff. The good news is that often the most effective way of developing your staff is not to pay for costly training courses that take your staff away from their day job.

When it comes to training or developing people, normally the first option suggested is "can we send them on a course?" A training course is often seen as an easy option to develop staff. The reason being that we kid ourselves that the person who has gone on the course will come back fixed. Not only are training courses expensive in terms of time away from the job, but often ineffective ways of developing staff. People only tend to develop well as a result of attending a workshop when they have active support back in the workplace to develop and hone their newly learnt skills. As we all know, this *active* support bit is often missing in today's accountancy practice. Research has shown that learning on the job is the most effective way for someone to develop. It's also cheaper and significantly more time-effective than sending someone on a course.

In a busy workplace, it can be easy to stop taking the time to review the progress of an individual. This review time is critically important as it gives your staff members the time to reflect on how far they have come and how they have developed. A great way to help staff members see how far they have come with their development is to make sure that they are all working towards a personalised development plan.

Name		
Objective:		
By when?	What?	Progress
31st October	Be able to run a quarterly review meeting with clients without help from others	Now running meetings by self, but still being observed by line manager
31st September	Run a performance and development conversation monthly with each member of team	Now happening and getting positive feedback from staff

Diagram 6.3 Example of a staff development plan

Retaining your good staff members isn't just about developing them. It's about making them feel valued, recognised and appreciated. This is more than just remembering to say thank you to staff for a good piece of work. It's about sitting down with them regularly on a one-to-one basis to see how they are feeling about life, work and stuff in general. In the next chapter, we will look at how to motivate your team and help them perform at their best.

Summary

Your firm structure will evolve as your firm grows. When you are aware of how your structure will change you can make good hiring decisions at the right time.

You can compete with bigger accountancy firms on working conditions, particularly flexible working, and the perks that you can offer them.

The best way to retain and develop your staff is to make a good hiring decision to begin with. Your staff want interesting work, career progression, but also to feel valued, recognised and appreciated. To help them progress their career look to provide opportunities for your staff to develop, remembering that the most cost effective and time effective development you can offer your staff is on-the-job training.

Action Points

- Take a long hard look at your firm's structure. Is it still fit for purpose both now and in the future? If not, what would need to change? How can you move towards creating your new firm structure? Map the steps you would need to take to evolve your current structure into your new structure. If your new firm structure requires you to take some drastic action to your current employees' roles and responsibilities, take advice from an HR specialist for the best way to do this legally.
- Create job descriptions for all your current and future roles in your firm. Include in these job descriptions the main responsibilities as well as what success looks like for an individual in the role.
- Ask your staff what they like about working for you and your firm, in particular what perks or staff benefits they really like. Use their responses to help you craft any future job adverts.
- Introduce personalised development plans for each member of your staff.
- Brainstorm with your staff options, without going on a training course, to help them get the development they want (and the firm wants them to have).

7

How to lead and manage your people

Topics covered in the chapter:

- How to build and develop a team
- What motivates people?
- How to give effective feedback
- How to set objectives
- How to implement good performance management systems

You can't become the owner of a one million pound practice without a great team around you, and great teams don't magically appear. They take conscious effort to build and nurture. This chapter provides the information that you need to build the right team to allow you to get on with growing your practice.

> “Great tech founder/CEOs tend to focus on What & Who: What product to build, and Who to hire/train/retain/motivate to build it.
>
> *MARC ANDREESEN*

How to build and develop a team

> “All of us perform better and more willingly when we know why we're doing what we have been told or asked to do.
>
> *ZIG ZIGLAR*

If you are going to grow your firm you will need a trusted team of people who you can rely on to do *the right things right*. These could be people inside your firm, outsourced support or other professionals you collaborate with on a client's affairs. This means you need to build and develop individuals and teams who will be able to service the firm's clients.

You can buy the fastest Formula 1 racing car in the world but with a weak team it will never win a race. However, with the best team in the world, you can buy a lesser car and the team will develop it into a winner. In other words, the quality of the team you build is just as important as the quality of the clients your firm wins. A motivated and capable team around you will consistently give you the time to work *on* the business, and avoid getting pulled back into the Work In/Work On Trap.

Typically a team – as opposed to a group of people – will share a mutual purpose; e.g. wow all our clients, similar performance goals and hold themselves mutually accountable. Identifying a One Big Focus for your firm and allocating Growth Tasks to every member of your firm is a great way to ensure that individuals and teams in your firm are all focused on achieving the firm's 3-year Growth Plan.

You will often hear the phrase 'high-performing team' used in conjunction with team performance. A high-performing team is one where:

- The team has shared values, with common work standards and behaviours.
- There are clearly defined roles and responsibilities for each of the team members.
- The whole team is focused on achieving the firm's 3-year Growth Plan, in particular the Growth Tasks to achieve the quarter's One Big Focus.
- There is a high level of respect and mutual trust within the team for the skills, knowledge and expertise that each team member brings along.

- The team is excellent at overcoming any obstacles to achieve their team's objectives.
- Open and clear communication is present between the team members, regardless of their location in the world. The daily Operational Huddle, as well as Rhythm Meetings, is a great way to get this open and clear communication.
- Effective decisions are taken at the right time by the right people.
- There is a collaborative and positive atmosphere between the team members.
- Conflicts are surfaced and resolved quickly and effectively.
- The team achieves superior results.

Typically as the owner of your firm and by default a team leader, you will be performing, at any one time, four roles within the team:

Direction setter: You will be working with your team to identify, clarify and build commitment to achieving the firm's 3-year Growth Plan and One Big Focus. Part of your role is to help the team identify the right journey for them as a team to achieve these.

Facilitator: You will be helping your team to work effectively and knit together as a high-performing team. This may include having difficult conversations to get people to perform well and work together.

Coach: Similar to any sports team coach, you will be working with the team as a whole and on an individual level to make sure that people have the right skills and behaviours for the work they are required to do.

Road-block clearer: You will be responsible for clearing any road blocks which are preventing your team from achieving progress.

Your team does not become high-performing overnight; it takes time, focus and energy to get it to this level. The Tuckman model of team development explains that as the team develops maturity and ability, and relationships establish, the leader must change and adopt different styles of leadership. In the model, there are five distinct stages of team development:

Forming

Storming

Norming

Performing

Adjourning

Forming

At this stage, the team is very new and freshly formed. Every time someone joins or leaves a team, the team reverts to this stage again. The team members look to the team leader for guidance and direction, plus clarification on each team member's roles and responsibilities. As a team leader, be prepared to be very 'present' with the team to communicate their purpose, objectives and facilitate any external relationships.

Storming

The team is becoming clear on its purpose and how to get there. However, there is still plenty of uncertainty and decision making may be slow within the group. Inevitably there will be some conflict as the people jockey for positions. Sometimes you may find that there may be power struggles and challenges to the team leader's authority. A team may never get through the storming phase where unresolved conflict is left to fester. It is the team leader's role to focus the team on its objectives and resolve relationship and emotional issues.

Norming

Only if conflict is resolved at the storming stage does the team move on into norming. The team now is fully committed to its mutual purpose and objectives. The dust has settled, meaning that roles and responsibilities within the team are now clear and accepted. Collaboration across the team is established. Unlike the storming stage, big decisions are taken as a whole team, whereas the smaller decisions are delegated to the appropriate people within the team. You may find that the team is starting to socialise outside of the working environment. At this stage the team is working together to develop its working processes and team dynamic.

Performing

When the team starts to display the characteristics of a high-performing team it moves into performing. The team leader role is still generally required as the team will still need ongoing coaching, delegation and guidance from the team leader. However, generally, the team is self-supporting; i.e. the team no longer needs much instruction or assistance as they are pretty much self-sufficient.

Adjourning

This is where the team breaks up as it has fulfilled its purpose. If the team has been particularly strongly bonded, the ex-team members may experience a sense of loss during this stage. As a team leader it is your role to celebrate the success of the team and facilitate team members' journeys on to new projects and roles.

What motivates people

To get your team to perform to the best of their abilities you will need to know how to motivate them; i.e. find out what makes them *tick*. Different things motivate different people and these may change as they grow older and their lives change.

The last chapter discussed what motivates accountants and the best ways to develop them. To recap, accountants are typically motivated by three things:

- Interesting work and career progression
- Empowerment and control over their work life
- To feel valued, recognised and appreciated

Being able to provide interesting and challenging work is not always easy within a small accountancy firm. This is because the work of an accountant is often fairly repetitive in nature. However, you do have some control over who does what in your firm. And can, therefore, provide work which interests and motivates your staff members.

For example:

- For each individual in your team do you know what kind of work they like and want to do more of? Do you know what expectations they have for developing their career? How can the growth of your practice help meet these expectations?
- Are you aware of the skills gaps in your team and as part of your 3-year Growth Plan? Do you have a plan in place for your whole team to be able to fill these gaps?
- What can you delegate from your desk to your team?

Making people feel valued is an interesting one because not everyone feels valued in the same way. Furthermore, you may not yet be in a position to have the budget to provide the salaries and perks your staff would like.

Here are some simple ways in which you can help people in your teams feel valued:

- Taking an interest in what they do both inside and outside of work

- Giving regular praise (when it is due)
- Showing individuals why their work and efforts matter
- Spending time with them during the working day to help them achieve their objectives
- Creating an atmosphere of mutual co-operation
- Truly listening to your team members' ideas and concerns – not just brushing them under the table.

Do not use timesheets as a substitute for good people leadership and management skills. They should only be used to assess the profitability of a job for a client and the capacity of the firm.

How to give effective feedback

Giving actionable feedback is one of the most powerful ways to develop your team and yourself. However, many accountants shy away from giving feedback, particularly negative feedback, to their staff, for fear of upsetting the apple cart or having to have a difficult conversation. So, what do we mean by *effective* feedback?

Effective feedback is feedback that:

- Creates and delivers a specific message based on observed performance.
- Describes specific behaviour so that a person can learn by repeating good behaviour or ceasing bad behaviour.
- Enables the receiver to walk away understanding exactly what he or she did and what impact it had on you or others.

There are many models or processes around on how to give feedback to someone. A good model is the Situation Behaviour Outcome (SBO) feedback model.

What is SBO?

The SBO model is a feedback model which can be used to structure both positive and constructive feedback. Its structure increases the likelihood the feedback will be received in a clear, non-defensive manner by the recipient. Other feedback models often require you to deliver both positive and negative comments. These models never tend to work very well because the person receiving the feedback always wonders whether the positive feedback is genuine, and only really hears the negative feedback.

The SBO model:

Situation	Describe where and when the observed behaviour occurred, and what happened. Be specific.
Behaviour	Describe what you saw or heard.
Outcome	Share with the individual the outcome or impact of the behaviour on you and/or on others.

When you describe someone's behaviour avoid interpretations and judgements such as '*You weren't listening to me.*' Simply describe the person's behaviour: '*When I was talking, you pushed your chair away from the table and gazed out of the window.*' Outcome is what you or others experienced. It can include work outcomes, client satisfaction, work team and/or the larger firm. Most often, it starts with '*I felt ...*' or '*I was ...*' or '*It appeared to me others were ...*'

Some examples of using SBO feedback:

Weak feedback:	*Janet, you were good in the client meeting today – thanks.*
Effective feedback:	*Janet, at the client meeting this afternoon* [**SITUATION**] *you demonstrated your knowledge of our retail client particularly well when*

you talked about the challenges of managing cash flow for retailers [**BEHAVIOUR**]. *The Client commented on your thorough preparation and that it showed a great understanding of her challenges. As a result I could see the Client opening up more about her business and the help she needed.* [**OUTCOME**].

Weak feedback: *James, the Client was unhappy – you didn't do what he asked.*

Effective feedback: *James, the Client was unhappy as you didn't get back to his query about VAT when you said you would* [**SITUATION**]. *I know you are really busy at the moment but by not keeping the Client updated on progress or managing his expectations* [**BEHAVIOUR**] *this led to the Client getting frustrated and complaining to me.* [**OUTCOME**] *Can we work through this together so that we can prevent this happening again?*

Some tips for giving feedback, which will be accepted first time around:

- Ask the other person first what they thought went well and not so well
- Praise in public, criticise in private
- Always ask permission to give the feedback; unsolicited feedback is rarely welcomed
- Wait until your emotions have calmed down, before giving feedback
- Use the SBO model to help you be specific.

How to receive feedback

Being the type of boss who people love working for isn't just about being able to give effective and timely feedback. It's also about being open to feedback yourself and then be seen to be acting on it. Receiving feedback yourself – particularly of the hard to swallow variety – is never easy to hear. The best way to view feedback is that it is a gift, but one where you can choose to act, or not. If you choose not to take any correct action, you need a very good reason to explain your inaction. You expect your staff to act on negative feedback, so you have to demonstrate the same willingness.

Creating a firm culture where feedback is expected and freely given all starts with you. The way you behave and what you view to be important will be mirrored in your firm's culture.

If you are fortunate enough to receive feedback from your staff, regardless of whether it is negative or positive:

- Always thank the person afterwards (whether or not you agree with it); people offering feedback are almost always well-intentioned
- Listen carefully to what they are saying, if necessary asking for clarification
- Resist the temptation to get defensive or clarify your version of events
- If you feel yourself getting emotional, request some time to reflect on the feedback before discussing it.

Setting objectives

Your role as leader of a team is to work jointly with each of your team members to set their objectives. Each member of staff will have 2 types of objectives. Their day-to-day job objectives, e.g.

process the VAT returns without any errors, and Growth Tasks. Their job objectives will come from their job description, whereas their Growth Tasks cascade from the firm's One Big Focus for the quarter.

You shouldn't need to pay staff more just to do their job. For example, offering your staff cash bonuses to get clients onto a cloud accounting package.

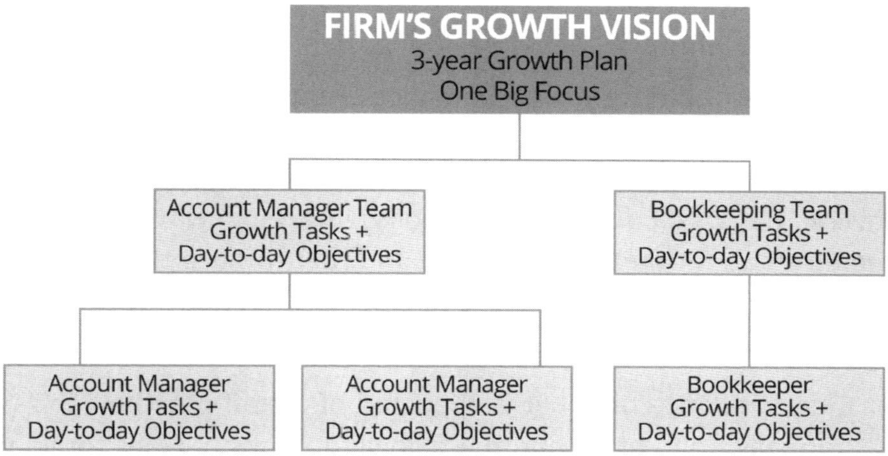

Diagram 7.0: How your team member's objectives relate to the firm's 3-year Growth Plan and the firm's One Big Focus.

How to implement a good performance management system for your firm

Implementing a performance management system for your firm has many benefits, both for you and your staff.

- It focuses individuals on what they need to achieve.
- It helps your staff know what you expect of them and how they can progress their career at your firm.

- It provides an opportunity for you and your staff to reflect on their performance to-date.
- It reduces conflict as everyone knows what is expected of them.
- It gives the team leader and team member the opportunity to privately share feedback on how well the firm and they are personally performing.
- It provides a mechanism to help your staff feel valued, recognised and appreciated.

Current best practice for performance management is not about having discrete points in the year where you and your staff member review their performance, i.e. the annual or bi-annual performance review. It's about having an ongoing dialogue with your staff members about their performance. In order to have this ongoing dialogue, your performance management system needs the following elements:

1. Clear guidance on what is expected of a staff member. This is normally done by having the following things in place for your firm:
    - A competency framework which details HOW you expect your staff to do their job.
    - Job descriptions for each role which detail WHAT you expect your staff to do and achieve, i.e. the responsibilities of the role and what success looks like.
    - A document which summarises the values of your firm and how these values play out in the day-to-day running of the firm.
    - Each member of staff having their own objectives to achieve which include Growth Tasks to help the firm achieve its One Big Focus.

2. An expectation that staff and their line manager will sit down regularly to discuss their individual performance, development and how things are going. Ideally this should be monthly. Or if the staff member is new or under-performing more frequently.
    - To facilitate this discussion, each staff member will have their own Work and Development Plan to record their progress.
3. Staff objectives, including their Growth Tasks, are reviewed monthly to see whether they need to be changed.
4. A procedure to be followed when staff members fail to achieve the performance standards expected of them. This typically looks like a manager sitting down with their team member every day or week to agree on what needs to be achieved, and what support they need to achieve this. If the staff member still under-performs despite the daily and/or weekly meetings about their performance, then formal disciplinary proceedings need to be started. Detailing what needs to go into formal disciplinary proceedings is beyond the scope of this book. An HR specialist can help you implement these for your firm.

You get the staff you deserve! How are you personally contributing to the quality of your staff members?

Summary

Your success at building a one million pound practice is intrinsically linked to your ability to successfully lead, manage and develop your people. Building a successful practice around you will free you up from working *in* the business and allow you to focus more of your energies on growth.

To get great members of staff who you can rely on, you will need to create a performance management system for your firm. This system will allocate regular time for each team member to:

- Review their work with their manager.
- Review their progress against their day-to-day objectives and One Big Focus.
- Reset any objectives if required.
- Help develop them to acquire new skills and progress their career.

Action Points

- Think about the teams you lead. What stage of team development are they at? What three actions will you do to increase the performance of each team?
- Have a private conversation with each of your team members to find out what they like about their role and how they would like to progress their career. Then take action on this conversation.
- Ask three people you trust and work with regularly for feedback on your abilities as a leader. Write an action plan for yourself to improve your effectiveness.
- Implement a performance management system for your firm.
- Set day-to-day objectives and Growth Tasks for each of your team members.
- Diarise regular conversations with your team members to find out how they are doing and what progress they are making on their day-to-day objectives and Growth Tasks.
- Work with a coach to help improve your people manage ment and leadership skills.

8

How to cost effectively resource your growing firm

Topics covered in this chapter:

- How to match your resourcing requirements to your predicted workload
- How to use apprentices effectively
- How to outsource your compliance work

Chapter 4 explored the pain and frustration of the Work In/Work On Trap. One way of avoiding this trap is always making sure you have the right level of resource in your practice. Given that this resource always costs money – sometimes money you don't have – this chapter shows you how to cost effectively resource your practice.

How to match your resourcing requirements to your predicted workload

Modelling your capacity needs means you can plan your resourcing requirements well in advance. This means you are less likely to get caught out by unexpected work coming through the door, but can also minimise the peaks and troughs in your firm's workload. You can take well-thought out decisions in advance to be able to cost-effectively service your clients' work. If you get your capacity planning fairly accurate, it becomes easy to increase or decrease your resource to match your needed capacity.

The best way to understand your current capacity requirements is to look at each client, understand what work needs to be done when, and then the likely time it will take to do. Then aggregate this up so you can see a top-level view of what capacity is required by month for your firm. Then look at the current resource available to you month by month, and identify the months where you have spare resource, and where you are under-resourced. Don't forget to consider when staff may want holidays or be out on study periods. This is often best done on a spreadsheet. Once you have done this it is now time to look at how these capacity requirements will change as your firm grows. Then overlay your current capacity requirements with your predicted future capacity requirements. Of course, it isn't an exact science, but it will help you identify the following:

- Where your firm has peaks and troughs in its workload.
- When you will need to bring in extra resource to handle the requirement for increased capacity.

This capacity planning needs to be done every month, forecasting capacity requirements for the next 12 months.

	Jan	Feb	Mar	Apr	May	Jun	Jul	Aug	Sep	Oct	Nov	Dec
Max hours available	693	693	693	693	693	693	693	693	693	693	693	693
Study leave and holidays	32	160	40	144	64	80	40	152	40	64	40	160
Actual hours available	661	533	653	549	629	613	653	541	653	629	653	533
Current capacity required	600	400	410	550	550	550	600	550	650	650	650	550
Forecasted capacity required	600	400	430	580	600	620	650	620	700	720	730	650
Spare capacity (hour)	61	133	223	-31	29	-7	3	-79	-47	-91	-77	-117

Diagram 8.0: Example of a 12-month capacity plan

If there aren't any consequences for a client to miss the deadlines set by your firm, then your firm is educating your clients that it is okay to bring their records in late.

Case study:
Case Study: Delia

Delia's firm was growing at a rate of 4-8 new clients every month, which equated to approximately £12k of new work being won each month. The majority of the work Delia was winning was from current clients recommending her to new clients. Delia built a capacity plan and modelled her likely future capacity requirements if she carried on winning clients at the same rate. She updated her capacity plan every month to add in the requirements of the new clients she was winning. From her capacity plan, she identified that she was likely to have a surplus of hours in March and not enough capacity from October onwards. To help smooth out the firm's workload she incentivised the new clients she won, with December year ends, to bring in their records in February and March. Delia started to look for a new team member in March so that they would be in situ and trained up in how the firm worked by the start of October.

Do remember that there is often a 6-month lead time from the point you decide to hire in a new member of staff until they are performing at the level you need them to be at. Very often firms fall into the trap of not anticipating when they will need a new member of the team. As a result, they often recruit in too late and over-trade until they get the new member of staff up-to-speed.

How to reduce the peaks and troughs in your firm's workload

In the UK, most businesses have their year-end in March (the end of tax year) or December (the end of the calendar year). This results in huge peaks in workload for firms as the deadlines to file the year end statutory accounts approaches.

Here are how the most efficient firms smooth out the peaks and troughs in their workloads:

- They agree with clients when the firm will service their work. Some firms even incentivise clients to bring their records in at a certain point in time.
- They prevent staff from taking holiday in peak time.
- They use accounts outsourcing companies (see later in this chapter) to service the peaks in demand or help them reduce their backlog of work.

How to use apprentices effectively

Hiring apprentices, particularly given the incentives businesses in the UK are given to hire apprentices, can be an incredibly cost-effective way of resourcing your practice. Particularly if you are looking for your first or second employee and your cash flow is tight. For example, in the UK, you can pay apprentices £3.50 an hour, rather than the current national minimum wage of £7.50. Apprentices are aged 16 or over, and combine on-the-job training with classroom-based study as they work towards a professional qualification, normally AAT in the UK. An apprenticeship can be between one and four years in length. Whilst it is more normal to take on a school leaver as an apprentice, it could be someone who is doing a career change or even an existing staff member.

If your practice has never taken on an apprentice before, it can be a daunting prospect. It's a big shift to go from school to the world of work. After all, these apprentices, whilst full of enthusiasm, often turn up knowing absolutely nothing about accountancy or the world of work. As we covered in the last two chapters, it's important to carefully choose and onboard your new apprentices. After all, they are a new member of staff just like any other member of staff.

Your new apprentice is going to be on a very steep learning curve. Leaving them to their own devices, i.e. not being ultra-clear about what you want them to do, could be an expensive way to let them make mistakes. Therefore, they will need very close supervision. Given that many apprentices are new to the world of work, it is best to assume that they know absolutely nothing. For example, they may not know that they can ask for help, or what is truly expected of them, or what is appropriate attire to wear to work, or what delivering great client service actually means in practice ... So, unlike your more experienced hires, you will need to be in contact with them more often, spell out what is expected of them more regularly, and create the time to guide them appropriately.

The last thing you probably have the time for is to spend lots of time supervising and developing your new apprentice. If it isn't you, it will need to be someone else within the firm. Your apprentices need a high level of supervision in order to make sure they are learning and doing the right stuff in the right way. Most apprentices will probably spend one day a week at college studying for an accountancy qualification. You will need to factor this into your resource planning and the fact that in the UK you need to pay them for when they are doing this training.

Your new apprentice is likely to be very keen and eager to progress. Just as with any other employee, you will need to show them how they will develop to become a valuable member of your practice. This means having a personalised training programme for them. However, this shouldn't be any different from any of your other members of staff.

Apprentices often work better when they can have a workplace buddy in a firm. Buddies might be former apprentices who are only a few years ahead of the apprentice and they are able to share the benefit of their experiences and help the apprentice.

Case study: Sian's Growth Story

I actively look to hire local school leavers as apprentices within my firm. I've learnt to expect that my apprentices are on a very steep learning curve for their first 12 months with the firm. This means that it is only after a year in the role that my apprentices start to become a very valuable member of the team. Before this point, the amount of supervision, training and handholding they require means they are cost neutral. Each of my apprentices is given their own personalised training plan to enable them to do all the different roles in the practice, e.g. payroll, tax returns, bookkeeping etc. They all, individually, spend time with their line manager at least once a week in the first few months they are with us. As they become more experienced and confident, they will sit down with their line manager once a fortnight. The pace at which our good apprentices pick up stuff is phenomenal. I often have to only tell them once and they have got it.

How to outsource your compliance work

Many accountancy firms use the services of an outsourcer to help them increase their firm's capacity. This can either be on an on-going basis or on a project basis. In the context of this book, as you grow your practice outsourcing your compliance work can free up your staff to take on more exciting work.

Case study: Bill

Bill was following his 3-year Growth Plan and had six accountants. To free up his staff and allow them to progress their careers, Bill outsourced two functions over the space of eight months.

His IT employee Chloe was actually a young school leaver who was technically capable of setting up and supporting IT when the firm only had 3 employees. But Chloe had no formal qualifications and she was nervous about the coming changes involving the cloud. By outsourcing IT support, Bill was able to give Chloe real advancement, plus a qualification at the local college.

Bill's accountants were getting frustrated that they didn't have enough time to truly deliver the proactive service or become the trusted advisor that they and Bill wanted them to. So, the firm started outsourcing their clients' Year End Accounts. This freed up over 50% of his accountants' time. Bill made sure his accountants were trained in how to deliver non-compliance services such as management accounts, cash flow forecasting and business planning. 12 months after Bill took the decision to outsource the Year End Accounts preparation, the advisory income for his firm had grown from £15,000 a year to £100,000 a year. His accountants loved being able to truly be the trusted advisor to the firm's clients.

What are the benefits of outsourcing?

The benefits of outsourcing are more than just being able to more cost effectively service your firm's compliance work. Outsourcing your compliance work can free up your staff to do more of the higher value stuff, like building strong relationships with clients, which you need them to be doing and they want to do. Given how hard it is in the UK to recruit in decent qualified members of staff, many firms are turning to outsourcing as a way of increasing their capacity without having to externally recruit. Working with an outsourcer can help you increase the services you offer. For example, you could use an outsourcer to cost effectively offer a bookkeeping service to your client.

Often firms find the act of defining their work processes, ready for outsourcing, to be hugely beneficial. After all, the last thing you want to do is outsource unwieldy or inefficient ways of working to your outsourcer. Mapping your processes is a fairly simple task to do in your firm's weekly Rhythm Team Meeting. To map a process follow these steps:

Step 1: Decide on which process to map

Step 2: Define the start and end of the process so that everyone knows what is in scope.

Step 3: Write down each individual step in the process on a post-it note. Identify on the post-it note who is responsible for each step of the process. If different staff members have different ways of doing things map both versions of the process.

Step 4: Identify ways that your firm could do the process better, simpler or cheaper. For example, could you invest in a new piece of software to automate part of the process?

Step 5: Agree on the new version of the process, that everyone will follow.

Step 6: For the new version of the process identify check-points through the process to allow everyone to easily see where a piece of client's work is in the process. For example, Sian's firm measures both the number of Year End Accounts the firm has to prepare, but also the amount of Year End Accounts that they can start processing because they have the clients' records.

As part of your process mapping you will need to consider how it will change when you decide to outsource. I.e.

- At what point in your existing processes will you send work to an outsourcer?
- What is the process to send and receive back work from the outsourcer?
- How do you keep control of what is being sent over to the outsourcer?
- What can you automate in the outsourcing process?
- How much do your clients need to be informed whilst the work is being outsourced?
- Who will contact the client and at what stage?
- How will queries that come back from the outsourcer for the client be dealt with?
- How do you make your processes more efficient before you start outsourcing?
- How will your outsourcer keep you updated on progress?

Case study: Sharon's Growth Story

In our weekly Rhythm Team Meeting we brainstormed our new client onboarding process. As we went through the mapping process we identified all the ways we could automate what we did.

I then gave a task to my team to take the basic onboarding process we had identified and find options to wow our new clients. My staff did a great job in putting in place more touchpoints with our new clients to help them feel really supported and wanted. All new clients now have a 3-month review to check that we are delivering on what's important to them, and how we can help.

As a result of automating our new client process, we have saved 4-6 hours per new client onboarded.

What sort of accountancy-related tasks can you outsource?

Any task which can be put into a process or systemised and needs little on-going input from your client can easily be outsourced. Accountancy outsource providers will offer the following services:

- Bookkeeping, both cloud-based and traditional
- Year End Accounts preparation
- Self-assessment personal tax returns
- VAT returns
- Corporation tax returns
- Management accounts
- Payroll
- Basic tax planning.

Why are so many firms extremely reluctant to go down the outsourcing route?

There are many bad news stories about outsourcing compliance work, however these are all normally based on poor handling by the firm in the first place. For success, there are three key things you must do:

1. You have to bundle up the work into an efficient set of steps. This means having a well-defined handover of information to the outsourcer, a clear set of instructions on the work to be done, a list of actions the outsourcer must take if they find a problem, and finally a well-defined handover of information back into your practice.
2. You have to find a rock-solid outsourcer, with a strong reputation and long track record of doing quality work. You must also ring their clients and get testimonials directly.
3. During the first months of outsourcing, you will need to appoint a transition person from your practice to keep a very close watch on the outsourcing, until everything is bedded in. The time spent by the transition person is your insurance, because you want a mutually successful relationship to continue for 10 years or more.

Case study: Sharon's Growth Story

I'd never really intended to outsource our compliance work. However, when a member of staff resigned in November and left before Christmas, I had a massive shortage of resource right at our busiest point of the year. As you can imagine I was pulling my hair out. If I wanted to grow my firm I needed to stop doing the day-to-day compliance work, like the VAT returns. Other firms, which I knew and trusted, were telling me how well outsourcing was working for them.

As a result, I decided to outsource the firm's VAT returns and bookkeeping to Global Infosys. They came highly recommended from other accountants I knew who used them. Global Infosys were really good in helping us start to outsource. They helped us map out the information flows and split of responsibilities between them and us. They even adapted to our ways of working. In fact, they helped us identify that our former member of staff hadn't been following our own firm processes! They taught us to treat them like a new member of staff and give them feedback after every piece of work to help them deliver jobs to our normal high standards. By outsourcing this compliance work, plus some automation of processes, we increased our gross profit by 28%, and our net profit by 119%. Our direct wages costs reduced by 10%. The great thing about outsourcing is being able to flex it up or down based on our busy or quiet periods.

How to get ready to outsource your compliance work

Outsourcing any of your client work is a big decision which should not be taken lightly. In many ways choosing to outsource is the equivalent of hiring a completely new team in your practice. Just as you would do your due diligence on a new team member, it is vital that you do your due diligence on any potential outsourcer *before* you press the button and send them work to complete.

Your due diligence needs to include the following:

- How will your outsourcer guarantee the quality of their work? What is their review process? What quality standards are they working towards?
- How does your outsourcer keep your clients' data secure? What systems and processes does it have in place to minimise the risk of a data breach?
- What office hours do they work? Do they work to your location's office hours?

- How will you access support from the outsourcer? Do they have a locally-based account manager? Can you pick up the phone and contact the person doing your work at any time?
- What software packages do they use – and are certified to use? After all, you don't normally want to be paying your outsourcer to learn how to use your software.
- What workflows do they use, and how will they adjust to your ways of working?
- What is the quality of their English, both for spoken and written communication?
- Do they have written and videoed references which you can check? Can you speak to their current clients?

Outsourcing most definitely is a huge change if you have never done it before. It is important to take the time out and talk to your outsourcer to make sure you are 100% happy with everything before moving forward. It's not something to be rushed. If you are having doubts when it comes to outsourcing why not pick a few Year End Account jobs from non-profitable clients, or work of low importance. That way you can iron out any kinks before committing fully.

You don't have to jump in headfirst to outsourcing, you can start off slowly. In fact, it's actually better to start slowly with outsourcing and then ramp up when everything is working properly. It can be tempting when the pressure is off to delay setting up an outsourcing relationship. However, you want to get this in place and working well before you hit a peak time. Just as it takes a new team member time to get up to full competence, it's the same for your outsourcer.

How to get your team to embrace outsourcing

Even if your staff may not personally have had a bad experience with outsourcing, they may have a perception that it will result in a loss of control and poor-quality work coming back from the outsourcer. Given everything that could be going through your staffs' minds, including a concern about their future job security, when you broach the subject of outsourcing, understandably you may face some resistance to outsourcing from your staff.

Often staff can be worried about using an outsourcer because they are concerned about loss of control and a reduction in quality. In extreme cases, they may be worried about the security of their own roles. It is important to allow staff to fully voice their concerns otherwise the resistance can come out in other ways and potentially sabotage getting outsourcing started. Take the time to talk to staff as a group. In these conversations, talk to staff about how outsourcing will help the firm with its 3-year Growth Plan, but also about the benefits to them personally, e.g. less grunt work, more capacity in the team, releasing them to service clients properly.

Once managers and staff can see it working and how it will work they are often more willing to embrace outsourcing. Therefore, plan to start small with outsourcing and gain full buy-in from staff before sending everything you can to your outsourcer. Often the best way to bring your reluctant members of staff on board is to actually show them how it works and the fact it can work very well (see Chapter 3 for more advice on how to get your staff supportive with a proposed change).

There will probably be within your team a real advocate for outsourcing who can see the benefits of embracing it. Find this individual and then train them up and make them your expert on outsourcing.

How will the structure of your firm change if you use outsourcing?

In the early days, there will probably be very little change with your firm. Most accountancy firms initially use outsourcing as an overflow resource to help cost-effectively resource up for their peak times. It is as the trust develops between you and your outsourcer, that you will confidently start to change the structure of your business. For example:

- Hiring a client administrator to liaise with your clients to get the information required for your outsourced team to prepare the accounts.
- Your staff have the time to be more proactive with clients, but also grow and develop their careers within your firm.
- You will need a smaller headcount overall and the profitability of your firm will rise
- Fewer people will be needed to manage the workflow of compliance jobs.

See Diagram 8.1 and Diagram 8.2 for a Before and After structure chart for an accountancy firm which has fully embraced outsourcing for all its compliance type work.

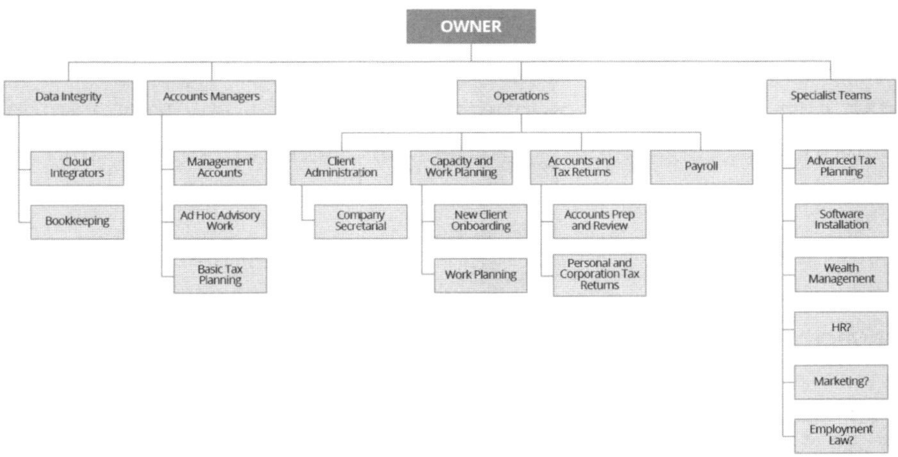

Diagram 8.1: Structure before outsourcing

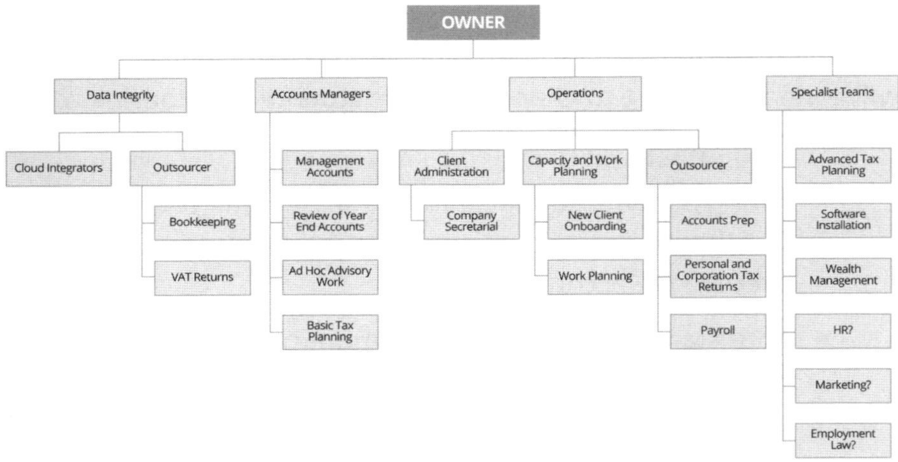

Diagram 8.2: Structure after outsourcing

Summary

If you plan your capacity and resourcing requirements in advance, you can take informed decisions in advance to cost effectively resource your practice.

Many firms choose to use apprentices to help them grow their own staff cost effectively. Apprentices are often very new to the world of work, and consequently will need far more supervision than an experienced hire.

Using the services of an accounts outsourcer is a great way to flex up and flex down your resourcing to cost effectively meet your firm's capacity requirements.

Action plan

- Create a spreadsheet to help you model your firm's resourcing requirements over the next 6–12 months. Identify what you can do now to reduce any periods where you are short on resource or have too much resource.

- Speak to other firms who regularly recruit, develop and retain their apprentices. What do they do well which helps them get the benefit of apprentices? Take a decision on whether hiring apprentices is the right thing to do for your firm.
- Speak to other firms who successfully outsource their compliance work. What can you learn from them? Take a decision on whether to try out outsourcing your firm's compliance work.

9

How to standardise your practice's way of working

Topics covered in this chapter:

- What to standardise?
- How to go about standardising your practice's way of working
- What technology should your firm invest in as it grows?

Standardising your practice's way of working enables you and your team to be hyper-efficient, consistently use best practice ways of working, minimise the risk of missing client deadlines or making mistakes on client affairs. This chapter takes you through what to standardise and how to go about standardising your practice's way of working.

Case study: Guy's Growth Story

My practice was growing by 40% each year. In real terms this meant that in 2 years I had taken my practice from £200k to £400k turnover. My 3-year Growth Plan always intended for me to standardise my practice's way of working. As circumstances would have it, I had to pretty much recruit in a completely new team as my practice doubled in size. I think this also contributed to me having far more grey hair. I've started to measure my practice efficiency by calculating my practice annual revenue divided by hours in the business; i.e.

$$\frac{\text{Practice annual turnover}}{\text{Number of hours worked by my employees per year}}$$

With so many new people in the team, I could see that our efficiency dropped off a cliff. My practice efficiency was running at £20/hour. We needed to get more efficient at delivering the work to the client. To do this the practice needed to follow a standardised way of doing client work. Once we had a standardised way of delivering client work, I could then delegate more of my responsibilities down to my team.

I won't lie, standardising my practice's workflows was one of the most painful things I have done. It was something I needed to get through. After all, once it's done, it's done. I used my coach to keep me accountable to getting each workflow completely standardised, so that everyone in my team worked the same way.

I firstly categorised my services into three different types: Book-keeping, Accounts and Advisory. Activities included completing a client's personal tax return or doing their monthly management accounts. For each activity, I looked at how we were currently doing the activity, and then what would be a simpler way of completing that activity. Then, in our weekly Rhythm Team Meetings, we tackled each activity in turn. As a team, we identified the most effective way of doing the activity and captured this. For each activity, we also produced a checklist. This checklist needed to be completed for each activity before anything could be reviewed or sent out to the client.

With the team coding up their time by client activity, I was able to see for the first time exactly how long each job was taking. It also enabled me to see who were the most efficient members of my team. As a result of standardising our practice's way of working, managing individual performance issues and all of the team consistently following the practice's way of working, we have nearly doubled our practice efficiency. I.e. from £20/hour to £37/hour.

Calculate your firm's efficiency

What to standardise?

What every accountancy firm does can be categorised into one of six different top-level processes:

Create It: Everything your practice does to generate a client lead. This will include all of your lead generation processes. (See Part 3 of the book)

Convert It: Everything your practice does to qualify and convert a client lead into paying client work. This will include your process for qualifying a new client enquiry, having a new client meeting, quoting for a new client, managing your firm's sales pipeline and onboarding a new client. (See Chapter 10 and 11)

Deliver It: Everything your practice does to deliver a piece of client work. This will include exactly how your firm delivers its services for clients. Some examples are Bookkeeping, Payroll, Tax Returns, Year End Accounts and Management Accounts. It will also include how your firm manages the workflow of your practice. That is, how you plan in and allocate client work to members of the team.

Get Paid For It: Everything your practice does to get paid for completing a piece of client work. For example, how you go from issuing a monthly invoice to getting paid by Direct Debit.

Cultivate It: Everything your practice does to get repeat client business or more business as a result of completing a piece of client work. These are all your Account Management processes.

People Stuff: Everything your practice does to ensure you have the right people doing the right things right. For example, recruitment, performance reviews, career planning, training and developing your staff.

To become a one million pound practice you will need to have nailed down your practice's ways of working for each of these six different processes.

Case study: Paul's Growth Story

I've always loved being with my clients and going out and winning work. It's why I get up in the morning and why I've been in practice for the last 30 years. I've never been interested in being the person who services the clients' compliance requirements. Reviewing a set of client accounts is not my idea of fun.

As a result, I'd put together standard *"Create It"* processes for how the firm went about winning work. I'd optimised these processes but also how we as a practice grew our client accounts, *"Cultivate It"*. I knew what worked and what didn't work. I found it comforting to know that if I ever needed to add in lots more new client work, I knew exactly what to do to make this happen.

The problem was that my operation needed some management time from me. My staff costs had escalated to 43% of my annual turnover. My *Deliver It* processes were not efficient. So, I decided – in conjunction with my team – to have a One Big Focus on reducing these staff costs back down to 35%. (In time, I plan to get this figure down to a more industry-leading figure of 30%) The thought of spending three months sorting out our workflow for clients work filled me with dread. I knew I would find every excuse going to avoid doing this work. It needed to be done if I wanted to scale my practice to one million pounds, so I outsourced this work.

My operations manager and I went to spend a couple of days with Inform Accounting to see exactly how they had standardised their *"Deliver It"* processes and workflow. I then paid for the person who set up Inform Accounting's *"Deliver It"* processes and workflow to work with our operations manager to do the same for our practice. Within three months I had finally done what I had avoided doing for decades – standardised how we delivered the on-going client work for our practice.

Case study: Sian's Growth Story

When I used to work in industry, bi-annual performance reviews and monthly performance conversations with my staff members was just something I did. After I set up my own practice I stopped doing this. I suppose I had just got lazy. After all, when you only have a handful of staff, this stuff seems less important as you are working so closely with each member of your staff.

My practice had grown, and over a period of 18 months I'd recruited in 4 trainees, who were a mixture of school leavers and graduates. They were bright, intelligent and super keen to progress in the firm. I rapidly began to realise that if I was to achieve my 3-year Growth Plan, and retain my new young members of staff, I needed to standardise how I supported their development and managed their day-to-day and long-term performance.

The first thing I did was put together a competency framework for my practice. My competency framework showed my staff what attitudes, behaviours or skills they would need as they progressed in my firm. I then put together job descriptions for all the roles and future roles in my practice. My job descriptions detailed exactly what each role was there to do and what I expected each role to achieve (including KPIs) for each of the six top-level processes in my practice. As my young team were rapidly progressing I implemented mini 3-month performance reviews. In these performance reviews, we spent a large proportion of the review identifying their gaps in knowledge and skills and what they needed to do to close the gap. In particular, what would be covered by studying for AAT or ACCA, and how they would develop on the job.

After I had done the first round of performance reviews with my staff, I was kicking myself for not starting them much earlier. My staff really appreciated the focused time I was spending with them. And I got much closer to my staff as a result. Since implementing regular performance reviews and monthly performance conversations no staff member has left my firm. My staff are working much more effectively as they know exactly what is expected of them.

If your firm doesn't have documented processes, templates and checklists for all your firm's compliance work, so that execution can be standardised, your firm will be inefficient.

How to go about standardising your practice's ways of working.

Standardising every part of your practice's ways of working is a major undertaking. As the saying goes, how do you eat an elephant? One bite at a time. It's the same with standardising your practice's ways of working. In time you will standardise all your practice's ways of working. However, at this point in time you only want to tackle the priority areas. Look at your KPIs? Where is your firm inefficient or under-performing? Which areas, if you standardised your practice's ways of working, would have the biggest impact to help you achieve your 3-year Growth Plan?

To standardise part of your practice's ways of working do the following steps:

Step 1: Identify what you want to achieve by? Do you want to eradicate mistakes? Process work more quickly? Increase your current capacity? The best areas to normally focus on are your firm's Bookkeeping processes, Year End Accounts processes and your onboarding new clients process. Identify the KPIs for your firm that will be impacted by implementing your new system.

Step 2: Measure, using the KPIs, how you are performing right now. This gives you the ability to see how your new standardised way of working is impacting your firm's performance.

Step 3: Map step-by-step how you currently do things.

Step 4: With the appropriate people in your firm, map how you want to do things in the future. Capture this new process.

Step 5: Implement any changes to your technology, e.g. automating a manual process, to be able to do the new process.

Step 6: Identify ways you can easily check that the new process is being followed correctly. This is often best achieved by checklists which need to be completed before an activity is started, or completed before an activity can be ticked off as completed.

Step 7: Identify additional KPIs to see how well staff are following the new system.

Step 8: In your weekly Rhythm Team Meeting for the next 4 weeks monitor the KPIs to see how well the new process is going. If the KPIs are Red or Amber then implement some further process improvements.

The next chapter of the book focuses on your firm's *Convert It* processes, in particular how your firm manages the process by which Leads turn into Clients.

What technology should your firm invest in as it grows?

Some tasks that take you hours could be done in minutes by utilising technology better. How are you educating yourself on what technology is making possible in your practice?

One of the best ways to make your practice's ways of working more efficient is to also invest in technology to help your firm do stuff better, simpler and cheaper.

Your technology choices split into technology that will help your clients run their business better; which in turn helps you service them more effectively. And then technology which helps you service your clients' work more effectively, typically by automating manual processes. Alongside your internal practice software that helps you do the normal compliance stuff like calculating tax returns for clients, you also want to identify a suite of software to help you manage your practice and deliver advisory services to your clients. For example, if you use Fluidly[1] as your tool to help clients seamlessly manage their cash flow, your firm can completely ditch using spreadsheets

[1] www.fluidly.com

to model and forecast cash flow. Thus, saving you and your client time and minimising the risk of having an error in your spreadsheet's formula. Or you could invest in a service such as The Gap 2014 Ltd which will help you systemise the way you market, sell and deliver advisory services to your clients.

When it comes to recommending cloud accounting solutions to clients, you want to encourage your clients to use your firm's preferred:

- cloud accounting platform, e.g. Xero, Quickbooks, Exact or Sage
- cloud bookkeeping apps, e.g. Receipt Bank, AutoEntry, Datamolino or Hubdoc
- cloud reporting and forecasting app, e.g. Fluidly, Futrli, Spotlight Reporting, Silverfin or Fathom

As well as these apps which you want all your clients to use, you want to recommend some sector specific apps. For example, cloud based EPOS systems for any retail clients your firm may have. It is cheaper to have your clients using your preferred accounting software packages as you can often negotiate a better licence fee from the software provider, and you only have one way of working across your firm.

Summary

In order to function effectively, your accountancy practice needs to standardise how it does the following six things.

- Create It
- Convert It
- Deliver It

- Get Paid For It
- Cultivate It
- People stuff

To get the best economies of scale, recommend just one type of cloud accounting or bookkeeping software to clients, e.g. bookkeeping app, accounts package.

Action point

- Calculate your practice's efficiency each month by dividing the practice's monthly turnover by the number of available hours each month. For any months where efficiency drops, root cause the reasons for the drop and implement an action plan to stop the drops happening again.
- If your practice's wage costs, including outsourcing fees, are greater than 30% of your firm's revenue, then have a One Big Focus for your firm to become more efficient. As part of the One Big Focus process map how your firm plans its workflow, prepares Year End Accounts and does your clients' bookkeeping. Identify ways for each of these areas to make these processes more efficient.

10

How to manage your firm's sales pipeline

Topics covered in this chapter:

- What you need to know about the business development process to sign up clients
- How to progress a Lead through to a Client
- How to spot that a Prospect is interested in working with you
- Creating a weighted sales forecast
- The importance of keeping in touch with Prospects and previous Clients

The last chapter talked about standardising your firm's working practices. This chapter is a deep dive into how to manage your firm's *Convert It* processes, i.e. everything that your firm needs to do effectively manage your firm's Sales Pipeline, so that you convert the right type of Leads into Clients.

This chapter uses the following definitions:

Tactical Marketing Plan: This is something that looks at the million pound practice that you want to grow, and converts that into a specific list of where you'll get new business, what activities you'll do to get it, and how much business you'll get from each type of activity. See Chapter 15 for how to create your firm's Tactical Marketing Plan.

Prospect: Someone in your niche market who could become a good Client for you.

Lead: Someone who has proactively contacted you to talk about your services, but they are not yet a Client.

Client: Someone who pays you an agreed fee for doing work.

Conversion Rate: This is your ratio of Leads to newly signed-up Clients.

How to spot a potential Lead

As part of your Tactical Marketing Plan you are measuring the number of Leads your firm generates by channel to market. (See Chapter 15) For this to happen, you and others in your firm need to know how to spot a Lead. Remember that the definition of a Lead is someone who has proactively approached your firm to explore whether your firm will be able to help them. Sometimes a Lead is obvious, For instance, you get an email or a tweet from someone saying *I think I want to work with you* (or something along these lines.) However, it isn't always that clear cut.

Before a Prospect will become a Lead they need to go through three tests. These are:

1. Awareness: do they know your firm exists?
2. Interest: do they know your firm can help them?
3. Evaluation: do they want to assess or trial your firm?

Very often, the Evaluation test will happen when you or someone from your firm meets them or talks with them over the phone.

Here are common signs to look out for that a Prospect is likely to become a Lead:

- They ask detailed questions about how you work with others.
- They are keen to know costs.
- They will relatively easily agree to a conversation or chat with you.

- They may look at your LinkedIn profile a couple of times over a period of a few months.
- They will frequently engage with you on social media or with the regular marketing emails that they send to you.
- They will ask interested questions about your services, and the typical results you get for your clients.
- They may recommend you to others and talk positively about you.

Case study:
Sian's Growth Story

Apart from Leads, which come from existing clients, all of our new Leads come from our website. Given our heavy and regular investment in producing regular valuable content and keeping the firm highly visible on social media, this isn't surprising. Leads either book a call with us via the website or send us an email via the website. Our website is on Hubspot, which means we can see exactly where on our website our Lead has been. This gives us great insight into who is a serious buyer and who is probably just fishing for a price. We find that we sign up most new clients on the basis of a phone call rather than a face-to-face meeting.

What is your firm's Sales Pipeline?

The Sales Pipeline is a concept to represent where your firm's Prospects, Leads and Clients are in the business development lifecycle. Now an important thing to remember is that all sales go through a number of steps. Sometimes they go through fast, sometimes slowly, and occasionally, like leaky pipes, some of the Leads will leak out.

Your role in pipeline management is to help the person through the key stages in the process to make it easy and logical for them, so they understand what's going on. When Leads know where they are at, and what will happen next, it minimises the number that drop out. Or to put it another way, it increases the conversion rate.

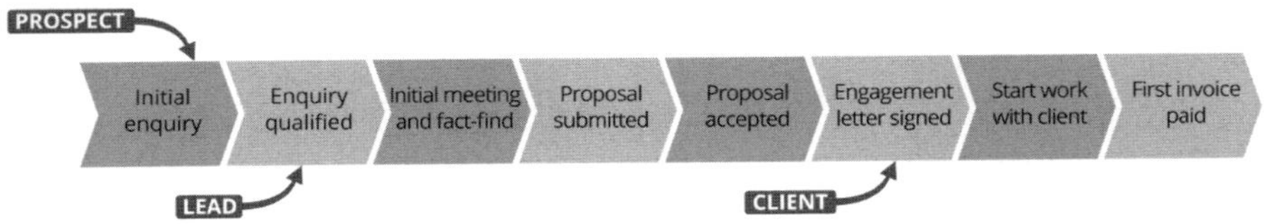

Diagram 10.0: Stages in a Sales Pipeline

Typical stages in your Sales Pipeline will be:

- Initial enquiry
- Enquiry is qualified; e.g. you decide that this is a Prospect your firm would like as a Lead
- Initial meeting and fact find between you and the Lead
- Proposal submitted
- Proposal accepted
- Engagement letter signed
- Start work with Client
- First invoice paid.

For a simple compliance Lead, there should be no reason why you can't provide, if requested, an accurate quote for them in the sales meeting.

What's a good conversion rate?

There is no right answer for what is a good conversion rate. For example, if your firm sells a very expensive, big ticket service, you would expect a lower conversion rate than a firm which sold a cheaper version of the same service. Part of the aim of your firm's marketing is to weed out unsuitable Leads before they take up your time, attention or resources.

A low conversion rate would be 5–10%. It is not uncommon for an accountancy firm who wins the majority of their new work from existing Clients to have a very high conversion rate up above 80%.

When you have established your firm's conversion rate from Lead to Client, the next task is to look at the amount of people who make it between each of the stages of your Sales Pipeline. You can then see where you have *big leaks* in your Sales Pipeline, and identify remedial action to fix those leaks to improve your firm's overall conversion rate.

If your Lead to Client conversion rate is over 80%, it's not because your sales skills are great. It's because your fees are too low.

Sales Pipeline management

When you know what you have in your Sales Pipeline and at what stage of the sales process it is, you can then do a multitude of things:

- Forecast your firm's future capacity requirements.
- Predict your firm's future income and cash flow.
- Identify when your firm needs to spend more time marketing to cover up periods of low demand.

You ideally want to be regularly producing a weighted sales forecast for your firm. A weighted sales forecast will identify the value of your Sales Pipeline, and will be weighted by the probability of the business converting, depending on the stage the Lead is at in your firm's pipeline.

For example, Sam identified these stages and conversion rates for his Sales Pipeline:

Initial enquiry – 30% conversion
Initial meeting and fact-find – 60% conversion
Proposal submitted – 75% conversion
Proposal accepted – 90% conversion
Engagement letter signed and money laundering procedures completed – 95% conversion
First invoice paid – 100% conversion

Sam had three live Leads, each worth £5k. They were at the following stages of his firm's Sales Pipeline:

Lead A:
Proposal accepted, work likely to start in March, but engagement letter not signed yet.
Weighted value of work = £5k x 0.95 = £4,750

Lead B:
Proposal submitted, but not yet accepted, work likely to start in April.
Weighted value of work = £5k x 0.9 = £4,500

Lead C:
Initial enquiry, work likely to start in April.
Weighted value of work = £5k x 0.3 = £1,500

He then combined these to produce his firm's weighted sales forecast for March and April:

March:
Lead A = £4,750

April:
Lead B + Lead C = £6,000

Sam then used this forecast to plan his cash flow and also to check that he had enough capacity to deliver the work in March and April.

Weighted Sales Pipeline exercise

How to follow up with a Lead without being pushy

Many accountants hate the thought of selling, as this implies in their mind that they need to turn into a pushy second-hand car sales person. Consequently, they have a very hands-off approach to their Leads, and often lose many potentially good Clients by this approach.

Your aim when managing your firm's Leads through your Sales Pipeline is to let them set the pace, but also design into your firm's sales process little acts of commitment from them to take them to the next stage in the process. These acts of commitment enable your firm to focus on the Leads who are committed to proceeding, and eliminate the *tyre kickers*. Tyre kickers is a name often used to describe the accountants' equivalent of the people who are just browsing in a shop.

Unfortunately tyre kickers can sometimes be mistaken for a genuine Lead, because they will exhibit some of the same signs that an interested Lead will. For example:

- Be very interested in what you charge, and what they get for that
- Want some free advice from you (rather than actually pay for your service).

Here are ways of getting your firm's Leads to commit to the next stage in the process, whilst also weeding out tyre kickers:

- Ask them what they see as the next step.
- Check very early in the sales process that they have the budget to afford your services. An easy way to do this is to have your prices on your website, i.e. "from x" and then

before your first meeting send them your very broad brush costs for the typical client or service you provide.

- When asked to submit a proposal ask the Lead to commit to a quick conversation to talk through the draft outline before you spend a large amount of time writing it. This allows you to find out which Leads are actually bringing the sales process to an end by asking for a proposal. Or if you use a quoting tool in your firm, use it in the sales meeting to build a live quote for them.
- Ask them how and when you should follow up with them if you have not heard anything.

If you are taking over 24 hours to get a proposal and quote out to a client after a sales meeting you will be losing business.

How to get a face-to-face or phone meeting with your Prospect

Most accountants find that they need to get their Prospect to commit to a face-to-face meeting or a telephone call before their Prospect will become a Lead. Testing the water by setting up a face-to-face or phone meeting can help you generate more clients in two ways:

- It helps to establish a relationship and a greater understanding of the Prospect, which may help your firm sell to them at a later date
- It may flush out a Lead.

Getting a face-to-face meeting is as simple as asking for one. Yes, really. Here are ways in which you can increase the likelihood of the Prospect saying *Yes*:

- Ask them after they have asked for some advice from you

- If you have been chatting for a while on social media, suggest a phone call to get to know each other better
- When a member of your network pops up out of the blue and starts chatting to you
- After they have given you some positive feedback
- Suggest a meeting on a certain date as you are *in their area*.

The importance of keeping in touch with Leads and ex-Clients

Depending on which study you are reading the cost of winning a new client is 5–25 times more expensive than keeping an existing one. However, when the Client engagement has finished it can be tempting to move onto the next piece of client work and forget about the Client. As a result, your Clients can go for long periods of time without hearing from someone at your firm. Not maintaining a regular dialogue with your firm's Clients is one of the biggest risk factors for Clients leaving.

That's not the only reason why keeping-in-touch helps your firm's business development effectiveness. As the book has already mentioned, the pace at which a Lead moves through the Sales Pipeline is not controlled by you, but by your Leads. Very often they may press *Pause* because of matters completely outside of their and your control. This could be any number of reasons, such as:

- Waiting for sign-off for a budget, or a new financial year to start.
- Key personnel have moved or gone on holiday.
- Poor business performance and resultant low cash flow stopping any non-essential spend.

However, if your firm has done everything right up until this point, there is no reason why the Lead may not press the *Go* button again. The challenge your firm faces is to stay in touch with this Lead until they are ready to press *Go*. This means standardising your firm's keeping-in-touch processes for A- B- and C-grade clients.

Chapters 13 and 15 will introduce you to the importance of staying in touch with your network, Leads and Clients. Here are some tips to help you and your firm stay in touch:

- Have a Relationship Plan for your A- and B-grade clients.
- Adjust your firm's Content Plan so it specifically includes how you will use your firm's blog, LinkedIn updates and tweets to stay in touch with your A- and B-grade clients.
- Ask your Prospects, Leads, Clients and ex-Clients what sort of information they would welcome receiving from your firm regularly.
- A monthly newsletter is better than nothing, however the more valuable and tailored your firm can make the content for the audience, the better.

As your Sales Pipeline grows you will find that you are juggling multiple Leads. It's very easy to take your eye off the ball and forget about the Leads in your Pipeline. Particularly if you are in your firm's busy season. Use a cloud-based CRM system, such as ActiveCampaign or CapsuleCRM, to keep your Sales Pipeline highly visible to everyone in your firm. Then in every weekly Rhythm Meeting review the Sales Pipeline and make sure each Lead has a next step allocated to it with a person assigned responsibility for the next step.

Summary

Every time someone agrees to buy a service from your firm, they go through a series of typically well-defined stages, called your

Sales Pipeline. Your aim is to seek small acts of commitment from your Lead to move them to the next stage of the Sales Pipeline and ultimately have them become a Client.

Your Leads control the speed at which they progress through the Sales Pipeline, and not everyone will go on to become a Client. Use your firm's keeping-in-touch processes to stay in contact with everyone, so that you maximise the chances that they become a loyal Client.

Action points

- Identify the stages of your firm's Sales Pipeline. Determine the percentage conversion rate for each stage of your Pipeline. Over the next 3–6 months measure the conversion rate of all your Leads and adjust accordingly the percentage conversion rate used in your Sales Pipeline.
- Invest in a cloud based CRM system for your firm so you can easily monitor your firm's Sales Pipeline.
- Identify every live Lead you are aware of, and add these into your firm's Sales Pipeline. Now calculate a Weighted Sales Forecast, i.e. the likely revenue your firm will bill over the next 6–12 months. What action will you need to increase your firm's marketing activity or your team's capacity to hit the Goals you identified in your 3-year Growth Plan?
- Set time aside each week in your weekly Rhythm Meeting to review your firm's Sales Pipeline and implement actions to progress Leads through the process steps.

11

How to turn your Leads into paying Clients

Topics covered in this chapter:

- How to qualify a Lead
- How to structure and run a sales meeting
- How to increase your Lead's motivation to buy, particularly advisory services
- What to do when faced with objections from your Leads
- Tips to help you write a winning proposal

The previous chapter dealt with the process side of successful selling. The fastest way for your firm to sustainably grow is to be able to sell both advisory AND compliance services to your clients. The quality of selling skills needed to sell advisory skills is much higher than the quality of selling skills needed to sell compliance services. This is why this chapter looks at the practical selling skills you will need to learn to convert the opportunities that come your way.

> “Half the battle is selling music, not singing it. It's the image, not what you sing.
>
> *ROD STEWART*

How to qualify a Lead

Possibly the biggest business development time waster is generating and progressing the wrong sort of Leads; i.e. the people who are never going to become a Client, or if they do sign up are not the type of Client that your firm wants. Your firm needs to make sure that when someone enquires about using your firm's services, they are likely to become a Client and a good fit for what your firm does. See Chapter 13 for how to decide on your firm's target market.

The firms that grow the fastest are often the firms which are most picky about the clients they will take on.

Case study: Paul's Growth Story

We are very picky about the type of Client we take on. This means we spend a lot of time qualifying our Leads. When we receive a Lead we ask him/her to fill out our Potential New Client Questionnaire and send us their last two years of accounts. We score their answers. If they score high enough we book in a short 15-minute conversation via the phone to check that we would be a good fit for them. Only after this conversation will I then go and meet them to bring them onboard as a Client.

As a result of this qualification process we probably qualify out half of our Leads every month. It may sound quite high, but we find that the nearer the Lead is to our Client Personas the better a Client they become for us.

When you are qualifying a Lead, and *before* you spend large amounts of time writing a proposal, you want to be finding out about the following four things, or DUFF:

- Decision maker
- Urgency
- Fit
- Funds

Decision maker

Very often the person who enquires about using your firm is not the ultimate decision maker. Whilst they may seem to have the right title to make the decision, it may not always be the case. For example, family owned businesses often need the approval of more than one family member to change accountants. As much as possible your firm needs to be talking to the individuals who are the budget holder, and have the authority to allocate funds. When you are talking with a Lead you will need to investigate who else may need to be involved to hire your firm.

Urgency

When someone buys a service from an accountant this normally represents a considered purchase. There is a high level of risk (be it money or reputation) as a result of using your firm's services. Therefore, before your firm allocates a large proportion of time to developing a piece of business, you need to make sure that the Lead intends to make a purchase and has a specific timeframe for doing so.

Fit

Not every Client and Accountant pairing will be a match made in heaven. Many an accountant has found they have signed up a Pain-In-The-Arse (PITA) Client due to a lack of rapport between them and the Client. As well as a good level of rapport, you need to make sure that the Lead has specific needs that your firm can solve. When your firm first speaks to them, these needs may not be easily visible. In fact, the initial *presenting problem* is often not what, after some investigation, your firm ends up solving. You have to determine whether your Lead is truly interested to learn what is possible as a result of using your firm's services, and is motivated to achieve this.

Funds

As early in the Sales Pipeline as possible you want to ascertain that the person has the financial capacity or access to the funds to buy from your firm. If they state that they don't have a budget for your firm's advisory services, this may not be a *Game Over* sign, but indicates that you will need to decide whether you want to educate them as to the value of your firm's services. In an early conversation with a Lead it often helps to let them know what your firm's services are likely to cost. In this early conversation, try not to be too prescriptive with your firm's fees, but let your Lead know the likely range of fees that they may need to fork out for. For example:

> *Clients with problems similar to yourself typically find that it will cost them between £5k and £10k a year.*

Your firm will be qualifying the Lead as they travel through the firm's Sales Pipeline. However, most qualification will happen before and during the first sales meeting. The next part of the chapter looks at how to structure and run a sales meeting with your Lead.

How to structure and run a sales meeting

Chapter 10 talked about ways to spot a Lead. A key indicator that they are interested in using your firm's services is that they will request a time to speak, either via the phone or in person. To help you and your firm get the best possible result from this meeting, follow this structure:

Before you meet:

- Agree time, date, duration and venue.
- Have a quick 10–15 minute phone call to qualify them as a good Lead for your firm and establish a loose agenda for the meeting.

- Ideally send them a couple of pieces of valuable content which demonstrate your firm's expertise and authority.
- If you can do, start a dialogue with them on social media.

A week before you meet:

- Check the meeting is still going ahead, and re-confirm time, date and venue.
- Check the agenda is still the same.
- Ask them whether there is anything that you need to prepare to help them get value from the meeting.
- Send them another piece of short valuable content, relevant to your meeting.

When you meet:

- Introduce yourself very briefly, i.e. in under a minute.
- Things may have changed since you last checked, so clarify how much time they have for the meeting, that the agenda is still appropriate, and what they want to achieve by the end of the meeting.
- Explain that you are keen to understand more about them, and the organisational reasons behind this meeting taking place, particularly *what has motivated them to talk to you about becoming their accountant?*
- Allocate **at least 50%** of the meeting time to listen and explore their problems.
- Summarise to check understanding of what you are hearing.
- Identify the risks for the client of doing nothing, plus the value your firm can bring to the client by working with them.

- Find out the criteria that they will use to select a new accountant.
- Uncover their timings and anything that will affect their ability to proceed quickly.
- Suggest some potential solutions, and cost these solutions if requested.
- Find out any resistance or objections they may have to working with you.
- Agree any next steps and ask when they would like you to follow up with them if you have not heard anything.

After you meet:

- Thank them for their time.
- Send a note summarising your understanding of what was discussed.
- Do your next steps from the meeting.
- Diarise when you should contact them next.

Quote a provisional fee for the first 3 months of your relationship with a new client. Then review the quote after 3 months working with the client. This way you will be able to give your client an accurate fee based on what it really costs to service them.

How to increase your Lead's motivation to buy, particularly advisory services

Selling advisory services as opposed to compliance services needs better quality sales skills.

As mentioned earlier in the book, unlike compliance services, your Lead does not need to buy advisory services. It is an optional spend.

Just telling your Lead that you offer advisory services, such as business planning, is not sufficient to get them to buy. Consequently, in the sales meeting you need to increase your Lead's motivation to buy. Here is how you do this.

Your Lead is currently in the As-is state. The first thing your questioning needs to do is establish the To-be state. What are their goals and aspirations? What is really important for them to achieve and why? Once you have helped them identify their To-be state, the next part of the process is to increase the distance between their As-is and the To-be state. After all, if it was easy to get to the To-be state they wouldn't need your firm's services.

Good questions to use to find out about the To-be state are:

- What is your business trying to achieve? How will that benefit you personally?
- What will become easier or better when you have achieved your business's goals?
- How will your life be better or easier when your business gets there?
- What was your vision for yourself when you set up your own business?
- If your business achieves its goal, how will that impact your partner and family?
- What will doubling the capital value of your business on exit mean for your pension pot and future retirement?
- What's the motivation behind trying to achieve …?

If you don't increase this distance in the sales meeting you will typically hear your Lead say things like:

- It's not a priority for us right now.
- We don't have the budget or cash flow for this.
- We think we can probably do this in-house.

Once you've increased the distance between a Lead's As-is and To-be it's then important for you to ground your Lead in their harsh reality. *Perhaps you could tell me a little about your situation.* Going back to their As-is brings your Lead back down to Earth with a large bump. This is your moment to really dig into their current As-is. For example:

- *Tell me about your profits and losses*
- *Do you really have enough profit to take the income you want out of the business?*
- *What have you tried and failed with?*
- *What are the weak links in your current organisation?*
- *What will happen if you can't overcome …?*
- *What is the impact if you do nothing or delay with …?*

When you are digging into the As-is with your Lead, it is important for them to be challenged in order to not be in denial about what is really going on for them right now. If you do this stage right you will escalate the pain they are feeling right now.

By increasing the distance between their As-is and To-be, and intensifying the pain they are experiencing right now, you stand the best chance of getting your Lead to agree to your firm being the solution they need to their problems.

If a Lead needs time to think about engaging your firm then you have normally failed to surface a potential objection to using your firm.

Case study: Guy's Growth Story

My firm was one of the very early adopters of the cloud. The cloud is helping us get to the point where we, as a firm, can truly deliver a real-time accounting service to our clients. This is often the reason clients opt to work with us. We received a lead from a supplier of one of our clients who was impressed with how they did all their finances in the cloud. Naturally, we had set up our client to work this way.

When I received the Lead I thought, from my initial conversation to qualify the Lead, there was the likelihood of a £10,000 annual recurring fee as they wanted Bookkeeping, Year End Accounts, Tax Returns and Management Accounts. In the business development meeting with the Lead it became apparent that their current accountant had got their business up onto the cloud but had made a huge mess of it. As a result, they were stuck. Their records were incorrect and they couldn't move forward with growing their business because they didn't have decent management information. Their Pain Point was huge and was really hurting them. They also didn't trust their current accountants to sort out the mess without another big bill. As a result of investigating their Pain Points and the aspirations for their business, the client ended up agreeing a £21,000 annual recurring fee and a one-off fee of £2,000 for me to go up to their offices to sort out their systems. If I hadn't have spent so much time digging into their As-is and To-be I doubt I would have come away with such a big fee from the Lead.

When it comes to proposing a solution to your Lead, you want to make sure that you turn the features of your service into benefits for the Lead. A feature is a fact about you or your firm's service – you can't deny it exists – whereas a benefit is something that your firm can *do* for the Client, that the Client wants. They are typically buying into the benefits of your firm's service, rather than its features.

When you understand the benefits that they really want and need, then you can tailor the features to help move your Lead to commit to buying from your firm. You can also propose solutions to help your Lead achieve their desired results. However, many accountants often struggle with features and benefits. Table 11.0 turns often used features into benefits.

Feature	Restated as a Benefit
We are a local firm of accountants	We are a local firm of accountants, which means that we are close enough to make it easy to have a face-to-face meeting when this is needed.
We are the only specialists for retail businesses in the county.	We are the only specialists for retail businesses in the county, which means that we are working with similar clients to you every day. We know the strategies which will help you grow your retail business, which KPIs to monitor like a hawk and which apps you can use in your business to take the headache out of your accounts and books.
We are a small firm	We are a small firm, which means that you will be a very important and major client to us, and receive a high level of personalised client service.

Table 11.0: Turning a feature into a benefit

The best way of finding out what is really important to your Lead, in order to turn a feature into a benefit, is to ask them. For example:

- What are the Top 3 criteria on which you select your accountant?
- If we work with you, what is the main result you want to achieve?
- What initially attracted you to us, rather than our competitors?
- What was it that your current accountant was doing that has prompted you to seek another accountant?

Case study: Sharon's Growth Story

When it came to sales conversations I was my own worst enemy. Somehow, I had got it into my head that we just needed MORE clients. Regardless of whether they were a good fit for us as a firm. I would often do all the talking in the meeting – and even discount my own fee quote without the client asking for a discount.

I worked with a business development coach who helped me get SO much better at really listening to what the client was saying, or sometimes not saying. I now spend at least half of any sales meeting focusing on the client, their As-is and To-be. I've stopped feeling as if I need to tell the client about all of our firm's services, or that I have to take on every Lead as a client.

As a result of these changes to how I run sales meetings with Leads, our conversion rate, for qualified Leads, is now over 80% and our average client fee for new clients is over £250 per month. Most new clients now take some kind of advisory service from us when they sign up.

What to do if you are faced with difficult questions from your Lead

Unfortunately good results with your clients are never guaranteed. You know that, and any potential client knows that. Consequently, whenever a Lead decides to work with your firm they will be risking their money, reputation and potential livelihood. As a consequence, they are always going to want to check out exactly what is involved in hiring your firm, and whether they believe that you can deliver what they want. When you are meeting your Leads, you need to surface these concerns and ask potentially difficult questions.

Luckily, the reasons why a Lead will decide not to work with your firm boils down to only three:

- They don't believe your firm is capable of doing the work.
- They don't believe that they are getting good enough value if they work with your firm.
- There is not a good relationship fit.

When you realise this, it becomes a little easier to anticipate their concerns, and how these will be articulated. For example, if you were asked *What sort of results you have achieved with previous clients?*, this is the Lead testing your capability to be able to help them. Answer the difficult questions by using one of your Credibility Stories (see Chapter 14). Whilst these difficult questions may not feel like it at the time, these are not because your Lead is being awkward, but normally they either want to be reassured about something or to find out the answer to something. Changing your mindset to view difficult questions as just a request for more information, helps you be more relaxed in a sales meeting. It also helps you see that things like *Your fees are quite pricey* as a signal that they are thinking that the price is higher than your competition.

A good technique to use to help identify what are your Lead's objections to working with your firm, is to proactively tell them some of the objections that other Clients had before they were signed up. For example:

Although our costs are higher, all of our Clients have remarked after implementation that they now realise that our solutions are robust, and therefore there is no tidy-up or refinement necessary afterwards.

When faced with one of these difficult questions, you want to let them know that not only do you understand why they feel that way, but that they are right, and others have in the past felt that way. In other words you are not being defensive, but reinforcing the fact that they are right. (Remember the Lead is the one who controls the buying process, and whether you disagree with what they are saying, they are the ones who will ultimately decide to hire you.) However, you also need to show to them that Clients who had been in exactly their situation, had managed to gain a positive outcome by working with you. This is called the Feel, Felt, Found technique.

> ***Feel:*** *I understand how you feel about doing tax planning.*
>
> ***Felt:*** *Many of my other Clients when they were in the same situation as you, felt the same way, and were wondering whether they should ditch tax planning altogether. They were really concerned that their actions would be viewed negatively if it got out into the public domain.*
>
> ***Found:*** *However, when we have worked with Clients in exactly the same place as you now, we have found that they have been able to significantly reduce their tax bill by us helping them find ethical ways to reduce their tax bill, such as R&D tax credits.*

Identifying the real barriers to using your firm's services

Within the sales meeting, your aim is to find a mutually agreeable solution to your Lead's requirements. Whilst they may raise many objections to using your firm's services, some of these may not hinder them signing on the dotted line. Your aim is to investigate which objections are 'real' and how to find a solution that works for both parties.

A great technique for doing this is the *If … then …* technique. Essentially, what you are saying with this technique is 'That's an important issue, so *if* we can resolve it to your satisfaction, *then* we can proceed to contract?' For example:

If *we can find a way of reducing our fees by 25%,* then *you will be happy to sign up as a Client?*

What happens if a client wants you to reduce your fees

Even if you have qualified your Lead correctly, there are still times when they will ask for a reduction in your fees. Unless you are in a competitive bidding situation, this isn't a showstopper, but sometimes a very good indication that you are about to sign them up.

Your aim at this stage of the process is not to arbitrarily reduce your fees, as this is educating your Client that every time they want a fee reduction, they just need to ask and your firm will do it. You need to establish exactly the value you are delivering to them; i.e. what it is that they really want, and what is non-essential. If you can cut the non-essentials from your packaged offering, then you can offer your Client a more bespoke package at a reduced fee. Your Client is happy, and you are happy because you have signed up a Client and not reduced your firm's profit margin or devalued what your firm does for Clients.

If you don't have the option to trim away parts of what your firm will do for the Client, you may find that one of these approaches may help eliminate the deadlock:

- Explain that the fee is what it is, and if they don't want to pay this fee you will happily walk away, no hard feelings. Sometimes this works, and they still sign up.
- Restate the benefits of using your firm's services and how this will help them achieve their organisational goals.
- Demonstrate to them why it costs so much and why you don't have the room to reduce your fees.
- See whether they would accept a more junior member of staff working on their account, in order to reduce the fee level.

- Use a Credibility Story (See Chapter 14) to illustrate how other Clients have also had doubts about your fees, but achieved great results, which justified your firm's fee.

Tips for writing a proposal

It is unusual for a Lead to become a client without asking for the accountant to provide a proposal. The invitation to write a proposal often brings you one step closer to a new client. A proposal, in its simplest form, is where you state what services your firm will provide, your firm's fees for doing so, and the objectives for working together. The form that your proposal takes could be as simple as:

Could you just send me an email outlining what we have agreed to do?

or a full *War and Peace* style document for a formal tender process. Here are some tips for making sure your proposals get accepted:

Send your proposal to your client within 24 hours of the business development meeting

The sooner your client can receive your firm's proposal, the quicker they can sign it off. Most clients are really impressed if their potential new accountant can get them a proposal within 24 hours, as this is far from the norm. Software such as Practice Ignition will help your firm automate the proposal process. Clients are more likely to accept a proposal if it mirrors what you were talking about in the meeting. There should be no surprises. If you can use your firm's pricing tool with the clients in the meeting, this will help reduce any friction in accepting your firm's proposal.

Quantify the results the Lead can expect from engaging your firm

Your Lead is buying results. Therefore, quantify as much as possible the likely results you expect they will get if they work with your firm. Ensure that these results are linked to the Lead's goals and aspirations.

Use a proposal document template

Having standard templates within your firm can help you and your team quickly produce a proposal for a client. Wherever possible use the firm's proposal document template to help you structure your proposal and cut down the time to write. However, do make sure that you tailor any standard pieces of text in the template to fit the piece of work your firm is bidding to win.

You can download a proposal document template from the Account ants Millionaires' Club website – http://www.accountantsmillionaire.club.

Keep the options to a minimum

It can be very tempting to present your Lead with a myriad of options and solutions in your proposal. This can have a similar effect to going into a shop, and being so overwhelmed by the choice, that you get caught up in the decision making, consequently walking out of the shop having not bought what you originally intended to buy. Aim to keep any options you suggest to your firm's standard packages for compliance and recurring services, plus your proposed solution if they want to take advisory services from your firm. Do not be tempted to give your Lead multiple options for advisory services. Your proposed solution for advisory services needs to have been agreed upfront in the sales meeting. If your Lead hasn't agreed to buy advisory services from your firm in the sales meeting they are not going to buy them just because you include them on the proposal!

Make sure that the proposal is readable

The proposal that you write should be simple and easy to read. Remember that your Lead may not be an expert in what your firm does, so eliminate jargon from the document. As you write the document, imagine you were sitting opposite the person and having a conversation. Aim to keep the tone of the document conversational, rather than dry, stilted and stuffed with corporatese.

Features and benefits

Wherever possible, go through your proposal document and turn any feature into a benefit for the Lead. The three benefits that your Lead will be interested in are:

- Saving them time
- Saving them money
- Reducing their risk in hiring you.

For example, instead of stating, *We are the local expert for …*, turn this into, *You know you will be in safe hands with us as we are seen to be the local expert for …*

Differentiate your firm

If you know that your Lead is considering working with other accountants, then you need to make sure your proposal articulates why the Lead should choose your firm, rather than your competitors. However, you need to do this in way that doesn't rubbish your competitors. When you are speaking with your Lead find out their top buying criteria for selecting an accountant. Then show in your proposal how your firm meets or exceeds these buying criteria.

Summary

Before your firm decides to pursue a Lead, you need to make sure that you have the agreement of the decision maker at their company, and the Lead:

- Has the budget to work with your firm

- Is the right fit for your firm
- There is enough internal urgency to want to move from their current accountant and pay for your firm's services.

Your role in the sales meeting is to get a detailed understanding of the Lead's problems and propose a solution that the Lead is motivated to buy. To do this you will need to increase the distance between their As-is and To-be states, whilst amplifying the pain they feel right now. When you propose a solution to your Lead make sure that you turn any features of your firm's services into benefits for your Lead.

Action points

- For the next three Leads who contact your firm, decide to pursue them based on the DUFF qualifying criteria of decision maker, urgency, fit, funds.
- Get out the last five proposals your firm submitted. Based on what you have learnt in this chapter, and which ones were successful, decide what you will start, stop or continue doing to get more proposals agreed by a Lead.
- In your next monthly Rhythm meeting brainstorm with your staff potential objections to using your firm's services. Then role play as a group using the Feel, Felt, Found model how to successfully handle these objections.
- When faced with an objection at a sales meeting, use the Feel, Felt, Found model to successfully handle the objection.
- If you have a Lead asking for a reduction in fees, see how you can repackage what your firm is offering to them so that they get the reduction, but your firm's profit margin is still honoured.

- In your next five sales meetings spend at least half of the meeting digging into the Lead's As-is and To-be, and increasing the distance between the As-is and the To-be.
- Get your next five proposals out to your Leads within 24 hours of meeting the Lead and them asking for a proposal of how they and your firm will work together.
- Take along a business development coach to your next sales meeting. Implement their recommendations on how you can improve your sales skills, particularly your ability to help increase the motivation of your Lead to buy from your firm.

PART III

Scaling up your practice

Now you have a firm foundation for growth it is time to scale up your practice. This isn't just about winning new business, it's about growing your business in a way which is predictable and scalable. Practices either typically decide to grow organically – by winning new clients and growing their existing client base – or by acquiring another practice. Neither way is better than the other. It all depends on your personal preferences.

If you decide to grow organically, and you are to consistently scale your practice over time, it is important that you don't give yourself sole responsibility for generating Leads. If you are going to work fewer hours with less stress, the responsibility for marketing and sales needs to belong to the whole practice.

This part of the book takes you through:

- How to successfully acquire another accountancy practice
- How to decide on your target market
- How to then make yourself irresistible to your target market
- How to create a marketing plan
- How to grow your existing client base and maximise referrals from your network
- How to get others to take responsibility for your practice's sales and marketing activities.

12

How to buy another accountancy practice

Topics covered in this chapter:

- What to do before you consider buying another accountancy practice
- What the key stages are in the acquisition process, in particular what due diligence to do
- How much to pay for an accountancy practice

So far, this book has been showing you to build a firm foundation in order to effectively and profitably grow your practice. Often the quickest – but not necessarily easiest – way to grow your firm is to buy another accountancy practice or book of fees. The profession is currently divided about the benefits of buying fees. For some firms buying another accountancy practice or book of fees was the best thing they did. For others, their troubles all started at the point they bought another practice and have been spending the intervening time sorting out the problems they inherited.

This chapter will help you take an informed decision about whether buying another practice or book of fees is a good growth method for you and your firm. The process of buying another practice is a separate book in its own right. So, this chapter will just give you an outline of what's involved.

It is recommended that if you intend to buy a practice or book of fees that you take professional advice rather than rely solely on the contents of this book.

What to do before you consider buying another accountancy practice

From this point in the chapter, for ease of reference the book will refer to buying an accountancy practice rather than a book of fees. It's still the same process to go through regardless of whether you are buying a whole practice or a discrete block of fees. Go back and look at your 3-year Growth Plan:

- Would your firm achieve the goals set out in that Plan quicker or cheaper by buying an accountancy practice?
- Have you got the appetite to gain funding to buy the practice?
- Will you be able to get funding to buy the practice?
- Do you have the available time, now or in the future, to do the due diligence and progress the sale?
- Does your firm have the capacity, either now or in the future to manage the transition as well as implement the handover plans for all the Clients you are buying?

If the answer is *Yes* to all 5 of these questions, it is first worth considering the pros and cons of buying a practice.

Remember that when you buy an accountancy practice, you are not just buying any old thing. You are buying a group of people that are used to working in a certain way with their accountant or their employer. It can be very tempting to take advantage of a *great deal*. For instance, an accountancy practice in distress being sold at a large discount. But if this purchase doesn't fit with your 3-year Growth Plan or your available capacity right now to handle the sale and transition, then it can be a very bad deal. It is very difficult to focus on growing your practice when you are in the process of buying or integrating another accountancy practice into your firm.

Pros	Cons
• You can pay for a practice in instalments spread over 1-2 years.	• You need funds to be able to buy the practice.
• You can sometimes be in control of how much of the practice you decide to take on.	• As part of the sales agreement you may be required to take on Clients which don't fit the profile of your firm.
• You can inherit some great staff members from the practice you are buying.	• You can inherit some poor performing staff members from the practice you are buying.
• You can put in place a claw back clause in the sales agreement which means you don't need to pay for any Clients who don't stay with you for the length of the claw back arrangement.	• There is no guarantee that the Clients or staff you acquire will stay with you. Or that the staff you acquired don't leave and take Clients with them.
• There is normally great potential to upsell more services to the Clients you acquire or process their affairs more efficiently.	• If the owner of the Client accounts is still in business or sets up another accountancy firm locally, you are at risk of losing Clients back to them.
• There is the potential to add in new services to your current firm offering which you can cross-sell to your existing Clients.	• You will need to transition the Clients and staff to your practice's way of working.
• It's a great way to add in fees to your practice without having to win each Client separately.	• Agreeing the sales and implementing the transition plan will incur large amounts of management time. It may have been quicker to win each Client separately.
-	• There may be restrictive clauses in the sales agreement which stop you from managing your new Clients and staff in the way you want too; e.g. not put prices up for 12 months.
-	• You are not normally allowed to speak to the staff in the practice you are buying before the sale is agreed.

Table 12.0: Pros and Cons of buying an accountancy practice or book of fees

You can buy a practice OR go after organic growth. You can't easily do both at the same time.

When you decide that inorganic growth is a good way to achieve your 3-year Growth Plan, the next stage in the process is to consider how acquiring another practice is going to help you do that. For example:

- Will your firm's overall cost of sales or overheads reduce, or your net profit margin increase by adding on more Client fees?

- Will you be able to bring in more expertise or specialisms?
- Will you get better usage of your current office space?

Once you know how acquiring a practice is going to help you achieve your 3-year Growth Plan, it's time for a reality check. Is now the right time to be buying a practice?

- Is your firm or are you financially stable enough to acquire a practice? And can you get financing from a bank if needed?
- Do you, and the wider firm, have the capacity to integrate the clients and staff into your firm? If you and your firm are working flat out at the moment, the firm will not have the capacity to integrate an entire practice.
- If you were to inherit new members of staff do you have the space in your current office for them?
- Who in your team can you give the responsibility of project managing the integration? And will they do a good job with minimal supervision from you?

On average it takes 5 months from start to finish to sell a practice. For practices with less than £100k of fees, this can be reduced to 3–5 months. For practices larger than £500k it can be longer than 6 months, particularly if the firm being sold is a multi-partner practice.

What are the key stages in the acquisition process?

Most sales of fees or practices are brokered by a specialist in accountancy firms. Each sale typically goes through four discrete stages.

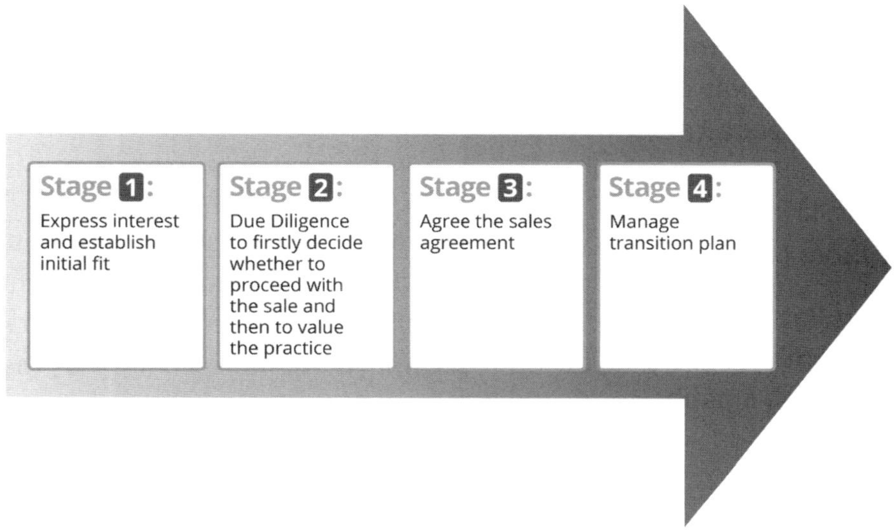

Diagram 12.1: Process to buy an accountancy practice

Stage one: Express interest and establish initial fit

In this stage buyers will express an interest in an opportunity to buy a practice. This normally involves you filling in a non-disclosure agreement, and profile of your firm. The broker will then send through an anonymised version of your firm's profile to the Seller. The Seller will then select potential buyers and the broker will arrange a 'face-fitting' meeting. Remember it is in the interest of the Seller to find the right buyer to allow them to maximise the capital value of their business on exit. It's also in your interest to buy an accountancy practice which is well matched to you and your firm. After all, you want to have a smooth and easy transition of clients and staff.

During this initial meeting or fairly soon after the meeting you will be given copies of the Seller's accounts, a schedule of all the client accounts to be sold and the value of these clients. Of course, client names are removed from this schedule.

It is at this point that you can choose to proceed to the next stage of the acquisition, Due Diligence.

Stage two: Due diligence

Buying an accountancy practice is a big undertaking. Therefore, it is essential that you do your homework to make sure that the deal you are entering into is firstly a good one, and secondly a good fit for your 3-year Growth Plan. Just as you use a surveyor to check that a house you are buying is sound, you need to check that the accountancy practice is also sound. After all, you can't easily go back after you have signed the Sales Agreement with the Seller. It's important that you verify every bit of information that the Seller tells you about their firm.

In the Due Diligence part of the acquisition it is up to you to ask for the information that will allow you to verify what the Seller is claiming. This should be enough to make an informed decision about the value of the practice you are buying. Be aware that you normally won't get access to information or people which could jeopardise the current or future capital value of the practice. For instance:

- Client names
- Interviews with staff

Due Diligence is split into two parts. The Due Diligence you undertake to make a decision to proceed with the sale, and then the Due Diligence you do to finalise the price you will pay for the practice and the Sales Agreement.

Information that you should expect to see to allow you to take a decision about whether to proceed with the sale will include:

- Revenue and profitability of the firm both now and expected revenue and profitability 3 years in the future
- Number of existing Clients

- Evidence for how the firm will grow over the next 3 years; i.e. existing Clients wanting more, referrals from existing Clients
- Net cost per £1 of revenue generated
- Age profile of existing Clients
- Staff numbers, profile and costs.

When you have taken an initial decision to proceed with the sale you are normally asked to sign a letter confirming you have the funds to buy the practice. You may be asked to sign a further confidentiality agreement and undertaking. For example, if you don't proceed with the sale that you are not allowed to poach staff from the Seller's practice.

The second part of your Due Diligence is where you want to dig really deep. A good broker may be able to help you with this part of the Due Diligence. If your Seller can't or won't provide an answer to your questions, and has no legitimate reason for doing so, then this should sound alarm bells. In your Due Diligence you want to check for the following:

- Risks and known liabilities, in particular claims or pending claims on the practice's professional indemnity insurance
- Copies of the firm's Top 10 Client files
- Book value and fair market value of the fixtures and fittings; e.g. furniture, IT hardware and software
- A full Client list, by year end, industry, service provided and fees
- Billing and cash collection; how promptly does the firm get paid for its services?
- A list of all Clients lost in the last year and reasons why they left

- Full financial records, including cash flow forecast, management accounts, income statement, Year End Accounts
- Total dividends or draws, by year, paid to the partners or owners of the business
- How well the firm can run without the Seller in place
- Any Seller quirks; that is, stipulations on what you can or can't do when you take on the practice. For example this could be that you have to buy the whole practice, not just cherry pick the Clients you want.
- What technology the practice is using.

For a detailed Due Diligence Checklist go to http://www.accountantsmillionaire.club

Stage three: Agree the Sales Agreement

The Sales Agreement is where you and the Seller set out the terms of the sale. As part of the agreement you and the Seller will decide on how and when you should pay for the practice. Paying in 2–3 instalments over a 1–2 year period is very common. The larger the practice the greater the chance of paying in 3 instalments over a 2-year period.

It is usual in a Sales Agreement to have a claw back clause. Claw back clauses are typically done in one of two ways.

1. For every Client the Seller's firm loses over a certain period – often between two and five years – this amount is taken off the selling price of the firm.
2. For every Client the Seller's firm loses over a period – often between two and five years – offset by the value of new Clients won by the Seller's firm, this amount is taken off the selling price of the firm.

As part of the Sales Agreement you need to consider:

- Which Clients you are buying and which you are not?
- What restrictive covenants the Seller is enforcing and how this impacts the value of what you are buying?
- For the transition plan, how will the Seller help you with this?
- The Seller's role after the Sales Agreement has been signed. How long do you need to retain them in the practice to ensure a smooth transition and handover?
- What will the Seller do to introduce you to the Clients you have bought?
- What will happen with the Seller's work-in-progress and debtors?
- Remuneration structure for the Seller to attend handover meetings and future queries or consultancy work.
- How you will pay for the practice. What you will pay on exchange, and when you will pay future instalments.

Stage four: Manage transition plan

You've just paid a large sum for an accountancy practice. It's important that you have a transition plan in place to realise the value of your purchase. Your transition plan needs to consider three main areas:

1. How to defend and grow the client portfolio. Expect to lose up to 15% of the client portfolio.
2. How to integrate any staff you have acquired into your firm.
3. How to move your new clients over to your firm's ways of working.

Probably the best way to describe your transition is to consider it akin to a marriage with children. Like any good parent you want to make sure that you are behaving in front of the kids, i.e. the staff and Clients affected. But also be certain that you are communicating the same messages to all the Stakeholders, e.g. Staff, Clients and the Seller.

Do not underestimate the timescale required to get to know the Clients you are inheriting. Part of the transition plan needs to include how the Seller will transfer the Clients to you. If you have a claw back clause in your Sales Agreement this will be a big incentive for your Seller to stick around to help you have a smooth transition. Clients are people at the end of the day and don't like to feel that they have been sold. However, they are likely to be very understanding. A good way of communicating the change to the Seller's clients is for the Seller to send each Client a letter explaining the change in ownership and suggesting a meeting between you, the Seller and them. In the letter make it clear when the Seller will be available until or if they will still be able to be contacted for the foreseeable future. There will be some sensitive Clients, and your Seller will be able to highlight them for you. Together with the Seller put together a special transition plan for these Clients. For example, getting the Seller to call them before they receive the letter to reassure them.

From your Due Diligence work you will have identified what the gap is between your fee structure and the Seller's fee structure. If your Seller's fees are less than your firm's fees it's worth keeping them static for a year in order to get the transition handled smoothly and a relationship built up with the Client.

When you buy a practice you not only need to consider the Clients you are buying but the staff as well. For example:

- How will you welcome them into your firm and train them into your ways of working?

- Will you need every new member of staff? How will you handle any redundancy or TUPE situations?
- Will you need to restructure how your firm operates when you integrate the Seller's practice into yours?
- How will you handle any discrepancies between pay or benefits for your new members of staff?
- How will you reassure your existing and new members of staff that their jobs are secure?

One of the potential risk factors when you buy a practice which comes with staff as part of the deal is how to avoid a staff member leaving and taking clients with them. If this did happen you would probably be covered financially by your claw back clause in the Sales Agreement. However, this could make a good deal into less of a good deal.

Case study:
Sian's Growth Story

In 2017, I bought a small accountancy practice from a local accountant who was over 70. Reading between the lines he probably would have sold up earlier if it wasn't for his daughter working in the business. Given the average client age I was able to pick up the accountancy practice for a low multiplier of gross recurring fees (GRF), and a decent claw back clause, as long as I agreed to take on his daughter, Catherine, into our practice.

As Catherine had been the day-to-day contact for most of her father's clients, it was really important to me that she felt wanted, but could quickly integrate into our practice. Adding an extra headcount wasn't a problem as we still had space for more people in our office. I was able to give the transition plan to a team member. Specifically, how to move our new Clients onto the cloud and work the way we wanted them too. Even though the Clients we inherited were on lower fees than my normal fee rates, we took a decision to keep their fees static for a year. These new fees will come into line with our current fee structure in the next 12-24 months.

Time will tell whether buying the practice was a good move. But at the moment we've inherited a great member of staff and added a decent chunk of fees to our Client portfolio.

How much should you pay for an accountancy practice?

Accountancy practices historically were valued on a 0.8–1.2 multiplier of GRF. Modern cloud-based practices are occasionally valued on a 6–10 multiplier of net profit. These factors – and this is not an exhaustive list – will increase the multiplier used with a practice:

- Amount of Clients paying monthly via direct debit or standing order. The higher the percentage, the higher the value of the practice.
- Practices which can prove they can run without the firm owner in situ
- Practices with a high gross and net profit margin
- Highly systemised practices
- Practices with a high proportion of revenue from Clients on the cloud and/or advisory services

- Practices based in or around London, or urban areas with a large density of accountants, can attract a higher multiplier
- Practices with motivated staff
- Practices with a young and growing Client base
- The availability of the Seller to help with the transition.

It is possible to buy a practice for a very low multiplier of GRF, for example 0.25. This would only happen if the owner of the practice was selling a practice where a high proportion of the Clients are selling up or exiting their business. Or if the owner wanted to get paid 100% upfront and/or didn't want to be involved in much of a handover.

Summary

Buying an accountancy practice is a big undertaking, but one which can help you rapidly grow to be a one million pound practice. Buying an accountancy practice is not the right growth route for every accountancy practice.

Most practices are valued between 0.8–1.2 times their gross recurring fees. This multiplier can be significantly reduced if the owner wants a quick sale and not to be part of the handover, or the portfolio contains a high proportion of Clients due to exit their business.

To get the most value out of buying an accountancy practice you will need to have a plan to transition the Clients and staff over. This will take up a significant amount of management time.

Action points

- Decide on whether buying an accountancy practice is a good way to achieve your 3-year Growth Plan. If so, when would be the right time in your plan to buy a practice?
- Talk with other accountancy firm owners who have bought a practice or a book of fees. What can you learn from their experiences?
- If you were to buy a practice identify what would be a good buy for you. That is, the type, number and size of Clients, whether or not to inherit staff.

13

Choosing your firm's target market

Topics covered in this chapter:

- Why your firm needs a niche
- How to choose your firm's niche
- How do clients now buy
- How to research your firm's niche
- How to create Client Personas for your firm

Most clients struggle to differentiate one small accountancy firm from another. After all, in the eyes of a client one set of accounts is largely similar to another set of accounts. And, when a client can't tell the difference between one firm or another, they invariably start to buy on price. This means that if your firm wants to win the bigger and better clients, you need to differentiate your firm from other accountancy practices. One way to win the bigger and better clients, and avoid clients buying on price is to choose to market your firm's services towards a niche.

When you have built your firm's reputation within a niche it allows your firm to spend less time on business development as well as reduce your cost of generating a lead. This chapter show you how to decide on your niche.

If you can't differentiate your firm in the eyes of the client, they will always buy on price.

Case study: Carl Reader

Carl, by his own admission, fell into accountancy, more by luck than judgement. Early into his career with Dennis & Turnbull, he was given the opportunity to look after a portfolio of approximately 30 martial arts schools. He took this opportunity and got to know the key players in the industry, adjusted their services to meet the needs of the industry, and through that learnt how to crack into a very niche industry.

Through his profile in the martial arts industry and relationships with the collection agencies who collect the fees from the school's owners, Carl has been able to grow his portfolio of martial arts clubs and schools to 250.

His expertise in servicing martial arts clubs and schools lead him to his next niche, franchising. As a result of helping one of their martial arts clients franchise his business, he gained an expertise in franchising. To help his client franchise his business, he attended a franchising exhibition in 2004. At this exhibition Carl realised that accountants either specialised in helping franchisors *or* franchisees. No-one in the accountancy world had yet looked at the franchising market place holistically, and how they could add value to the franchisor and franchisee by servicing both of them.

Carl used his first big franchising client win, Stagecoach Theatre Arts, to prove his credibility in the franchising market place. After winning Stagecoach, Carl attended as many franchising events as possible, did talks on franchising and built relationships with franchising consultants and bankers specialising in franchising. When Dennis & Turnbull discovered that their conversion rate for new franchising and martial arts schools was nearly 100% compared with a 33% conversion rate for local business, they stopped actively marketing to local businesses. Dennis & Turnbull find that every new client who comes to them from the franchising or martial arts school marketplace, tends to have arrived pre-sold on the basis of at least two recommendations.

What is a niche?

The dictionary defines *niche* as:

- A situation or activity especially suited to a person's interests, abilities, or nature
- Relating to or aimed at a small specialised group or market.

When this book refers to a niche, it is referring to those definitions. That is, where your firm's particular passion and technical talents are used to cater for one particular specialist audience. Without a niche, clients will see you as identical to other accountants and the risk is that it leaves a client no alternative but to buy on price. And when clients only buy on price, they will look for the lowest fee they can get, thus putting pressure on your profit margin.

Let's take some examples of where firms have chosen a niche:

- Cornish Accounting are known as experts in pubs, restaurants and hotels. They attract hospitality clients from all over the UK.
- Standard Ledger are an Australian firm who only work with tech start-up businesses.
- Savoir Faire, as the name suggests, specialise in French businesses who want to do business in the UK.

If your firm's marketing is built to appeal to everyone, it will appeal to no one.

Case study: Phil

Phil is an accountant who specialises in independent retailers. Over the last few years he has built up very strong relationships with a handful of other retail specialists, including a lawyer and retail branding expert. Two-thirds of his referrals each month come from these retail specialists. These referrals convert 90% of the time.

Why your firm needs to commit to its niche:

- It helps your firm be referred and recommended more often
- It helps your firm's marketing materials be more effective
- It enables you to differentiate your firm from other accountancy practices
- It allows you to tailor your firm's service to what your clients want and need, making it easier to convert prospects to clients
- It helps you to form strategic alliances
- It allows your firm to charge premium fees
- It minimises client churn

Case study: Paul's Growth Story

My practice is based in Bodmin in Cornwall. Cornwall is a highly rural county with a large number of hospitality and leisure-based businesses. As my practice grew I gained a reputation for helping people in that niche – restaurants, pubs and hotels – to grow.

I'm still very much a generalist with a specialism in hospitality businesses, so I work with all the small businesses within 35 miles of Bodmin. However, 10% of our clients are hospitality businesses and this figure is increasing. The hospitality businesses we win are typically our bigger clients and they use our in-house bookkeeping service, as well as our technology knowhow – Deputy and Receipt Bank – to handle their back office burden.

Once a quarter I team up with other Cornwall hospitality specialists to run hospitality-focused events. The last time we ran one of these events we generated 6 leads of which we converted four into clients.

Why do accountants resist adopting a niche?

Given that focusing your firm's marketing on a niche is the most effective way to win new clients, particularly the bigger and better clients, you'd be forgiven for wondering why so many firms decide to remain a generalist. There are typically four reasons why this is:

- They don't want to risk losing their existing clients by adopting a niche

- They are concerned about turning away business, particularly if they don't get many good client leads. This is often the case in the early days of running a practice.
- They don't want to offend a client or introducer by not accepting a referral
- They don't know where to start

Many accountants worry that if their firm starts marketing to a niche then they will alienate their existing clients who don't belong within that niche. But remember, your firm's marketing is not aimed at your existing clients, just the new ones that your firm wants to win. If your firm is delivering a great or even extraordinary level of service, your existing clients probably couldn't care less about your niche. However, you may find that to deliver the right level of service to your firm's niche clients, you need to exit some long-time clients.

By focusing on a niche, your firm's marketing will be optimised to attract the right sort of clients – the ones that your firm really wants to work with and find rewarding in more than just the fiscal sense. What would you do if somebody else approached your firm or if your firm got given a referral outside of your target client? You would decide if your firm had the capacity to take them on, or not. You don't have to turn them away; your firm just doesn't market to them. Most clients and introducers are not offended if you tell them that the referral they have for your firm is not a good fit for your practice.

Understandably, it's one thing to say that your firm has a niche and another to actually commit to it and capitalise on your firm's niche. Read on to the next part of this chapter to find out how to find and decide on your firm's niche.

Still happy to take on any client for your firm? If so, you are just storing up a problem for the future.

How to find and decide on your firm's niche

The hard part of finding a niche is identifying and choosing one that you and your staff are passionate about, are confident that there is enough of a market which will be motivated to buy your services, and can make a good living from.

Your firm does not have a niche if it specialises in entrepreneurs, small businesses, SMEs, or owner-managed businesses.

Examples of poor niches	Examples of good niches
Accountant specialising in Owner-Managed Businesses (OMBs). This is what most mid-tier and small firms of accountants specialise in.	Accountant specialising in working with owner-managed financial services businesses
Accountants specialising in entrepreneurs. An entrepreneur could be Richard Branson, founder of Virgin, or someone with a jam making business who only sells a few jars to friends every month. It's not specific enough.	Accountants specialising in working with growing independent retailers.
Accountant specialising in local businesses turning over up to £20m. Do you really want the tiny businesses, startups and sole traders? And could your firm cope with a £20m business? Would it get the service it requires from your firm?	Accountant specialising in local businesses turning over less than £2m.

Table 13.0: Comparison of poor and good niches

To help you draw up a short-list of potential niches you could adopt, go back to the results of your Client Portfolio Analysis. Look for clusters of similar type clients, as these clusters make great candidates for your firm to focus on.

Case study: Sharon's Growth Story

As one of the early adopters of the cloud, we traditionally won new clients because of our cloud-based knowledge. We cultivated a reputation as the experts in helping your small business run on the cloud. This expertise was a big enough differentiator for us to win both local and national clients supported by a small amount of social media marketing. Now that the rest of the marketplace is catching up with us, being an expert on the cloud side of things is no longer enough to differentiate our practice from our local or national competitors. As a result, we started to look at focusing our marketing on sector specialisms.

We did a Client Portfolio Analysis and looked for particular clusters of clients. When we did this we realised we had several sector specialisms. These are retail, particularly food retail, security experts and businesses being run on the move. Our marketing is now all targeted to these types of businesses.

It's still early days in our journey to build our sector specialisms, and for the time being our known cloud accounting expertise is still enough help us cost effectively generate leads.

With these clusters in mind, ask yourself:

- Which of the clusters are you and your team really passionate about?
- Which of the clusters is there a really good fit for the way you and your firm work, in particular your fee levels? For example, if your practice is a late adopter of cloud-based technology, is focusing on technology businesses a good fit

for your firm? Or if your minimum client fee is £2000, do you really want to target startups?

- Which of these clusters do you and your firm already have credibility in the external market for? For example, which clients arrive already pre-sold? Which clients does your firm win regularly purely by word of mouth and existing client referrals?

A good choice for a niche will be one where all of these four conditions are satisfied:

- You and your team are passionate about the type of work or business.
- You or your firm are seen to be credible for this type of work.
- There is a big enough market for your firm to grow into a one million pound firm
- There is a good fit for your firm's strengths and what the niche wants from their accountant.

If you are struggling to decide on what one or two niches to focus your firm's marketing on, try plotting a graph with the axes Reward versus Passion. Then plot your candidates for a niche onto the graph. The best candidates for your firm's niche will be the ones where your passion *and* the reward level is high.

Choose Your Niche exercise

Researching your firm's niche

Before your firm can actively start to market to your niche, you need to put yourself in your clients' shoes and understand what is going on in their world. The best business developers never sell to their clients, they help them buy. You can only do this if you have a deep understanding of their world. It can be very tempting to skip this step and just assume you know what they want, need and are interested in.

Case study: Lilia

Lilia was really struggling with her lead generation. The only clients she seemed to be able to attract in were the sole traders and very small limited companies.

So, she did a Client Portfolio Analysis and realised that she had a large core of coaches, trainers and consultants. She set out to really understand their world. After doing five informational interviews she realised their top challenges were getting paid on time and being able to run their business from wherever they were in the world.

So, she reorganised her services to particularly appeal to coaches, trainers and consultants. Almost instantly she started to generate leads who were prepared to pay double her average fee to get help to be paid on time and run their business on the move.

There are many different ways you can get to know clients within your firm's chosen niche:

- Reading the trade-related press, blogs, on-line forums and articles
- Following companies and individuals from your niche market on social media (LinkedIn, Twitter, Facebook, Instagram etc)
- Reading on-line forums

- Reading the websites, blogs, reports and white papers provided by your competitors
- Signing up for newsletters/blogs from your competitors and people in your niche market
- Attending relevant industry events, such as conferences and seminars
- Interviewing people who work within the industry, particularly your existing clients
- Running focus groups for people within the industry or customers/clients of your niche market
- Sending out a survey or questionnaire. You will get a better response rate if you share anonymised results of the survey with all participants.

What you want to find out in your research

You want to understand what your firm's Prospects are thinking and are interested in, as they go through their Buying Journey to find an accountant. Prospects tend to have five discrete stages in their Buying Journey:

1. Everything is fine

This is the stage when your Prospect has no need of your firm's services. It could be that everything is absolutely fine without a proverbial cloud in the sky. Or that if they do have problems they need to fix they are already working on them with an internal resource or another accountant or supplier.

2. I know I have some problems

Your Prospect has now moved on to knowing that he or she has a problem. Now this could be a minor niggle which they are happy to ignore, or a full-blown crisis, which they need to fix right now. Part of your research will establish what problems they are motivated to solve, and which ones they are motivated to solve by using an accountant. When you know the problems they are coming up against, you can bet that they will be consciously or sub-consciously looking for answers to their problems. If your firm's content (See Chapter 17) will help them find the answers or demonstrate to them that they have a problem that needs to be fixed, you will have started the process of generating a Lead.

A Lead is normally defined as a Prospect who has identified himself or herself to you as being interested in using your services. The types of problems that clients will be driven to buy your services for are called Pain Points. The reasons why they decide to do something about these Pain Points will often be rooted in a deep-seated emotional rather than rational reason. For example, a business owner is unlikely to buy more advisory services from an accountant because they want to grow their business. The real reason they want to grow their business will be more emotional, such as "*I want to double the income I can take out from my business so I can send my children to private school*", and therefore they need an accountant.

3. I have decided what I need to do about my problem

Now that your Prospect has found answers to his or her problem he or she will have a clear idea of the outcome they want. This could be as simple as do nothing, or sell my business. At this stage, they may not have decided exactly how they will solve their problem. What they have decided is the desired outcome they require. A typical Prospect at this stage will have very rational questions they want to answer, such as:

- Who can help me fix my problem?
- How much will it cost?

- What are the risks with choosing each particular course of action?
- What are the steps in the process to fix my problem?

4. Finding people to help me and choosing the right solution

It is at this point that most Prospects will actively look for an accountant to help them decide on the right solution to solve their problem. They will then spend time with a selection of accountants to refine their ideal solution and decide who is the right person to help them achieve it. If the Prospect has been engaging with you or your firm much earlier in their journey, it is very likely that they will actively make contact with your firm to see how your firm can help them.

Part of your research will help you identify the services your firm needs to offer to attract clients. A way to stand out from your competitors is to name your firm's services in language that your ideal clients will instantly see how it helps them.

For example:

- The Brand New to Business Package
- The Established Small Business Package
- Time Saver Maximiser
- Cash Flow Maximiser

5. Taking the decision to buy

The Prospect has now decided on a solution and the accountant they will use to help them achieve their desired outcome. Very often this point in the buying journey is known as the 'closing the deal' part of the process. Your research in this stage ideally will find out how to make it easier to close the deal. Will your firm need to offer a guarantee? Maybe your firm needs to think about its payment terms? If your firm is offering tax advisory or business advisory services will some element of a conditional fee agreement help more clients sign up?

Can your firm's clients explain to people why they should choose to work with your firm rather than another firm? If they can't, your firm has a problem.

Doing research interviews on your niche

Even if you think you already know your firm's niche inside out, doing research interviews will still be an incredibly valuable use of your time. Here are some tried and tested tips to get agreement to do these interviews:

- Don't make it about you and what you need. Your reason for doing them is to understand the niche and their business in more depth so you and your firm can better tailor your services to that niche.
- Don't ask for too much. Most people will say *yes* to a 15-minute or even 30-minute phone call. Go with the availability in their diary, not when you have time to talk.
- Send the questions in advance and keep them short and open-ended.
- Don't give any hint of wanting to sell to them. Make this absolutely clear from the outset.
- Offer to send a summary of your findings to them.

Here are some good questions that have been used very successfully in niche research interviews with prospective clients and current clients:

- What are the top 3 challenges you are working on right now in your business? How are they impacting what you do at an individual, functional and organisational level?

- What are the top 3 barriers to growth that you are facing right now?
- Given the benefit of hindsight, what do you wish someone had told you 1–2 years ago?
- What 3 ways is technology changing your business but also your clients and customers' expectations?
- What are the 3 biggest shifts in your marketplace, which may change the way you do business?
- At what point, or what would need to happen, for you to use the services of our firm or someone similar to us?
- What 3 things do you see as the biggest threat to you and your business's future success?
- If you were in my shoes, who else would you recommend I ask these questions to?

Research interviews are not something that you do once. They become more powerful if you do one or two of them each month. The insight they bring you will help you polish and hone your marketing. From personal experience, it is not unusual to flush out some new Leads as a result of doing the interview.

Research interview exercise

Identifying your firm's Client Personas

Now you have a very clear idea of what your firm's niche is and the world your firm's ideal client inhabits, it's time to draw up Client Personas for your firm. Client Personas are fictionalised representations of your ideal client(s) and these help you bring them to life. They are there to focus your firm's marketing strategy, in particular the messages your firm puts out into the marketplace.

For each Client Persona, give them a name and answer these questions:

- What are their business or personal challenges?
- What are their particular accounting challenges?
- What sort of accounting and business questions will they be looking for answers to?
- What's their background?
- What's their employment history?
- What's their family situation?
- What are their goals and aspirations in life?
- What are their hobbies and interests?
- Where do they spend their time – both physically and online?
- Who are they well connected to?
- What size and shape is their business?

Case study: Richard

Richard's accountancy firm specialised in IT companies, with a key specialism in helping startup IT companies to grow. He did his research and identified the 5 life stages of an IT company: idea, developing, launch, validating and maturing. Richard decided that the right clients for his firm to target were clients who were in the developing, launch and validating stages. Richard identified a different Client Persona for each of these stages, who were representative of the type of clients he wanted to win.

One of his Client Personas was Nicki. She was 35, a mum of a 2-year-old, who decided to launch her software company after a series of redundancies from her former life as a marketing consultant. Nicki's software business at this point in time is self-funded. Her business has just launched and she is madly hustling trying to get early adopters to try out her software. Her goals are to focus on getting some early stage growth, but it is too early to say whether the business is going to take off. She is considering going for funding to help her business grow faster.

Richard used these Client Personas with his web designer, copywriter and social media person to formulate the copy and look and feel for his website, but also plan his firm's content going forward.

Client Personas exercise

Summary

The first step to winning clients is to identify a niche to focus your marketing. The best niche for your practice is one which passes these four tests:

- Passion
- Credibility
- Fit
- Market size

The best ways to win the right sort of clients is to help them buy. This means really understanding their world by doing your research and creating Client Personas to focus your marketing on.

Action points

- Look at the results of your Client Portfolio Analysis and identify any potential niches for your practice. Then do the Choose Your Niche exercise in the Workbook.
- Find two online magazines or blogs in your firm's niche area and start subscribing to them now.
- Do five research interviews with your firm's ideal client.
- Create Client Personas for your firm's ideal client and share these with your team and any suppliers you use to help with your firm's marketing.

14

How to make your firm irresistible to your niche

Topics covered in this chapter:

- How to choose your firm's service offering for your niche
- What needs to be in your firm's marketing tool kit
- What needs to be included on your website

You have decided on a niche to target with your firm's marketing. It is now time to make your firm irresistible to your niche. Being irresistible is like getting ready for a date. You want to have appeal and attractiveness to the person you seek. But you also want to say the right thing and you want to present the best possible version of yourself. This chapter shows you how to prepare your firm for a successful date with your ideal client.

Deciding on what services your firm will offer

Typically your clients will be driven to buy your firm's services by a Pain Point, i.e. a deep-seated emotional rather than logical reason. This may seem counter-intuitive at first. The initial impulse to hire your firm is always an emotional one, then backed up by logical and rational reasons to buy your services. Your research will have helped you already to identify the Pain Points which will be the underlying reason why your niche market will want to buy your firm's services. These Pain Points will form the basis of the services you offer to your clients. It is very tempting to think that you already know the Pain Points for your clients. After all, don't most clients want to save tax and grow their business? Or work less and still enjoy a decent income from their business. If your research hasn't gone deeper than this, then it is time to go back and do more research with representative clients from your Client Personas. What are the *real* Pain Points for your clients?

For example,

- Sarah, who ran a training business, was struggling to pay herself a decent income as her business had a really poor cash flow. This was because her business had a lumpy pipeline of work combined with long payment terms from her corporate clients.
- Mohammed was desperate to grow his retail business and expand beyond his original store. He needed to get access to funding to finance the expansion of his retail business.
- Timothy was 60 and had run his own business for the last 30 years. As a result he'd neglected to build up a pension fund for his retirement. If he was going to have a comfortable retirement he needed to get the best possible value for his business on exit.

If you think that all your firm needs to offer advisory services is "have a process to follow", then you have completely underestimated what it takes to become an advisory-led firm.

Case study: Robert

Case study: Robert was a manufacturer of lithium-ion batteries. His internal accountant was able to handle the UK tax system, but now they were exporting to the USA and some North African countries. The accountant needed to run five different sets of accounts and at any one time the accountant was stressing out and taking time off work. Robert found himself being dragged in to answer tax questions, at a time when he needed to stay focused on gaining more export markets. His pain became so great that he needed to outsource all the tax work, which he did. It seemed such a logical decision, but the driver was his emotional pain. As it unfolded, his own accountant became the liaison person between the service provider and Robert's business, and everyone's stress levels lowered.

The 5 Whys exercise in the Workbook will help you drill down to the real Pain Points that will motivate your niche market to buy from your firm.

📖 5 Whys exercise

📖 Pain Points exercise

How to package up your services

Most small accountancy firms sell a mixture of compliance services, one off ad hoc pieces of work (for example a mortgage application), and advisory services. That's a huge amount of different options for a client to choose from. By bundling up your firm's services into fixed price monthly packages, your clients can choose a package that best fits their requirements. Neuroeconomics expert, George Loewenstein, found that buyers prefer to make just one purchase rather than purchase multiple different services. This is because multiple purchases create multiple purchase decisions and can ramp up any potential buying friction. Whereas only having to take one purchase decision and buy a bundle of services, means only one purchase decision and therefore, less potential buying friction. At the end of the day, only having to make one purchase decision, rather than being presented with a list of options, is much less hassle for most people.

The services which work well in a bundle are the on-going recurring services that most of your clients will need. These are normally compliance or reporting type services. Examples include:

- Year End Accounts
- Bookkeeping
- Tax returns
- Management accounts
- Quarterly meeting

Your aim with your firm's packages is to offer them with ascending price tags. Your firm's packages will have included services, such as a director's personal tax return, but also the opportunity to add in optional extras, such as an additional director's personal tax return. By having an ascending price tag and optional extras, it gives you the accountant, the opportunity to upsell a higher priced package. The best way to name your firm's services is not to call them bronze, silver, gold. This is because nearly every small firm accountant seems to do this. It's to better to call them something that actually means something to your client.

There are two ways of structuring your packages.

Budget, Good, Best

When presented with three options, clients tend to opt for the middle option. After all, no-one likes to be seen as cheap, or buy a package with all the bells and whistles that they just wouldn't use. When a client knows and trusts your firm it becomes much easier to move them into a higher priced package over time.

Minimum, Normal, Open-ended

Your Minimum service is the most stripped back service you can provide to a client and still make a profit. It only includes the basic accounting services, e.g. Year End Accounts, corporation tax, personal tax return, etc. Your Normal service is what you would like most of your clients to take and is tailored to your Client Personas' requirements. Whereas Open-ended is typically your Normal package with tailored added extras to match requirements of the bigger spenders of your Client Personas.

Case study: Sharon's Growth Story

Our packages used to be called Bronze, Silver and Gold. We did some research on what our clients wanted and needed, and identified three Client Personas. We then built our packages around the needs of each Client Persona.

Our basic package is called Support Me. It's for the clients who just want us to manage the basics and keep them legal with their financial affairs. Our most popular package is our middle package Guide Me. This package is for our clients who want to be guided in the right direction so they have the right advice to stay in control of their taxes. Our top-level package is called Grow Me. It's for our clients who are growing businesses who need our day-to-day support to provide them with the key advice and numbers to drive their business forward.

Now that we have given our packages names our clients find it much easier to identify which is the right package for them. Because we have explained the purpose behind each package, we have a higher proportion of clients opting for Guide Me and

Grow Me. Who would have thought that just naming your package levels so it meant something for your clients would have made such a difference to getting clients onto the higher package levels?

	Support Me	Guide Me	Grow Me
Year End Accounts and corporation tax return	✔	✔	✔
Monthly Payroll	✔	✔	✔
Meetings per year	✔	✔	✔
Directors' Personal Tax Return	✔	✔	✔
Companies House Confirmation Statement	✔	✔	✔
Discounted Xero and Receipt Bank Subscriptions and Support	✔	✔	✔
24/7 Xero Support	✔	✔	✔
Registered Office Address	-	✔	✔
Quarterly VAT returns	-	✔	✔
Quarterly Xero Healthchecks	-	✔	✔
Business and personal tax planning	-	✔	✔
Monthly/Quarterly Management Reports	-	-	✔
Monthly/Quarterly Business Strategy Session	-	-	✔
Your own virtual FD	-	-	✔

Table 14.0: Kinder Pocock's service packages

Case study: Paul's Growth Story

To cater for our local small business clients, we put together three packages: Survive, Adapt and Evolve.

Our Survive package is our cheapest package and has been designed for startups or the everyday small or family business owner, whose business is stable and under £200k. We know these businesses don't need much more than the basic compliance services, and to have the peace of mind that we are always at the end of the phone if they need us. Personal service is still very important to our firm regardless of how much they are paying, so our clients who take our Survive package still get unlimited advice and phone calls. We know that our commitment to high client service is one the many reasons so many of our clients have been with me from the day I started the practice.

Our Adapt package was built for our local businesses who are growing and developing. Most of our clients take this package. This package gives our clients reassurance that the accounting and bookkeeping fundamentals – VAT returns and bookkeeping – are all taken care of, as well as twice yearly performance reviews.

The Evolve package is for our ambitious business owners who need their compliance stuff sorted but regular financial advice. Clients who take this service get quarterly performance reviews, annual tax planning, annual budget setting and annual cash flow forecasting. It is very common for our clients to start on our Adapt package and 6–12 months later move up to our Evolve package.

As well as our standard packages, we have a rate card which we send to our clients every year, which details all the ad hoc services they may want from us which are not included in their monthly package.

	Survive	Adapt	Evolve
Year End Accounts	✔	✔	✔
Director Personal Tax Return	✔	✔	✔
Company Secretarial	✔	✔	✔
Xero Subscription	✔	✔	✔
Fee Protection Insurance	✔	✔	✔
Unlimited Advice And Phone Calls	✔	✔	✔
Basic Bookkeeping	-	✔	✔
Half Yearly Management Pack	-	✔	✔
Half Yearly Performance Review	-	✔	✔
VAT Returns	-	✔	✔
Quarterly Management Pack	-	-	✔
Quarterly Performance Review	-	-	✔
Annual Budget Setting	-	-	✔
Annual Cash Flow Forecasting	-	-	✔

Table 14.1: Cornish Accounting's service packages

How to package advisory services

Unlike compliance services, advisory services are optional for the client. For example, there is no legal or regulatory reason for them to do advanced tax planning or have a cash improvement session. As a result, the biggest competitors of your advisory services are inertia, and the client thinking they can do it without any help from your firm. This is why packaging up advisory services and offering three or more types of packages just doesn't tend to work. Most advisory services are a one-off high-priced service rather than lots of little services. Creating a bundle for advisory services just complicates the buying process by giving the client too many options. This can lead to them never quite deciding which package to take. With advisory services, you want to sell your client a solution to their problem. Your suggested solution is likely to be a programme of activities, not three different packages for them to choose from. For example, if your client wanted to grow then they may buy business coaching services from your firm to help them achieve their business growth targets. A typical business coaching programme would look like this:

Start with a diagnostic, goal setting and action planning session
Followed by coaching and accountability calls to achieve goals

You would then build the amount of contact time in your proposed coaching programme to your client's requirements and budget.

How to deal with your fee level on your firm's website

Dr Robert Cialdini did some research on analysis paralysis and human behaviour when it came to spending. He discovered that people are more likely to take action when minimal parameters are set. This means that if you leave your fees off your website, then this can stop people contacting you.

On a more pragmatic level including fees on your website helps to qualify out any client who is unsuitable for your firm. It gets rid of the client enquiries who email your firm or ring your firm just to ask for a price, i.e. the hyper price sensitive clients who you don't want to be working with.

The best way to include fees on your website is talk about *"from £xx".* Give a minimum fee level rather than an absolute fee level or a likely potential range of fees.

Create your service offering exercise

Most clients are savvy enough to realise that it is unlikely that they will get your firm's services for exactly the 'from' amount quoted on your website.

How to differentiate your firm from your competitors in the eyes of your ideal client

If a potential client asked you today, why they should buy your firm's services rather than another firm, could you answer this question succinctly? This isn't about having a USP (Unique Selling Proposition), just a clear statement on why your Prospect would choose to work with *your* firm.

Case study: Sian's Growth Story

I never aspired to set up a traditional accountancy firm. That's why we do some things differently in our firm. We don't rely on a referral network to generate new business. Our investment in content marketing, and how we get our content in front of our target market, is our main route to market. This means we attract in a very different type of client. Our clients value the fact that we are prepared to do business via the phone or an online meeting. They don't need to come into our offices every time they want a meeting. They like that we are able to properly guide them on what technology to use to take full advantage of the cloud. We are certainly not representative of the traditional suit-wearing pale, male, stale accountant. We don't just give everyone the same management reports, we tailor them to the needs of their sector first. And then, if required we tailor them to their individual business. This is why we are finding that our biggest growth area is for ecommerce and technology businesses.

Very often it is not the service you offer, but *how* your firm delivers those services that will help your firm to differentiate itself. After all, for most accountants it is very hard to differentiate themselves based on the services they offer. For example, producing one set of Year End Accounts is pretty much the same service regardless of which accountancy firm you use. Like Sian, you need to be able to articulate *Why You* in your marketing messages. Use the Why You exercise in the Workbook to help you think through what features and how they are delivered you want to offer to your clients.

📖 Why You exercise

Your Firm's Marketing Toolkit

If you want to attract the bigger and better clients who are prepared to spend more, you will need to make sure your marketing material is all designed to attract the Client Personas from your niche market which you drew up in the last chapter.

Your Firm's Marketing Toolkit will include everything your firm will require to attract in your Client Personas. Depending on your firm's circumstances, it will include some or all of the following:

- Credibility Statements
- Credibility Stories
- Website
- Business card
- Biographies of all your client facing members of the team
- Professional photos, including a head and shoulders shots of all your client facing members of the team
- Social media profiles of the firm and your staff, especially LinkedIn and Twitter
- Templates for slides, documents and handouts
- Client list, testimonials and case studies.

Credibility Statements and Stories

As the saying goes, your reputation precedes you. However, you can actively help people to quickly grasp what your firm is all about, in particular the type of results you help your clients achieve, by the statements and stories you use. These are what we call Credibility Statements and Stories. Much of your Firm's Marketing Toolkit will be based on these.

Credibility Statements demonstrate your firm's credibility. These could be:

- The amount of a certain type of client you work with
- The professional qualifications the people in your firm hold
- The relevant experience your staff have gained
- Awards, honours, certifications, prizes and professional recognition your firm has received
- Who your staff have worked for previously
- The length of time the firm has been in existence
- The books and articles you have written
- When your firm or people from your firm have been featured in the media; e.g. radio or TV appearances, quotes in the national, trade or local press.

Your Credibility Statements typically are easily memorable, repeatable and normally short statements, which allow anyone talking about your firm to instantly convey your credibility.

Here are some real examples of Credibility Statements:

Guy Robinson: Former partner at BDO LLP and Moore Stephens
Kinder Pocock: Practice Excellence's Client Care Award Winner 2017
Sian Kelly: In the past, she's worked for Next plc, Marston's Brewery and Compass Group

Paul Miller: He's the founder and has run Cornish Accounting for the last 23 years

📖 Credibility Statements exercise

Identifying your Credibility Stories

Credibility Stories illustrate what your firm does, who are your clients and the results that your firm has helped your clients achieve. They are succinct and unlike most stories have no middle. You may have heard them being called war stories or sales stories.

A typical Credibility Story will firstly explain why the client initially hired your firm and the Pain Points they were suffering before they hired you. Then the story will include a short statement about the work you did together, before talking about the happy ending for the client, as a result of using your firm's services.

This is an example of a Credibility Story:
A client started to work with us. They were incredibly stressed and working far too many hours in their restaurant business. Often a regular 60–70 hour week. They needed to have a greater personal income from their business, but didn't know where to start. We began by getting their financial records up to date. It was at this point that we realised our client had a real problem with their cash flow. Unless they took drastic action, they were going to run out of cash within 6 months. We worked closely with our client to put in place a plan of action to reduce their overheads and cost of sales. It was touch and go for a while, but within 6 months the client was in a much better position. Their cash flow was now healthy, the bookings for their restaurant were significantly up, net profits were up by 50% and they were working more like a 50-hour week.

These Credibility Stories can be used in proposals, presentations, sales meetings, your firm's website, articles and your LinkedIn profile.

They can be used as the answer to any of these standard questions that you will receive at a networking event:

- How's business?
- What do you do?
- Got any interesting client work on at the moment?
- What does your firm specialise in?

Your Credibility Stories will need to be tailored to the document you are writing or for the person you are meeting for the first time. For this reason, you will need a minimum of three Credibility Stories, which illustrate the type of clients your firm works with, i.e. representative of your Client Personas, and the value you bring to them.

Credibility Stories exercise

Website

The state of your firm's website is a very good indicator of the type of clients your firm attracts. For example, if your firm's website is built to attract in creatives, your firm will tend to attract in creatives. If your firm's website screams about your firm's low prices, your firm will attract in highly price-sensitive clients. If your firm's website is fairly bland and devoid of personality, and only talks about working with small businesses, don't be surprised if your firm struggles to win clients.

The Hinge Research Institute found that over 80% of Prospects will check out your website before they contact you. Today's clients expect their accountant to have a website. Before a Prospect has contacted your firm, assume that they have checked this out in advance. Only having an entry in a directory, or a LinkedIn profile page or business page on Facebook is not a good substitute for your own website.

A good website for an accountancy firm is:

- Written specifically for the Client Personas you want to be working with. This means including images and copy that they instantly identify with.
- Answers the question, why should we choose to work with your firm?
- Making it easy for Prospects to get in contact with your firm: phone number, social media profiles and email address at the top of each page.
- Up-to-date and visually pleasing. It shouldn't look as if you built it 5 years ago.
- Mobile-responsive; the website design easily fits on a mobile and a desktop computer.
- Aligned with how clients buy, so has an About Us Page, Contact Us Page and includes all the information Prospects will want in order to take a decision as to whether to get in contact with your firm. This will include photos and bios of all the client-facing members of your team, client testimonials, details of your firm's services, in particular your packages and an indication of how much it will cost to work with your firm.
- Full of well-organised, easy-to-find and easy-to-navigate valuable content tailored to the requirements of your Client Personas. This is normally via a well-written and up-to-date blog and downloadable assets such as guides, checklists, templates, calculators.

Case study: Diana

Diana placed a huge amount of value on the fact that she was the cheapest accountant locally. It was like a badge of honour. Until she realised that this was only leading to her attracting in very needy and price-sensitive clients. So, she looked through her clients and identified the ones she really enjoyed working with: coaches, trainers and consultants. She created three different Client Personas for these types of client. Then she completely overhauled her packages of services and website in order to tailor it to her Client Personas. Her website very clearly heroed the type of work and results she got for these Client Personas. Within two months of the new website going live, her monthly Leads had increased from 2 to 10. She was converting 70% of all her Leads and her average fee for new clients had more than doubled to £3000.

Business card

A business card is still the world of business's preferred way of exchanging contact details. You and all your client facing staff members will need their own business card.

What needs to go on your firm's business cards:

- Name, firm name and job title
- An email address
- Phone numbers, preferably a direct line
- Your firm's logo
- Your firm's website address

The back of your firm's business card is a valuable piece of real estate. You can choose to add the following to the back of your firm's business card:

- A list of the services that you offer.
- A blank space for people to add notes on when they meet you.
- Valuable resources for your niche market. E.g. a calculator for tech start-ups to help them identify how much cash they have left.

When buying your firm's business cards do think about the impression you want to give when you hand over your card. A professionally designed, clean, new, high-quality business card will leave a very different impression to poorly designed, cheaply produced, scuffed, ripped or dirty business card.

Biographies

The purpose of a professional biography (Bio) is to help tell an individual's story in a way that:

- Emphasises their credentials
- Allows your audience or reader to get to know a bit more about them.

Typically, your Bio is made up of Credibility Statements. A professional Bio written for a social media profile is normally written in the first person, as it is believed that this makes you seem friendlier and more approachable. By contrast, a professional Bio written for a magazine, brochure, program or proposal is normally written in the third person, as this is perceived to be more business-like.

Here is Sian's Bio on her website:

Sian Kelly ACMA BSc Managing Director

A Chartered Management Accountant since 1995, Sian now heads up the Inform Accounting team. In the past, she's worked for Next plc, Marston's Brewery and Compass Group plc, where she was Financial Controller. Oh, and she even worked at Disneyland for a year. Sian has helped a number of businesses grow from start-ups to well-established companies, working hand in hand, guiding them through the sales process. Away from work, her leisure time is mainly spent with her three children, who give her the ringing endorsement of being 'really nice'.

Here is Sharon's Bio on her website:

Sharon Pocock FCCA, MD and Principal Accountant
Sharon established Kinder Pocock Chartered Certified Accountants in 2005 following 15 years working in the accountancy profession. Her aim then, as now, was to offer professional yet straightforward advice and support to small and new businesses. Sharon speaks in plain English and won't confuse you with fancy jargon!

Having recently celebrated 10 years trading as Kinder Pocock, Sharon continues to support her clients both old and new, as their businesses grow, and says "I love getting involved with my clients' businesses, and it makes our work here at Kinder Pocock all the more worthwhile to know how much our clients appreciate what we do."

Sharon is also Xero UK's Most Valued Professional 2016!

🕮 Bio exercise

Professional photos

At some point in time you and your team will be asked for your professional photos, and perhaps photos of your workplace. They could be for:

- Photos on the website
- An avatar for social media
- A proposal
- Publicity
- An article on the firm's blog
- An event they are going to be speaking at.

It is worth engaging a photographer who specialises in portraiture to take these photos for you and the team. These photos will follow you and your team everywhere, so it is worth the time and investment to get them just right.

A good professional photo will:

- Capture your best side
- Be properly lit and processed to showcase you rather than the background
- Represent the brand or image you want to portray
- Will not have you square on to the camera
- Make you feel good about yourself.

Social media profiles

More and more Prospects are not just checking out an accountant's website, they will also look at their social media profiles as well. At the time of writing, LinkedIn, Twitter, Facebook and Instagram are all social media sites to consider as part of your mix.

With all the work you have completed on your firm's Credibility Statements, Credibility Stories and Bios, plus your photos, you now have all material you need at your fingertips to fill in your profiles on these social networking sites.

Social media site	Good for...
LinkedIn	Meeting business owners as well as Financial Directors and Financial Controllers.
Facebook	Facebook is excellent for keeping in touch with current and ex-colleagues, as well as maintaining a local presence.
Twitter	Twitter is a great place to keep up-to-date with what is going on, plus meet and form relationships with journalists.
Instagram	Instagram is great if your ideal audience would identify themselves as a creative or are particularly visual.

Table 14.2: Strengths of different social media sites

Tips for filling out your profiles:

- Do upload your photo to your profile. You will seem more credible and authentic with a photo than without.
- Remember to include important keywords in your profiles, as very often your clients will search for someone like you using keywords.
- Don't leave your profile blank, as this will result in people assuming that you are potentially not worth contacting
- Include links to your social media profiles on the bottom of your emails.

For more help on what to put in your LinkedIn, Twitter, Facebook and Instagram profiles, visit http://www.accountantsmillionaire.club.

Templates for slides, documents and handouts

It's often the little things that can stop your firm getting a referral or new client enquiry. One of these little things can be as simple as the look and feel of written material that your firm shares with people.

A graphic designer can create for your firm a set of templates based on the brand and image you want to consistently present to the outside world. Having these set up as standard templates can save huge amounts of time in the future.

Client list, testimonials and case studies

Without breaking client confidentiality, these will show future clients who your firm has been working with and the types of results your firm has helped them achieve. On a website, they will help generate new client enquiries. The best case studies and client testimonials will:

- Include facts and figures to demonstrate the impact of your firm's work with a client.
- State any potential objections to using your firm's services and how these were not a problem.
- Be attributed to a real person's name and photo.

Summary

In order to make your firm irresistible to your niche market you need to have created a service offering which helps solve your Client Personas' challenges. To help sell compliance services or recurring services (such as management accounts) to your clients, bundle these into packages with ascending price tags.

Your firm will need to have its own Practice Marketing Toolkit. This will help any Prospect get consistent messages wherever they bump – virtually or physically – into your firm.

Action points

- Decide on what services your firm will offer by doing the 5 Whys and Pain Points exercise.
- Package your compliance or recurring services up into three or four packages, each with an ascending price tag.

Name these services something which will resonate with your Client Personas.

- Take a long hard look at your firm's marketing materials; e.g. your firm website and social media profiles. If they are not focused on the requirements of your Client Personas then hire a marketing expert to redo your marketing materials so they are tailored to your Client Personas.
- Make sure that every client-facing member of your team has a professional headshot photo and a business card.
- Create a template for your firm's documents, proposals and presentations.
- Make sure every member of your firm has completed profiles on the social media sites which they use for business.

15

How to create and resource your firm's Tactical Marketing Plan

Topics covered in this chapter:

- How to create your firm's Tactical Marketing Plan
- Pros and cons of different routes to market
- How to outsource your marketing to others and what to outsource first
- How to get your staff to take responsibility for business development

Up until now in the book, you have been focusing on everything you need to do before you turn on the tap and generate Leads. The next 3 chapters look at exactly what you are going to do to generate these Leads, in particularly getting more work from existing Clients, content marketing, social media marketing, networking and referral marketing and using events.

A Tactical Marketing Plan is something that looks at the million pound practice that you want to grow and converts that into a specific list of where you'll get new business, what activities you'll do to get it, and how much you'll get from each type of activity.

Conversion Rate: This is your ratio of Leads to newly signed-up Clients

Building your firm's Tactical Marketing Plan

It's now time to create your firm's Tactical Marketing Plan. What your firm will actually do to generate a ready supply of Leads. Using a

Tactical Marketing Plan, and the focus it provides, is an essential tool if you want to grow to be a one million pound practice.

Top-Level Lead Summary

CHANNEL	MONTH 1		MONTH 2		MONTH 3		MONTH 4	
	Budget	Actual	Budget	Actual	Budget	Actual	Budget	Actual
Existing Clients	3	4	3	2	3	-	3	-
Wed Networking Group	2	3	2	1	2	-	2	-
John - Bank Managers	1	0	1	2	1	-	1	-
TOTAL	6	7	6	5	6	-	6	-

Activity Plan Per Channel

EXISTING CLIENTS		
What?	Who?	When
Call each A-Grade Client every 2 months to see how they are getting on	Client Managers	On-going
Continue analysing results of clients satisfaction survey every month, discuss results in monthly Rhythm meeting	Client Managers	On-going
Maintain current new client onboarding process including the 3-month meeting to discuss how the relationship is going	Client Managers	On-going
Continue analysing results of clients' satisfaction survey every month, discuss results in monthly Rhythm meeting	Client Managers	On-going
Continue exit meetings with clients who are leaving and discuss reasons in the monthly Rhythm meeting	Client Managers	On-going

Diagram 15.0: Tactical Marketing Plan

Case study: Max

Max ran a small accountancy practice which was turning over £50k. He was struggling to balance business development work and his chargeable time. He put in place a Tactical Marketing Plan for his firm. He and his one member of staff split up the responsibilities on the Tactical Marketing Plan. They reviewed how they were progressing with the plan every Monday morning during their weekly Rhythm Team Meeting. As a result of keeping very focused with their marketing they reduced the amount of time they spent on business development by a third. Within 12 months they had quadrupled their number of monthly Leads, and trebled the size of their practice.

If your firm has a Tactical Marketing Plan, you will find that you avoid some of these common mistakes that accountants make with their business development:

1. Not knowing how many Leads they need to fuel their practice growth.
2. Unable to identify what marketing inputs are having the most effect, for the least amount of effort. Consequently, their marketing is fuelled by random acts of marketing, underpinned by a large dollop of hope.

To build your Tactical Marketing Plan you will need to know:

- Your Conversion Rate for Leads to new Clients expressed as a percentage
- The average value of a new Client assignment
- Your revenue target.

These three figures then allow you to identify the number of Leads you require.

Number of Leads = revenue target/(average value of new Client assignment x conversion %)

The next stage to build your Tactical Marketing Plan is to decide on which channels you will use to generate the Leads you require. How many will come from:

- Existing Clients (See Chapter 16)
- Content Marketing (See Chapter 17)
- Social Media Marketing (See Chapter 17)
- Referrals from introducers, existing Clients and your network (See Chapter 18)
- Running physical or virtual events (See Chapter 19)
- Other routes to market, such as SEO or Pay Per Click advertising

See Table 15.1 for an analysis of the benefits of each route to market.

Marketing Channel	Relative effectiveness for a Growing Accountancy Practice (out of 10)	Pros	Cons
Existing Clients wanting more	9	• Cheap • Can be easily delegated to members of the team	• Difficult to scale up or down • Can't be outsourced
Existing Clients referring the firm	9	• Cheap • Can be easily delegated to members of the team	• Can't always rely on Clients to refer work to the firm when you need more work • The quality of Leads generated may be poor • Can't be outsourced
Content Marketing	7	• Can easily be outsourced or delegated to members of the team • Helps to increase Lead Conversion Rate	• Content generation takes time or money • Difficult to trace a Lead when produced by content marketing
Social Media Marketing	7	• Can easily be outsourced or delegated to members of the team • Cheap • Helps amplify and spread the reach of your firm's content	• Very easy to waste a large amount of time talking to the wrong people on social media • Difficult to trace a Lead when produced by social media marketing
Networking and referrals	7	• Cheap • Low skill level required • Members of staff can also go out and network	• The quality of Leads generated may be poor • Very time consuming • Can't be outsourced
Running physical and virtual events	7	• Excellent Lead generator with a high Conversion Rate • Easy to track Leads generated by events	• Can be expensive to host a physical event • Can be difficult to get people to turn up to an event
Email marketing	6	• Can be outsourced • Low cost if you have a well targeted email list • Great way to find out what services your Clients may be interested in	• Need a well-targeted email list to get decent results • Can be time-consuming to build a well-targeted email list
Search Engine Optimisation (SEO)	5	• Can be easily outsourced • When your website is search engine optimised it is easy to maintain it at the top of its ranking	• Low Lead Conversion Rate • Difficult to get high quality Leads without using an external marketing expert
Paid digital advertising, e.g. Pay Per Click, Facebook Ads, LinkedIn Ads	5	• Can be easily outsourced • Can be switched on, off or scaled up when required • Good way to build up an email list	• Low Lead Conversion Rate • High risk of wasting money on generating Leads • Difficult to get high quality Leads without using an external marketing expert
PR	5	• Can be easily outsourced • Great for growing awareness of your firm's brand	• Difficult to trace Leads produced by PR • High cost of hiring a PR specialist
Print Ads	2	• Can be easily outsourced	• High cost and no guarantee of Leads generated
Direct Mail	5	• Can be easily outsourced • Can be highly targeted to your ideal Client	• You need someone to follow up on any mailing you send out to maximise its effectiveness
Telephone marketing	3	• Can be easily outsourced • Easy to identify when producing Leads	• Low Lead conversation rate • Can produce poor quality price-sensitive Leads

Table 15.1: Advantages of each channel to market

When you have identified where your Leads are planned to come from, you need to decide on the action you will take to generate the Leads from each channel. To improve the accuracy of your Tactical Marketing Plan you will need to:

- Measure the number and quality of Leads coming through each channel
- Calculate the Conversion Rate for each channel
- Adjust your Tactical Marketing Plan as you get more understanding about the ROI of each channel.

Tactical Marketing Plan exercise

Deciding to stop taking on new clients for a fixed period of time may be exactly what your firm needs in order to sustainably grow. Remember you are in charge of how fast your firm grows.

How to outsource your marketing to others

Business development, particularly if you decide to use networking as one of your routes to market, is a time-consuming activity. To maximise your available capacity to grow your firm as well as increase the capital value of your firm on exit, you need to be able to delegate or outsource your business development responsibilities.

Outsourcing your marketing to an external supplier gives more benefits than just releasing your time. For example:

- At much less than the cost of employing a marketing executive you can get an entire team of marketing experts.
- Your outsourced marketing expert can give you the outside perspective on your business as well as valuable insight. For example, this could be understanding who is visiting your website.

- External marketing experts will allow you to decrease your cost per Lead.
- You get to focus on what you are really good at, which for accountants isn't normally marketing.

Case study: Sian's Growth Story

My Growth Vision was to build a one million pound practice which could be run by me during school hours. It was, therefore, important that I could find a way to market which didn't need me personally to run it. As a result, I invested heavily in organic SEO, social media and producing highly valuable content.

I outsourced production of the firm's content to my outsourced Marketing Director and social media marketing on Facebook, Twitter and LinkedIn to my sister. She does 2–3 days a week for us making sure that we have engaging 'light' content on our firm's Facebook page, and our freshly written blog posts are regularly shared on the firm's LinkedIn page, as well as individual fee earners LinkedIn accounts. She mirrors our Facebook and LinkedIn content on Twitter.

Once a year, my outsourced Marketing Director, my sister and I sit down to draw up a 12-month Content Plan. In the Content Plan we identify the key themes for the year for our sectors – retail and ecommerce, technology and hair/beauty salons, as well as key seasonal dates. We then break down these themes into blog post ideas and ebooks, which people can download for free from the website, in return for their email address.

My Marketing Director is responsible for producing all the valuable content as well as keeping our website up-to-date. We find that if we blog less than once a week our website drops down the ranking for local searches for accountants.

Our investment in content marketing and social media isn't cheap. When you add in the cost of salaries, our marketing spend each month is normally between £2–3,000. However, apart from referrals from existing Clients, all our Leads come from our content and social media marketing. For every pound we spend on marketing, we have calculated that within 12 months we normally generate fees worth 2–3 times our marketing investment.

To outsource your marketing to an external marketing expert:

- Be very clear at the outset what success looks like and how this will be measured, e.g. your KPIs. Check that any potential marketing expert has got experience helping other accountants achieve the results you want.
- Agree with the metrics, software and reports that your external marketing expert will provide. Make sure that they are prepared to talk you through the reports they send to you.
- Have an agreed Tactical Marketing Plan with clearly defined responsibilities for people in your firm and your external marketing experts.
- Set up diarised and regular communication – at least once a month – to check on progress, review results and decide on next steps.
- Check that they are committed to continuous professional development. Many of the marketing tools available are rapidly changing. You are paying for your marketing expert to keep you abreast of these developments.

- Check the Client references they provide you with and ask to see examples of their work.

Good marketing tasks to outsource first include either routes to market where there is a high level of technical skill needed, for example Pay Per Click marketing, or where you can hire low cost labour for highly repetitive and time intensive tasks, such as social media marketing:

- Creation of your firm's website and keeping it updated
- Content creation, in particular blogging
- Social media marketing
- Search Engine Optimisation for your website
- Pay Per Click marketing, especially Facebook Ads
- Press releases

Marketing tasks which are not suitable for outsourcing:

- Networking
- Account Management

Case study: Paul's Growth Story

Going out and hustling for clients is one of the things I love doing. As a result, I've always had all the business development responsibilities for Cornish Accounting. I attended a workshop on social media marketing and was influenced to properly commit to social media marketing.

I was working flat out and didn't have the time to run the social media accounts for the firm. And to be honest, I didn't really have the inclination to do this either. So I outsourced writing blog posts, Twitter and Facebook updates. For £120 a month my outsourced social media expert writes a blog post a week and also distributes these via the firm's social media channels. I help by sharing articles with him that I know our Client Personas would value. We trialed this approach for three months and found that the number of Leads we generated doubled. Understandably we have carried on with social media marketing since this point.

How to get your staff to take responsibility for business development

Everyone in an accountancy firm is responsible for business development. From the cheerful and friendly receptionist who helps to start the process of a Prospect feeling good about working with your firm, to the trainee who calculates the Client's tax return right first time, and keeps the Client regularly updated on progress. The more your staff understand the connection between their day job and how this helps your firm keep, grow or win more work, the more they will want to take a part in business development.

Firstly, you need to tell your staff what you want them to do. It's no good hoping they will want to get involved with business development. This means including their *Create It*, *Convert It* and *Cultivate It* responsibilities within their Job Description and giving them Growth Tasks to help the firm win work.

Your staff will need training and support to learn any new skills, such as how to spot an opportunity for more work with an existing Client. These new skills should form part of the Work and Development Plan which you discuss regularly.

Over the next four chapters the book will do a deep dive into the top four channels to market for accountants; growing existing client accounts, content and social media marketing, generating referrals and using events.

Summary

To predictably grow the size of your firm's Client portfolio you will need to have a Tactical Marketing Plan. Your plan will detail exactly what your firm will do, via each marketing channel, in order to grow. As part of the Tactical Marketing Planning process you will measure the effectiveness of each marketing channel, and adjust the plans accordingly.

As your firm grows you will need to outsource more of your marketing to external experts, or delegate more business development responsibilities to your staff.

Action points

- Start your Tactical Marketing Plan and identify how many Leads a month your firm needs to achieve the growth targets set out in your 3-year Growth Plan.
- Look at what marketing your firm is currently doing. Identify what responsibilities should stay in-house and what would be better served now and in the future by outsourcing part of your marketing.
- Get recommendations of good marketing experts who service accountancy firms.
- Spend time with each member of your staff to help them understand how their role contributes to the firm winning more business.

16

How to grow your firm's existing Client base

Topics covered in this chapter:

- What do Clients really want from their accountant?
- How to deliver Extraordinary Client Service
- How to smoothly onboard new Clients
- How to upsell more services to Clients
- How to reduce Client churn

The easiest way to win more work is via your firm's existing Clients. Depending on which study you are reading, the cost of winning a new client is 5–25 times more expensive than keeping an existing one. Research done by Bain & Company showed that increasing client retention rates by 5% increases profits by 25–95%.[2] Existing Clients, if your firm delivers extraordinary service and can demonstrate the value of your firm's services, will buy more services from your firm and recommend your firm to others. This chapter shows you how to consistently delight your firm's Clients, so they become your firm's easiest and most cost-effective route to winning more work.

What do your Clients really want from your firm?

Whilst the way Client Service is delivered may have changed for accountants, the fundamental principles of Extraordinary Client Service haven't. Namely,

- Accessibility
- Responsiveness

[2] http://www.bain.com/Images/BB_Prescription_cutting_costs.pdf

- Treating the Client with respect and being easy to deal with
- No mistakes
- No surprises, particularly with bills
- Deliver to time and on or under budget
- Value for money.

Once again, your firm's Clients are the ones who set the expectation for what is deemed to be an extraordinary level of service around accessibility and responsiveness. Do you know what this is for your firm's Clients? Response expected within 24 hours? More importantly, at the start of a client relationship do you set expectations for what service level they can expect on the package they are buying?

The type of Extraordinary Client Service that gets your Clients to routinely refer your firm to other potential clients doesn't happen by chance. It is normally underpinned by a culture and ethos of Extraordinary Client Service. This includes:

- Good communication protocols so that all the team from the owner to the trainee working on the accounts know exactly what the Client wants and needs.
- KPIs to measure and monitor how well the firm is doing on delivering Extraordinary Client Service.
- Empowerment of all staff to be able to do the right thing by Clients. For example, if there is a mistake on a piece of Client work, anyone can refund some of the Client fees without needing to get senior management sign off. After all, there is nothing worse than being told *I'll need to ask my manager if we can do that.*
- Processes, checklists and systems, which help every member of the team deliver a good job to Clients for every single piece of work that goes out the door. (See Chapter 9 for how to systemise part of your practice.)

Clients don't want a meeting to talk about their Year End Accounts. They want a meeting BEFORE year end to help them plan for the year ahead and sort out their tax planning.

Case study: Sharon's Growth Story

Our internally designed Client Happiness Survey is sent to Clients following completion of major work. With only three questions it's really quick and easy for them to complete. Our survey drives improvements throughout the firm. The survey responses told us that our Client Service Standards were slipping. We had also noticed that our Client churn, which was historically next to nothing, was creeping up.

As a result, I analysed our firm's processes and systems and set about changing them so they were truly client-centric. One of the big improvements we made was to change our client administrator role into a Client Co-ordinator role. We gave our Client Co-ordinator the responsibility to help our Clients feel loved and contacted regularly whilst keeping them organised. Our Client Co-ordinator manages a Client Contact calendar, built in-house, which reminds us when we need to contact Clients for key deadlines, but also ad hoc *keeping in touch* conversations, where we have no agenda but to help understand our Clients' world, and make them feel valued.

We have completely overhauled our Client Onboarding process which is now automated through Google Forms & Sheets, Practice Ignition and Xero to ensure that Clients feel loved, contacted and supported during their initial 3-month period with us, and beyond. All new Clients have a 3-month review to check that we are delivering on what's important to them, and how we can help.

At our weekly Rhythm Meetings, we:

- Review our KPIs for Client Service. These include the % of Clients who would recommend us, turnaround time and reasons for any Clients leaving.
- Check we have actioned any Clients requests we received in the week.
- Share examples of where we have delivered Extraordinary Client Service for a Client.
- Review the root causes for any Client complaints or mistakes and how we can make sure this never happens again.

My team were initially uncomfortable with sharing examples of Extraordinary Client Service that they had helped deliver. But when they could see how important it was to both me *and* the future of the firm, they slowly but surely started to share examples of how they had delivered Extraordinary Client Service. As we began to share more examples, this had the knock-on effect of helping every team member routinely deliver Extraordinary Client Service to every Client every day.

We use cloud technology exclusively throughout the firm, and our aim is to only work with Clients using cloud technology. We believe that budget shouldn't be a problem for Clients to benefit from the cloud (efficiencies, automation, real-time accounting), so we onboard and train clients for free on Xero and Receipt Bank. We regularly help them automate their business by identifying and assisting with the installation of other online apps; e.g. iZettle and Chaser.

As a result of all the changes to how we worked with our Clients, 92% of our Clients will recommend us and 46% of all new work comes as a result of a Client Referral.

How to deliver Extraordinary Client Service?

Word-of-mouth business is often the cheapest type of new business to generate but the hardest to reliably generate. Bain and Company[3] discovered that 60–80% of Clients who describe themselves as satisfied do not go back to do more business with the company which initially satisfied them. This means that gone are the days where Clients would routinely recommend your firm to others just because your firm did a good job. Doing a good job is what is expected, not what will get you Client referrals and word-of-mouth business.

In order to reliably generate word-of-mouth business, your firm needs to routinely deliver Extraordinary Client Service. This means not just doing a great job with a Client but going the extra mile. This extra mile is normally something that is unexpected, personalised to the Client and typically very cheap or free to provide.

For example, how about:

- Keeping a stock of mobile phone rechargers in your office for when Clients visit, so that they can charge their phone while they meet with you or your team.
- Taking note of your Client's dietary preferences, so that you can always offer them a hot beverage and something to eat which they can eat/drink and will enjoy.
- Having some umbrellas in the office so you can walk Clients out to their cars when it is raining.

[3] http://www.bain.com/Images/BB_Prescription_cutting_costs.pdf

- Sending them birthday cards or anniversary cards of when they became a Client.
- Introducing them to one potential Client or referrer every six months.
- Sending them a small gift, relevant to the work you are doing, after your work is completed.

Extraordinary Client Service exercise

How to onboard new Clients quickly and effectively

Given the time and effort it's taken to win your firm's new Client, the last thing you or your firm wants to do is create a bad first impression. The tone of this first impression often persists right the way through the length of your working relationship. This is the time when the Client is most unsure about your firm. The banking industry[4] have found that new customers are 3 times more likely to leave in the first 90 days after opening an account. Therefore, get the onboarding right and you will find that the Client sticks around and becomes a great advocate for your firm's services. In fact, in a survey conducted by BAI, it was found that 75% of all cross-selling happens in the first few months of new customer acquisition.[5] Get it wrong and it's going to be a tough working relationship which probably won't last for long. Get it right and you will have created the best first impression for your new Client to start to regularly refer your firm.

Remember all those promises you and your firm made to your firm's Clients in those new business meetings *before* they came on board as a Client. You know the ones:

[4] J.D Power & Associates Annual Survey of Retail-Banking Customer Satisfaction
[5] BAI: "Quest for Deposits: The Ninety Day Window of Opportunity"

We're proactive
We give you a personal service
We are accessible and responsive.

You need to make sure that in the first few months of your working relationship your firm *really* delivers on these promises (and then carries on delivering on these!).

Onboarding new Clients is so much more than just getting them set up on your firm's systems and the regulatory stuff done; e.g. money laundering checks. It's where your firm focuses on your new Client feeling loved and wanted during their first year with you. This means:

- Setting expectations on how your firm and they will work together.
- Training them on the systems your firm wants them to use.
- Diarising 3-monthly meetings to check on how they are doing.
- Potentially setting them up on new systems to help them work more effectively.

Key parts in the onboarding process

1. Updating the team about the new Client's requirements

You know what the Client wanted to buy. You also probably know some of the details of how they like things to be done. These are normally captured in the sales meetings you had with them and your proposal to them. However, how much of this stuff does anyone else in your firm know? All your notes about the new Client need to be accessible and communicated to your whole team. There is nothing worse than getting a great Client through the door, just for a team member to muck it up because they hadn't been told something really important about the Client.

Unless your firm is just you, other members of your team will be working with this Client at various points. This means that you need to have a systemised way of updating your team about the new Client. It's not just what the Client is doing right now and the services they are taking from the team. It's the detail and colour about the Client including the aspirational stuff. Things like they have three other companies (*and we want to get them too*), or they are really worried about timeliness as they had to pay fines to HMRC last year. This is best done by having a team briefing about the new Client.

2. Create a process for onboarding Clients and appoint someone to be responsible for the process

Your firm most likely has a checklist to ensure the main legal documents are returned. But, who is responsible for this checklist? Who chases up missing bits and when? How do you as the practice owner know when stuff is slipping in the onboarding process? This is why you need a documented onboarding process for your firm. When you have documented your onboarding process it gives you the insight to quickly identify which parts of the information flow can be automated. The less manual input to do in your new Client onboarding process, the quicker the process and the less room for errors.

The responsibility for your new Client onboarding process normally sits with the person in your practice who looks after Client administration. This person needs to:

- Know where every new Client is in the process
- Coordinate the response from your firm
- Chase the Client if they are slow to get information to your firm
- Flag up any problems to you or another member of staff.

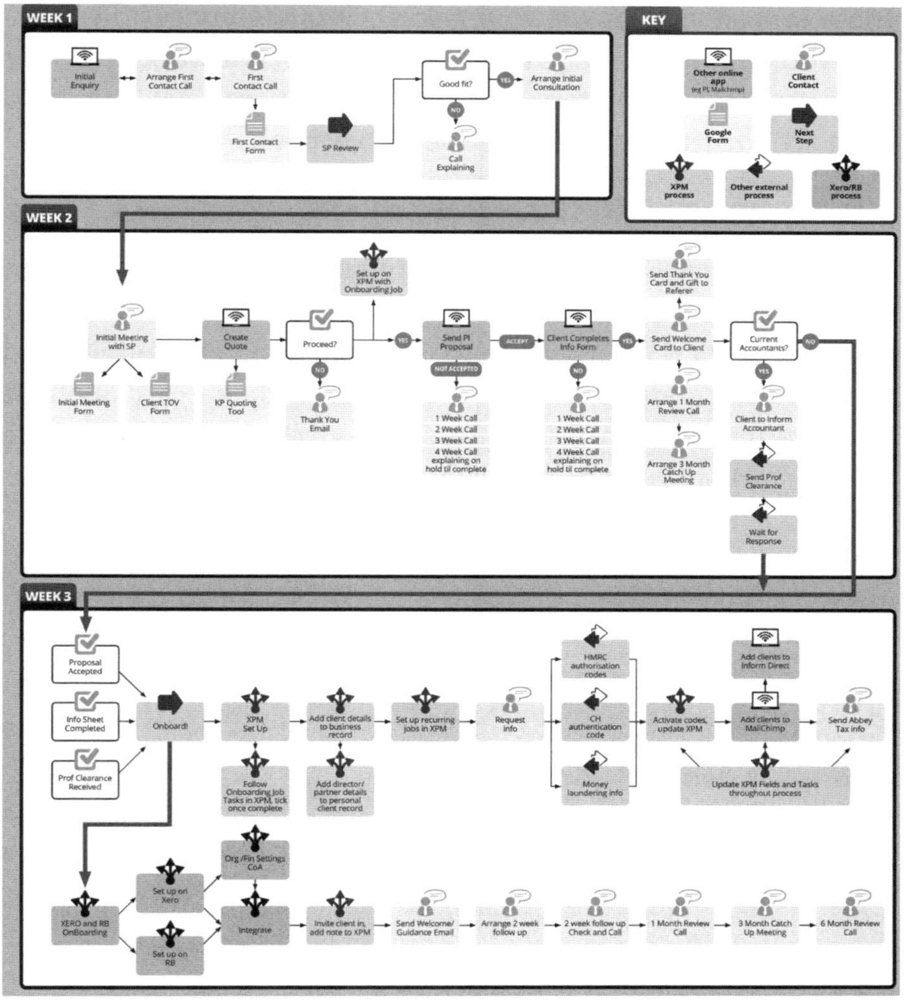

Diagram 16.0: Kinder Pocock new client onboarding process

3. Introducing your new Client to the team working on their business

Your new Client will want to be able to put names to faces of the people they will be working with at your firm. Therefore, get the relevant team members, including the junior members or receptionist, to give the new Client a call to introduce themselves.

These calls are a great way to set expectations with new Clients on how your firm will manage their Year End Accounts work, how your firm will ask them for information and what your firm will do to help them achieve their business/personal objectives.

4. Help your new Clients feel really special

In the sales conversations you had with your new Clients, you will have set some expectations about how your firm will work with them. If you want the new Client to start to refer your firm then you will need to exceed these expectations. Merely meeting their expectations at this stage means you're setting up a problem client. Are there simple little things that could help your firm exceed expectations now? For instance, a *Welcome Pack* (done differently, rather than a simple list of all the staff names), a small gift, or handwritten welcome card (personalised with a team/office/motivational photo on the front).

Case study: Paul's Growth Story

It's really important to us as a firm that we win the sort of clients that we want to work with. In fact, every new Client for our firm has to fill in a questionnaire to allow us to check that they are a good fit. Given the time we spent in qualifying new Clients, when we do win a new Client we really want to roll out the red carpet.

Each new Client gets:

- A handwritten card from me welcoming them to the firm.
- A short personalised video clip from me thanking them for signing up to our firm.
- A Welcome Pack with a list of team members and their contact details, our rate card for ad hoc work, a schedule

of key dates for their business, a list of what we have agreed to do together.

- Personalised management reports showing how their business has performed over the last 12 months.

How to upsell more services to Clients

CEB/Gartner did some research[6] which identified that 88% of salespeople believed the best way to grow existing Client accounts was to do great work for them and deliver Extraordinary Client Service. This perception is the accepted wisdom amongst accountants. Do a great job with Clients and they will reward you with loyalty and buy more from you.

However, the CEB/Gartner research[7] identified that delivering Extraordinary Client Service is a great way to *retain* your Client accounts, but not grow them. They found that there was no correlation between account managers who grew a Client account and the level of service they provided. This means that if you want your Clients to take more services from your firm you need to do more than just provide good or Extraordinary Client Service. The CEB/Gartner research[8] identified three specific behaviours which will increase the likelihood that Clients will buy new products or services from your firm:

- Being a critical friend to your Client to show them how they can improve their business
- Creating a vision for your Clients to show how they can improve their business

[6] CEB 2017 Account Growth Diagnostic
[7] CEB 2016 Sales Customer Panel
[8] CEB 2016 Sales Customer Panel

- Demonstrating the return on investment (ROI) they get from using your firm's services.

In other words, if you want Clients to buy additional services from you, your firm needs to create an exciting picture of how you can help the Client improve, how that can happen and the ROI. This is another benefit of focusing your firm's services on the needs of your Client Personas; it will be easier to find additional services your Clients want to buy.

Chapter 13 talked about Clients buying your services when they have a Pain Point. It's the same when it comes to upselling your services to Clients. No amount of love is going to convince a Client to buy more from you if they don't have a Pain Point which needs to be resolved. Use the results of the Client Portfolio Analysis that you completed in Chapter 5 to help your firm identify which Clients (your A- and B-grade Clients) are more likely to want to take more services from your firm.

In order to identify Pain Points that Clients are motivated to solve, your firm will need to systemise non-transactional type conversations with Clients. That is, conversations which don't focus solely on the current work at hand. This is often called account management. It's these conversations where your fee earners find out about how the Client is doing, the challenges they are facing and what goals they have set for themselves. Any Client which your firm has graded A or B, will need to have more of these conversations timetabled; that is, once a quarter rather than the once a year for C- or D-grade Clients. Your fee earners will need to be developed so that they can spot upselling opportunities.

Each of your firm's A- and B-grade Clients will need to have their own Account Plan. This is where your firm identifies opportunities to grow the Client account, and how it plans to realise these opportunities. Account Plans for A-grade Clients should be reviewed quarterly and B-grade Clients twice a year.

How to reduce Client churn

The best way to grow your existing Client accounts is to minimise the amount of Client churn your firm experiences. To do this:

- Measure the number of Clients your firm loses on a monthly basis. Record the reasons why each Client leaves.
- Do an exit interview with each departing Client to dig down into the real reasons why they are leaving and what your firm could have done to prevent this.
- Root cause with your team the reasons why a Client has left and what the firm did to cause this. Put in place an action plan to eliminate this happening again.
- Systemise how your firm delivers good and Extraordinary Client Service.
- Ask for Client feedback after each piece of major work you do for them. Root cause any problems with your team and put in place corrective action to eliminate any problems with your firm's Client service.

Summary

The easiest and most cost-effective way to grow your Client portfolio is to get existing Clients to take more services from your firm, and minimise your Client churn. This means having a system for:

- Getting regular feedback from your Clients and acting on the feedback received
- New Client onboarding
- Account management
- Wowing your Clients by delivering Extraordinary Client Service.

Action points

- Add to your firm's Tactical Marketing Plan how much work your firm will generate from Clients wanting more services from your firm.
- Use the results of your Client Portfolio Analysis to identify your firm's A- and B-grade clients.
- Create an account management system for your firm which systemises how your firm will have quarterly non-transactional conversations with its A- and B-grade Clients.
- Create Account Plans for all your A- and B-grade Clients. Start reviewing A-grade Client Account Plans quarterly and B-grade account plans twice a year.
- Process map your new Client onboarding process and appoint someone in the firm to take responsibility for new Client onboarding. Look at your process map and identify ways to automate the process but also increase the *Wow* factor for new Clients.
- Introduce a Client Satisfaction Survey to distribute to Clients after doing a major piece of work for them. Every month review the survey responses and put in place an action plan to correct any areas of concern.
- Start recording the reasons why Clients are leaving your firm. Root cause the reasons and put in place an action plan to eliminate the cause, and thus help minimise Client churn.
- Start exit interviews with Clients to get a deeper understanding of why they decided to leave your firm.
- Train your fee earners to be able to spot opportunities for the firm with existing Clients.

17

How to use content and social media to market your practice

Topics covered in this chapter:

- What is meant by Valuable Content
- How to use content to demonstrate your firm's expertise
- The different types of content
- What to put in your Content Plan
- How to use social media to market your practice

One of the best ways to negate the need to go out and win clients is to use Content Marketing and social media to attract them in. Unlike networking, these routes to market don't require you to personally drive them or spend high amounts of time in order to generate Leads. This means that you can easily outsource them to external marketing experts. This chapter helps you identify the content your Clients will find valuable and which social media platforms you and your firm should have a presence on.

Having a presence on social media is no longer optional for accountancy firms.

What is meant by Content Marketing?

Content Marketing is where you use content, normally in conjunction with social media, to market your firm. Content is any information which has been written, videoed, recorded or shared such as:

- White paper
- Blog post

- Article in the press
- Quote in an article
- YouTube video
- Podcast
- Comment in LinkedIn discussion
- Tweet
- Webinar
- A book
- A page on your firm's website.

Anyone can write and share content, whereas *valuable* content is anything that your firm shares which your Client Personas will find interesting and useful. For example, if you are an accountant who specialises in working with retailers, anything you can write on how to avoid high levels of obsolete stock would be valuable.

The Internet has permanently changed how people buy accountancy services. A client can find at least five local accountants by a simple Google search. Today's modern world moves at such a pace that clients want answers now – not three days later, not at next month's event. This is why people turn to the Internet first to get answers to questions, problems, challenges and opportunities.

Another consequence of a time-poor lifestyle is people's reduced tolerance for old-style marketing. The *Buy This Now* message just doesn't work. And, it definitely doesn't work on social media! Prospects want to take the sales process at their own pace, not the accountants' pace. This is why accountancy firms, who are prepared to give an instant quote in a new business meeting, have a higher conversion rate than accountants who want to go away and put together a quote over the next week. Prospects want to be able to do their own research, rather than rely on what the accountant is saying. The answer to this marketing conundrum is Valuable Content – content that will inform, help, entertain, and provoke the target audience. As Sharon Tanton and Sonja Jefferson in their book *Valuable Content Marketing* said:

If you regularly share this type of information you will draw people to your business – the company that inspires, understands and offers clear answers is the obvious place to turn when the time comes to buy.

To help your firm increase its marketing effectiveness, it will need to build up a library of Valuable Content that helps your firm get found, and emphasises the firm's credibility.

The three ways to create your content

Accountants are commonly known as numbers people. As a result accountants often shy away from writing. This and a lack of time are normally the biggest barriers accountants have to sustainably producing Valuable Content. Luckily, there is no rule that says only you or your staff have to produce content for it to be effective. With planning it is possible to efficiently produce content.

Generate

This is content that your firm has created from scratch. This could include:

- Blog posts written from fresh and not adapted from anywhere else
- Updates on LinkedIn, Twitter and Facebook where you and staff members post where you are, what you are thinking, what you are about to do, or pose a question to your followers
- White papers, reports, guides, workbooks, etc.

- Calculators, e.g. for tax calculations
- Video interviews with you and your staff
- Conversations on Twitter and Internet forums.

Recycle

This is repurposed or repacked content, which your firm has adapted from its original form. This could include:

- Publishing (with permission) another person's blog post onto your firm's blog or vice versa
- Repackaging a white paper or report into several blog posts
- Audio transcribing an interview, podcast or webinar into several blog posts.

Curate

This is where you filter or select/share other people's or your firm's content, that you think your network, contacts, Clients or social media followers will find valuable. This could include:

- Tweeting a link to a blog post or article (whether or not it is your own firm's article)
- Retweeting someone else's content
- Sharing a link to a blog or article on LinkedIn
- Including copies of presentations, video clips, white papers, reports and guides on fee earner's LinkedIn profile
- Sending out a valuable article to targeted people in your network
- Using a newsletter to share interesting articles on a theme.

What is a Content Plan?

A Content Plan is where you develop a framework for the Valuable Content you will produce.

MONTH	January	February	March
Guides, Reports, White Papers	*Guide to tax planning for solicitor practices*	*Decisions needed in order to bring in a new equity partner*	*Tips for successful mergers*
Blog Posts	*7 ways to minimise tax bill* *Case study on client*	*6 tips to make a good lateral hire* *10 tips to grow your own equity partners case study on clients*	*10 ways to merger your firm successfully case study on clients*
Newsletter	*Focused on saving tax*	*Focussed on how to bring in new equity partner*	*Focused on issues surrounding merging firm*
Linkedin	*New blog status updates* *Discussions based around on new blog posts*	*New blog status updates* *Discussions based around on new blog posts*	*New blog status updates* *Discussions based around on new blog posts*
Twitter	*Practice management tips for solicitor firms* *Links to blog posts* *Links to articles in Legal Week & The Lawyer*	*Practice management tips for solicitor firms* *Links to blog posts* *Links to articles in Legal Week & The Layer*	*Practice management tips for solicitor firms* *Links to blog posts* *Links to articles in Legal Week & The Lawyer*

Diagram 17.0: Example of a Content Plan

A Content Plan helps you to think about and schedule your firm's content in advance. This has many benefits including:

- Allowing you to align your content production with your firm's Tactical Marketing Plan, particularly campaigns
- Saving time as you and others in your firm are not thinking about what to write all the time
- Enabling you to outsource your firm's Valuable Content production

Before jumping into writing a Content Plan, it is always worth taking a step back, to think about some important questions that will help your firm save time in the long run.

- What is a realistic expectation for your on-going content creation? As a minimum, to get any meaningful traction, your firm needs to blog at least once a month, and maintain a daily presence on its preferred social media sites.

- Where are your Client Personas looking for information?
- What sort of questions or problems are your Client Personas looking to the firm to answer?
- What content can be created by you, other people in the firm and by outside (independent) sources?
- What infrastructure (e.g. blog, email marketing software) do you have available to help deliver the content?

Planning Your Valuable Content

> “Many professionals write boring technical articles, when really they should be starting with the simple things which worry their typical clients.
>
> *ALAN STEVENS, THE MEDIA COACH*

The purpose of your Valuable Content is to help your firm find, sign up and keep Clients. Each new Client that your firm signs up will typically go through a similar process, often referred to as the marketing and sales funnel[9]. Your content will keep the right Prospects and Client Personas in the funnel, and progress them through to being a loyal Client. Your marketing and sales funnel needs to be mapped so it aligns with your Client Personas' Buying Journey.

[9] The Marketing and Sales Funnel is adapted from Dr. Philip Kotler rational decision making models

Look at each stage in the marketing and sales funnel:

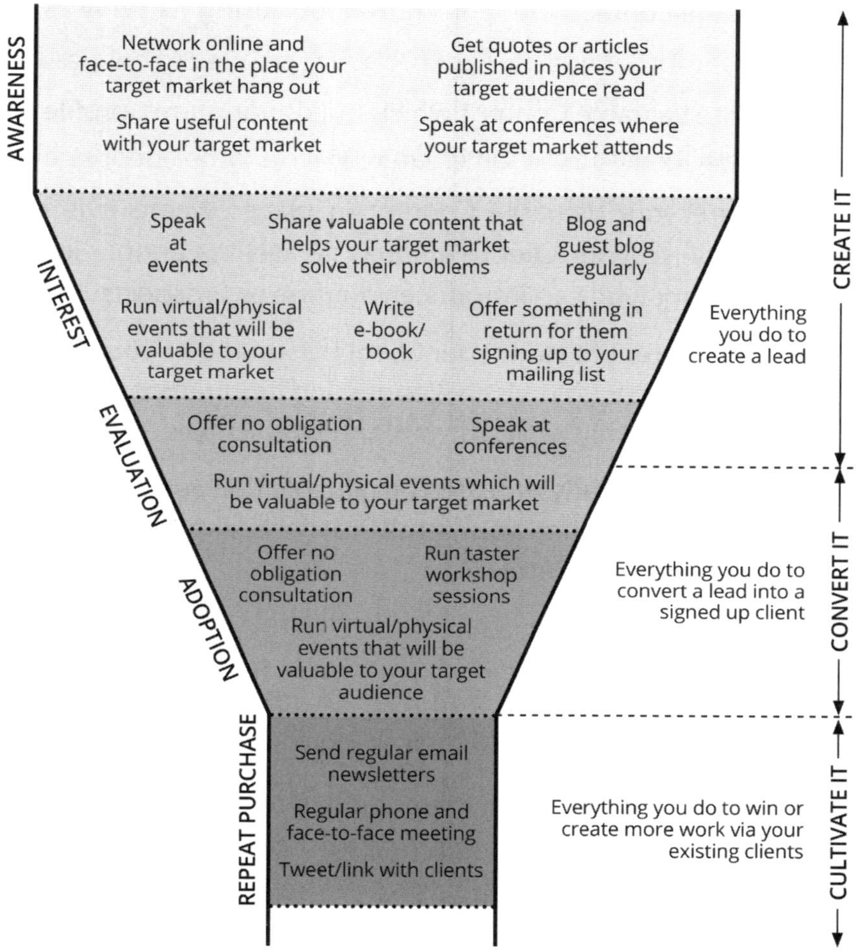

Diagram 17.1: The marketing and sales funnel with ideas of what your firm could be doing at each stage of the funnel to help progress someone to a loyal Client.

Create it

This is everything your firm does to generate a Lead from a Prospect who has made contact with your firm about using its services. For example:

- Write Valuable Content which builds your firm's profile and visibility with your Client Personas
- Share your Valuable Content in places where it is most visible to your Client Personas, as well as people in your network who can introduce your firm to Prospects
- Use content to show your Client Personas that your firm can help them with their challenges and requirements, and that your firm truly walks its walk and talks its talk
- Provide a steady drip feed of Valuable Content, and use it to stay in touch with your firm's Prospects until they are ready to contact your firm.

Convert it

This is everything that your firm does to convert the Lead into a signed-up Client who has paid their first invoice. For example:

- Assist with qualifying the enquiry your firm has received. Is it the sort of client your firm wants to work with?
- Anticipate and overcome objections Leads may have to working with your firm
- Build confidence in your firm in the eyes of Leads
- Provide a steady drip feed of Valuable Content, and using it to stay in touch with your firm's Leads until they are ready to buy.

Cultivate it

This is everything your firm does to win more work from your Clients, either through them recommending your firm to others, or buying more services from your firm. Therefore, your firm needs to create Valuable Content which:

- Is written and presented in such a manner that Clients will feel it is easy to forward the content onto other people
- Keeps Clients interested by demonstrating how your firm is leading change and advancing its expertise
- Maintains a high level of Client Service, even if your current engagement has finished.

📖 Content Plan

Case study: James

James runs an accountancy firm which has a niche in the leisure sector.

He thinks about his Clients in terms of the three stages they might be in: Prospects, Leads and Clients. He prepares Valuable Content materials for those groups.

For the Prospects who were not near to a buying decision, he writes a *Simple guide to hiring temporary staff and avoiding the pitfalls*, which is actually in eight parts so that he can drip feed this to audience on social media. The parts appear in his blog, and he also places some in a trade magazine.

James also arranges for these eight parts to be featured in a local lawyer's regular newsletter to their hospitality clients. They told him that they were willing to help because the content was so valuable. Importantly, what he had written was not blatantly pushing his services, but they did contain his name and contact details at the bottom.

For his Prospects who were nearer to a buying decision, he wrote a longer set of articles, many of which gave case studies showing how to get more value for money from agency staff. To access these articles, the readers needed to click through to his website and sign up for his free weekly email tip. Again, James was determined not to *sell*, but rather to offer valuable information.

Realising that some Prospects wanted to 'see' James rather than read articles written by him, James sourced YouTube clips to make for more compelling content. Some was from the Internet, and some others were testimonials from Clients he videoed himself. As he was behind the camera, the cost of producing these testimonials was low.

Finally, for his Clients, he wanted them to stay with him and to talk about his services to others. He did some proprietary research into the most cost effective way for leisure companies to recruit agency staff. He shared this information with his Clients and invited them to bring along a guest to a seminar he was hosting to discuss the implications of his research for them.

Tips to save time with producing and sharing content

Here are some tips to save time producing and distributing content:

- Schedule or automate the everyday content that your firm shares on social media as much as possible, using tools such as Buffer, Hootsuite and MeetEdgar

- Give your staff ready-made posts for them to share on Twitter and LinkedIn
- Get into the routine of checking into your key social media sites daily
- Aim to engage fully with a handful of sites rather than barely engaging with many sites, groups and communities
- Plan to produce 80% of your firm's blog posts in advance before your planned publish date.

The How, What, When and Why of blogging

One of the key pieces of infrastructure for your firm's Valuable Content is your firm's blog and it is important to maximise the effectiveness of the blog.

A blog is a form of website, where you can self-publish articles. Clients now expect their accountant to have a website with an integrated blog. Your Content Plan will guide what content your firm needs to write about, and your blogging schedule.

A blog post is not like a magazine article or feature. It is often shorter and more informal in nature than those types of articles. The ideal length of a blog post is 300-500 words; i.e. long enough to provide something of value, but short enough to be digested in three to five minutes.

The point of a blog is to help Prospects see past the commercial literature and help connect with you and your staff as people. Your firm's blog is a great tool to build up trust and credibility with your Prospects, showing your firm understands them, and that your firm knows what it is talking about.

A blog is a fantastic destination point to showcase your firm's credibility and demonstrate your thought leadership to your

Prospects, as well as keep in touch with your firm's existing network and Clients. When your niche market 'meets' you and your firm in the online world, they are often interested to know whether you and your firm are the real deal or not. A well-maintained blog – which your firm directs people to read either via Twitter or a link on a forum post – is the easiest way to build up your firm's credibility.

Your firm's website page rank in Google is heavily influenced by how much fresh content is on your website. As a blog is dynamic and users can interact with the website, Google is more likely to place a greater weight on that blog rather than on a static website. This means that maintaining a keyword-rich blog is vital for effective Search Engine Optimisation. Owning a website that features highly in the search engine ranking is a way of generating Leads for your firm.

Here are ideas for what your firm can blog about:

- Case studies, e.g. how you helped a client move from a desktop accounting package into the cloud
- Testimonials and achievements of happy Clients, e.g. how you helped a client automate their financial processes by putting their business on the cloud
- What a Client or you learnt whilst working together, e.g. on a custom install of a piece of software
- Interviews with experts inside and outside of your firm, e.g. a Cloud Integrator on what type of apps all businesses should be using
- How-To articles, e.g. how to use a new feature on an accounting package
- Introductions to new team members
- Responses to news items or articles, e.g. if a software vendor merges with another software vendor

- Anything that highlights your firm's credentials, e.g. if your firm has become a Platinum or Gold partner to a popular financial app
- Book reviews which are of relevance to your Client Personas
- Presentations your firm has prepared for seminars
- Video clips of you or a staff member presenting at a seminar or conference
- New products or services that your firm is starting to sell, e.g. if you have recently become accredited in a particular app
- Thought for the day, e.g. your top tip for saving tax.

How to maximise your effectiveness with blogging

Writing blog posts can suck away your precious time. Your aim when producing a blog post for your firm is to make each word count. Here are some ways in which you can do that:

1. Use a Content Plan to work to a schedule, so you can divide up the responsibility for producing blog posts. Remember that you don't need to be the person who writes the blog post.
2. Use the Pain Points you previously identified for your firm's Client Personas as themes across the year for your firm's Content Plan.
3. Integrate your firm's blogging with your firm's keep-in-touch strategy.
4. Use your firm's blog posts to educate your firm's potential Clients and existing Clients on what they should be talking to your firm about.

5. Use Google analytics to help you track what subjects people are most interested in and use this knowledge to influence your firm's Content Plan.
6. Ask your firm's Clients what they are interested in finding out about at the moment.

Case study: Jean

Jean owns an accountancy firm which specialises in helping advise family-owned groups of companies. She saved one of her Clients £8 million pounds in inheritance tax. (She also got permission from the Client to blog about how they managed it.)

Once she had written the blog post, she started to spread the content via social media and included a link to the blog post on her email footer.

She then went through her Client, intermediaries and Prospect lists and found people who might have an interest in inheritance tax planning. She sent a personalised email through to each of these people, sharing the blog post with them, and asked them whether they or their Clients had thought much about inheritance tax planning.

Many people ask the question, *How often should my firm's blog be updated?* The right answer is based on how often your firm's niche audience expects to read your blog. Remember that you, personally, don't need to be the sole person writing your blog. This responsibility can be easily outsourced or divided up between your staff members. If Content Marketing is going to be one of your firm's main routes to market prepare to be blogging at least once a week.

The rest of this chapter now looks at how to use social media to market your practice.

How to use social media to market your practice

Social media is a great tool to help your firm:

- Share Valuable Content with your Prospects
- Stay visible with your existing and potential Clients and wider network
- Search for new clients for your firm
- Amplify the reach of your firm's marketing messages
- Be found by Prospects or journalists
- Expand your knowledge about your Client Personas businesses and the world in which they operate.

For the right client base Facebook or Instagram may be a great place to win clients.

The best way to routinely win business using social media is to remember the 4Cs model. Where, in order to win new clients via social media your firm needs to:

- Share Valuable **Content**
- Have a presence in the **communities** (LinkedIn, Facebook, etc.) where your Client Personas hang out
- Join in the **conversations** on social media with your firm's Clients and Prospects
- Have social media as part of your firm's Tactical Marketing Plan. That is, have a **call to action** which brings your Prospects one step closer to becoming a Client

Diagram 17.3: The 4Cs Model

Potential Clients normally want to interact with a person rather than a corporate entity. This means as part of your firm's social media marketing activity, you will need to define what activity your firm will undertake, and what activity fee earners within your firm will undertake on social media. Your firm will get more traction on social media if your staff maintain a high level of visibility there. The right platforms for your firm and staff to belong to will depend on where your Client Personas hang out. However, as a minimum, your firm needs to have:

- A business page on LinkedIn

- Fee earners to have a LinkedIn account and Twitter account
- A business page on Facebook.

Social Media Marketing works best when your firm – whether via the firm or fee earner's accounts – has a consistent presence on social media. Whilst social media may be a low-cost way of marketing your firm, to do it properly means investing in high quality Valuable Content which is shared regularly. The best way of consistently sharing it is to have a Content Plan for your practice. (See earlier in this chapter)

Your firm's usage of social media will dominate your firm's online footprint, and be the first impression you make when Prospects meet your firm online. Get this wrong and you could easily damage your firm's credibility. Here are some dos and don'ts to make sure social media works for your firm, rather than against you:

Do:

- Hang out online where your Client Personas hang out.
- Engage in conversation rather than solely broadcasting out your thoughts, content and own material.
- Train your staff on how you expect them to behave online, as their public and private social media usage will impact how your firm is viewed.
- Be polite and remember your manners. You don't know who could be listening to your conversation.
- Try to be helpful rather than just pushing your own opinion or services.
- Think before you post anything online: *Is this helping my firm build a strong and positive reputation?*
- Speak to someone online as if they were standing next to you.

- Apologise if you receive negative comments online and offer to take the conversation offline.
- Remember that everyone is entitled to an opinion and you can't please everyone all the time.
- Let your personality shine through, but don't go off-message.

Don't:

- Swear, moan or whine. Remember that sarcasm can also fail online.
- Post online when excessively tired or drunk.
- Post anything you wouldn't be happy if your mother, a journalist, boss or good friend read it.
- Fight out your personal or professional battles on social media. A tweet-sent-in-anger can definitely lose your firm clients and tarnish your reputation.
- Share everything about your life, warts and all. Some things are best left unsaid.
- Be completely black and white with your opinions or thoughts, always leave room for some grey area.

When it comes to social media you can outsource the creation and scheduling of content really easily. You can also outsource engagement on your firm's business pages. Outsourcing the engagement on social media on your personal social media accounts, and your staff's personal social media accounts is often a false economy. Your Prospects want to build up an emotional connection with you and your staff.

How to use advertising on social media

Using Facebook, Twitter or LinkedIn or any kind of advertising is a job to outsource to the experts. It is a specialist area and beyond the scope of this book.

Benefits of using social media advertising:

- You can easily track how well your activity is doing, and the return on investment for using it.
- You can switch social media advertising on and off. You can start to generate Leads immediately via social means.
- It is really easy to target your adverts so only your exact Client Personas see them.
- It can be a very affordable way of generating good quality Leads.

Disadvantages of using social media advertising:

- Unless you are incredibly targeted with where you place your adverts, much of the audience you reach won't be interested.
- It is easy to create adverts and then forget about them, which can waste money.
- It takes a large investment of time and cost upfront to optimise your content, audience targeting, visuals and copy.

Summary

Valuable Content and Social Media Marketing are great ways to market your practice without you personally needing to drive the marketing activity.

Valuable Content and Social Media Marketing work well when your firm:

- Produces regular Valuable Content which is widely shared on social media
- Tailors your content to different stages of your Client Personas' Buying Journey.

Action points

- Subscribe to 3 newsletters and follow well-known influencers for your Client Personas. Regularly share their content on your firm's social media profiles.
- Decide on the right social media sites for your firm to maintain a presence. Aim to keep this to three or less social media sites.
- Decide on which parts of content marketing and social media marketing your firm will do in-house and what your firm will outsource to others.
- In a Rhythm Meeting with your team brainstorm what content the firm could share on social media, and how everyone in the firm can help to amplify the firm's reach on social media. Capture on an action plan what everyone has agreed to do.
- Produce a Content Plan for your firm. In your Content Plan identify themes which align with your Client Personas' Pain Points.

18

How to maximise referrals from your firm's network

Topics covered in this chapter:

- How to build a Networking Strategy for your firm
- How to systemise how your firm wins referrals
- How to reliably generate referrals from introducers; e.g. bank managers
- How to consistently generate decent Leads by attending a professional networking type of group

After winning more work from existing Clients, the main route to market for accountants is via referrals from existing Clients and their network. This chapter will show you how to systemise your firm's referral generation so you can easily predict how many quality Leads your firm will get by referral each month, in order to achieve your 3-year Growth Plan. It will also show you how to maximise the number of referrals your firm gets by involving your staff.

Building your firm's Networking Strategy

Effective business networking is the process of finding, building and maintaining mutually beneficial relationships. Your firm's Networking Strategy details how your firm will use networking to achieve its 3-year Growth Plan.

When a firm relies on referrals for new business there is often a lack of coordination and accountability between members of the firm about who will do what. As a result, opportunities get missed or there is a duplication of effort. Or staff don't understand why they need to develop a network and hence deprioritise this in favour of the work on their desk. That is why your firm needs a clear and concise Networking Strategy. It allows you to make the decisions as to *what* networking activities you and others in your firm will do. It is your firm's *plan* for connecting to important people. It's also your way to make sure that you are not the sole person in your firm who can generate referrals via their network.

There are five steps involved in creating a Networking Strategy for your firm.

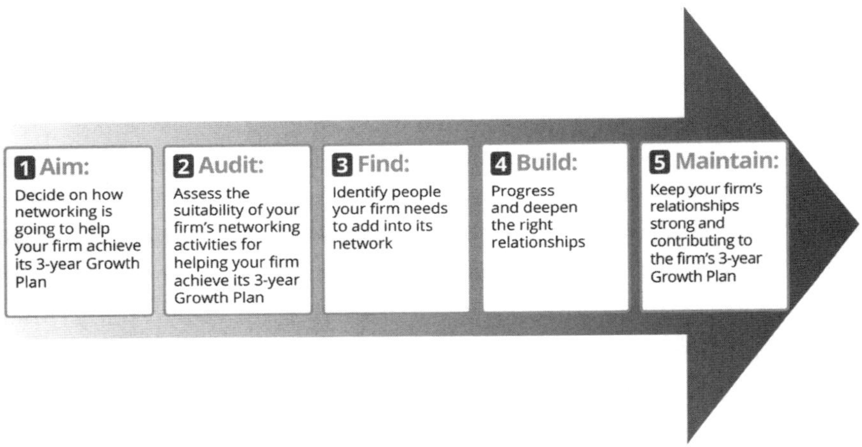

Diagram 18.0: The 5 steps to building a Networking Strategy for your firm.

Step 1: Goals

Go back to your Tactical Marketing Plan. How many Leads does your firm need to generate each month in order to achieve your 3-year Growth Plan? How many of those Leads do you want to come via referral, either from existing Clients, known introducers, membership of a networking group, such as BNI, or from your wider network? These targets will form the basis of your Networking Goals.

For example, Keyur looked at where his Leads had come from over the last 6 months for his firm. He discovered that per month on average he got:

- 2 from existing clients recommending his firm
- 2 from his network of local bank managers and lawyers
- 1 via his staff members who were building up their own network.

To achieve his 3-year Growth Plan, Keyur decided he needed to double the amount of Leads his firm gained by referral. To increase the capital value of his firm, it was important to Keyur that his firm wasn't heavily reliant on him to generate Leads for the firm. So, he set the following monthly Networking Goals for his firm:

- 4 Leads from existing clients recommending his firm
- 2 Leads from his network of local bank managers and lawyers
- 4 Leads via his staff members.

Networking Goals exercise

Now that you have your big Networking Goals identified, it is time to consider the next stage to building your networking strategy: Audit. This is where you review who is already in your firm's network.

Step 2: Audit

Many people think that they have to build a network from scratch. Actually, every single member of your firm will naturally have their own network. You may be surprised just exactly who your staff are connected too. There may be some excellent contacts already there. For example, Arun's Senior Account Manager, Jyoti was a long-term member of her local hockey club. It was only after sitting down with a member of the club, David, during the club's annual Christmas party, that she realised David was a senior decision maker in a company that her firm wanted as a Client.

Part of your role is to make sure that the right people are talking to the right people about the right things. This is why the second stage of building a Networking Strategy is to do a networking Audit. After all, you don't want to change anything that is working.

The best way to do a networking Audit is to draw out your firm's Network Map. Begin by literally mapping out your firm's ideal network. It's an exercise that will really help to focus individuals in your firm on *who* they want to meet, and how these people are going to help your firm become a one million pound practice. A Network Map will help you and your staff visualise their networking time. It also beneficial in helping them prioritise their networking activities, because they now truly understand why they are networking and why it is important to the future firm growth.

Networking Map exercise

Once you have completed your firm's Networking Map it is now time to critically look at the effectiveness of everyone's current networking activities. This is best done as a whole team together in a monthly Rhythm Meeting. The Networking Activity Effectiveness exercise can help you do this. For example:

- What activities are you and your staff doing – such as membership of a professional networking group – which are helping the firm connect with the right types of people; i.e. hubs?
- What activities are you and your staff doing which are helping grow your practice?
- What activities are not working for you or your staff?
- What activities should you or your staff start doing right now?

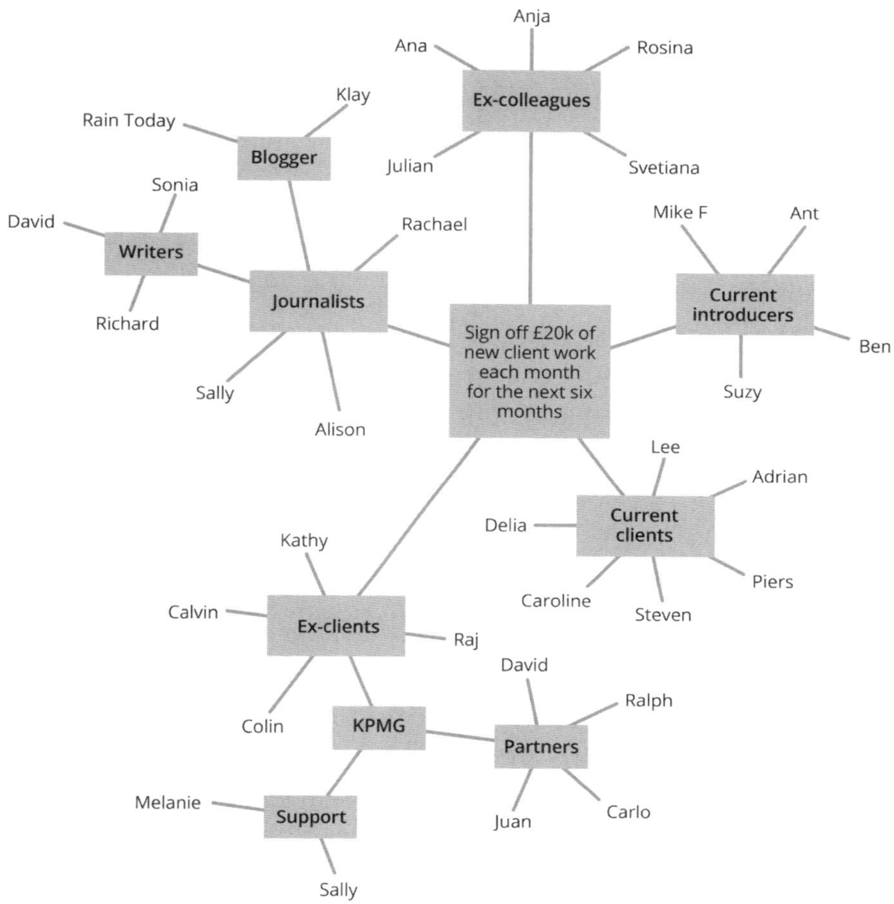

Diagram 18.1: Example Networking Map

📖 Networking Activity Effectiveness exercise

Step 3: Find

Now it is time to identify the gaps in your firm's Networking Map. Who do you need to add into your firm's network to help achieve your 3-year Growth Plan? This is likely to be well-placed introducers who can reliably generate referrals for your firm month in, month out.

Case study: Lisa

Lisa's small firm specialised in working with financial services companies regulated by the Financial Conduct Authority (FCA). Unlike most small practices her size, Lisa had taken the decision to build a revenue stream of audit work, because any FCA-regulated business needed to have an annual statutory audit. Lisa's best source of Client referrals came from the managers in a local practice with a large financial services client base, which wasn't able to audit FCA-regulated businesses.

Finding People exercise

Step 4: Build

Once you have identified *who* your firm needs to meet, then you need to categorise them. In the *FT Guide to Business Networking*, there is a simple A-, B- and C- grading system where:

A-Lister: Someone who is likely to be able to help your firm become a one million pound practice in the short term. These will include your firm's A-grade clients, which are your big and/or growing clients of the firm or clients who regularly introduce work to your firm, or introducers who regularly introduce work to the firm. Typically, these introducers will include financial advisors, bank managers, lawyers, business coaches and HR advisors.

B-Lister: Someone who is able to help your firm become a one million pound practice in the medium and long term. Likely to be a B or C-grade client, i.e. a small client who occasionally refers work to the firm, or an introducer who occasionally may refer work to the firm.

C-Lister: Someone who is unlikely to help your firm become a one million pound practice in the medium and long term. These will include your D-grade clients.

In your Networking Strategy, you need to decide on what your firm will do as a result of meeting an A-, B- or C-Lister. It is worth connecting with everyone on LinkedIn and Twitter, even C-Listers, as your or their circumstances may change.

You want to have in place a Relationship Plan for all your firm's A- and B-Listers. A Relationship Plan:

- Details what you know about the person and what more you want to know about them
- Contains who is the owner for the relationship, i.e. the Relationship Lead
- Contains the desired level of contact you want
- Indicates what you would like to achieve because of your relationship.

Relationship Plan exercise

Don't be tempted to be the Relationship Lead for all your firm's A- and B-Listers. If your staff, particularly your fee earners, are going to develop and allow you to work less in the business, they need to develop their relationship management skills. Help them develop their skill-set by initially making them the Relationship Lead for some of your firm's B-Listers. Then as they become competent as a Relationship Lead give them some A-Lister relationships to lead.

It's all very well having Relationship Plans for the folks who matter to your firm, however, your firm needs to implement these plans. Every month review all of your firm's Relationship Plans with the Relationship Leads during a monthly Rhythm Meeting. Check that

RELATIONSHIP LEAD	*Della Doe*		
NAME	*John Brown*	LINKEDIN & TWITTER	*www.linkedin.com/in/johnbrown @jobrown*
PHONE	*01234 567 8910*	WEBSITE	*www.johnbrownllp.co.uk*
EMAIL	*jobrown@johnbrownllp.co.uk*	ADDRESS	*Business House, 100, Any Street, New Town, AB10 9CD*
ROLE	*Owner*	COMPANY	*John Brown LLP*

FREQUENCY OF CONTACT	*In person: every 6 months, phone call: quarterly, email: monthly, twitter account: monitored daily*
CURRENT AND DESIRED RELATIONSHIP LEVEL (Out of 5)	*Current - 3, desired - 4*
THEIR GOALS AND OBJECTIVES	*Double the size of their revenue and maintain profit margin in next 2 years. Bring on board 2 new assistant solicitors and develop their niche and reputation with local and regional professional service firms*
THEIR INTERESTS OUTSIDE OF WORK	*Golf, fine dining, Spurs supporter*
FAMILY SITUATION	*Married with 2 teenage children, Stephen (13), Alex (15)*
HOW CAN I HELP THEM?	*Make introductions to our professional services client base, jointly run seminars together*
WHAT CONTENT DO THEY WELCOME ME SENDING THEM?	*Our monthly articles for our professional services clients*
RELATIONSHIP NEXT STEP	*Organise next lunch and bring along a client which they would like to meet*

Diagram 18.2: Relationship Plan

all of your Relationship Leads have three months of the right level of contact planned into their diaries.

Recommendations for A-Listers:

- Start a Relationship Plan for them, and diarise next steps from that Plan.
- Allocate a Relationship Lead who is responsible for implementing their Relationship Plan for each of them.
- Aim to speak in person to them at least once every three months.
- Actively find ways to help them. For example, sending them articles which they will find useful.
- Make at least one introduction and/or referral for them every three months.

- Include them in a List on Twitter which is checked every day by the Relationship Lead.

Recommendations for B-Listers:

- Start a Relationship Plan for them, and diarise next steps from that Plan.
- Allocate a Relationship Lead who is responsible for implementing their Relationship Plan.
- Aim to speak to them in person at least once a year.
- Find something useful to send to them at least every three months.
- Add them to a Twitter List which the Relationship Lead checks regularly.

Case study: Paul's Growth Story

I was always taught that the way to win new Clients for my accountancy practice was via my network. Although our hospitality sector was growing, we still have 90% of our client base within 35 miles of Bodmin. In order to be the first-choice accountant locally I maintain very strong relationships with all the local introducers; e.g. bank managers and partners in local law firms. These are the firm's A-Listers which I am the Relationship Lead for. These relationships normally deliver 4–6 new Leads every month. I've known many of these introducers for years and years. Initially I started with a Relationship Plan for each these Introducers. This has led to a well-formed habit of meeting every month for lunch or over a beer after work. I typically book the next meeting with an introducer at the end of our meeting – that way the relationship doesn't slip. Yes, this is a big investment of my time as I normally am meeting 1-2 of them every week. But this is just what I have done for the last 20 years!

My relationships are so strong with my local introducers that I will share my Prospect list with them and vice versa. If I act for one of their Prospects I will do my best to make an introduction to my introducer. They will do the same for me.

I am now helping Ant, my son, to build up his own network of local introducers. These are local B-Listers, but typically the up-and-coming future partners in the local law and professional services firms.

Deepening A-Lister Relationships exercise

Step 5: Maintain

Without regular communication, your firm's relationships will slip back and lose their usefulness. Therefore, a key part of your firm's Networking Strategy needs to be how to stay in touch with the people who matter, i.e. A-Listers and B-Listers.

One of the best ways of keeping in touch with the important people in your firm's network is through sending them and sharing with them valuable content. This could be articles or recordings made by you or others. Go back to Chapter 17 and revisit your Content Plan. What will you use from your Content Plan to stay in touch with these people? Go back and look at your Content Plan, and if necessary change it to identify what content you and your Relationship Leads will share regularly with the firm's A-Listers, and by what channel.

How to generate referrals via your firm's network

Having a network is one thing, but using it to build a predictable marketing machine for your firm is quite another thing. Your firm's Networking Strategy will get your firm talking to and in front of the right people, but if you and your staff don't say the right things, then your firm will miss out on opportunities to generate referrals.

Be specific

In Chapter 13 you identified your firm's niche and Client Personas. However, to really reap the benefits of having a niche, your firm will need to commit to it. Therefore, when you and your staff are networking, use the Credibility Statements and Stories you created in Chapter 14. These, rather than claiming to be all things to all people, will help your firm stand out and be memorable to your Client Personas.

Being specific is more than just being committed to your niche. It is also about being specific with your requests about who you and your staff want to be introduced to. If you have done your homework in Chapter 13, and drawn up your Network Map, you will know exactly who your firm wants to be introduced to and why.

When it comes to generating quality referrals from introducers who are connected to other local accountants (e.g. bank managers and lawyers) it is vital that you differentiate your firm from the other local accountancy firms in order to get the referral. This means telling your introducers about your Client Personas, and how and why your firm will deliver them a great service.

Case study: Harrison

Harrison realised that the Clients who his firm served best were hyper-local, i.e. within 15 km of his office, and tended to be micro businesses, typically no more than £300k in turnover. He built his firm's service offerings around the needs of these Clients.

One of his firm's best referral sources was a local bank manager who would send him on average a good Lead every month via a referral. Harrison banked at this bank, and offered to his Clients the same accounting packages that the bank recommended for micro businesses. Unlike his local competitors, Harrison really wanted to work with local micro business. The bank manager knew this, and could see how Harrison's firm was set up to deliver a great service to his local micro business Clients. As a result, he gave to Harrison all the referrals to local micro businesses who wanted a new accountant.

Stay visible

Being seen in all the right places, whether online or offline is a major component for referral generation. When your introducers are well connected to other accountants it is vital that your firm's Relationship Leads remain top-of-mind for them. This means regular 1:2:1 conversations, emails and activity on social media. Your firm's Networking Strategy will make sure that you and your staff are networking and being seen in all the right places.

Take the initiative

One of the best ways of generating referrals is to proactively ask for them, as well as introductions, which may lead to business. However, many of us, particularly staff members who are new to networking, don't feel we can ask, perhaps because it looks like we are being too pushy. Remember you are not directly asking for more business from them, just for their help. Most people don't give a referral or offer to make an introduction, based on a request phrased something like this:

> *I wonder whether you could help me? I'm looking for <insert the type of people you want to meet> who would also benefit from <insert the value you bring>.*

This type of approach only normally works if you are talking to a fellow member of a professional networking group. The reason why it doesn't work is people generate referrals or introductions in response to a problem which needs to be solved; rather than a direct *Who do you know?* type request. This means that if you want to ask someone for a referral or introduction, you need to involve them in a brainstorming type discussion. Which would go something like this:

> *I wonder whether I could pick your brains and chuck around some ideas on what you would do if you were in my position and wanted to win more Clients like you.*

Here are good opportunities to ask for a referral from an existing Client:

- When a Client gives you good feedback
- At the end of an assignment which has gone well
- When the Client has recognised that your firm have gone over and above the call of duty for them.

When Clients or people in your network give you or your staff members referrals or introductions, ask their permission to use their name when making contact. Or even, suggest that you could prepare an introduction for them to use via the phone or email.

It's not your clients' responsibility to generate referrals for your firm.

Collaborate with your firm's A-Listers

Working together with other professionals who share the same niche market as your firm can be one of the most powerful ways to generate referrals. Who do you know who has a similar type of client base to your firm, but offers a different service? For example if your firm has a niche in retailers, how about finding lawyers who specialise in retail, shop-fitters, consultants specialising in retailers, wholesalers or commercial property agents?

Niche	Potential A-Listers
Retailers	Lawyers who specialise in retailers, shop-fitters, retail consultants, wholesalers, commercial property agents
Law firms	Litigation funders, specialist software vendors to law firms, bank managers
Recruitment consultants	Invoice factoring companies, specialist software vendors to recruiters, HR consultants

Table 18.3: Examples of potential A-Listers for accountants

In the early days of your relationship you may want to help each other out with little things such as:

- Writing blog posts for each other's firm.
- Quoting them in an article.
- Recommending them in your firm's newsletters.

As the relationship, trust and credibility builds, it's worth thinking about bigger things you can do together, such as:

- Launching a joint service or product.
- Running a marketing event or campaign together.
- Systematically introducing all your new Clients to them, with an easy incentive to use their services.

Collaborate exercise

Case study: The Franchise Surgery

The Franchise Surgery is a series of surgeries for existing franchisors to come in and speak to professional advisors who specialise in franchising. The surgery was co-founded by Carl Reader, an accountant who specialises in franchising. For each surgery, they tend to get 6–10 franchisors. Every professional advisor in attendance normally comes away with invoiceable business from each surgery session.

Educate

If you want your existing Clients and introducers to act as an unpaid sales force for your firm, then they will need educating on how to spot a potential client, how much this is valued by your firm, and what to do next. Go back to Chapter 13 look the Pain Points you solve for your firm's Client Personas. How can your network physically see, hear, taste or even smell that someone needs your services? What are the sort of comments they will say?

For example, someone who may be ready to change their accountant will say things like:

- *I'm not sure what my accountant actually does to justify what he is charging me.*
- *My accountant only seems to get in touch with me when she wants her bill paid or Year End is on us.*
- *I'm unhappy with the current level of service I am receiving from my accountant.*

- *My business is growing rapidly and I think it may be outgrowing my current accountant.*
- *I'm hearing that I could be reducing my tax bill by claiming R&D tax credits, but my accountant never mentioned these to me.*

Your firm also needs to educate its network that giving referrals is a good thing. Do this by saying thank you. For example:

- Send them a handwritten note saying thank you
- Give them a gift
- Give them a referral in return
- Buy them lunch or a drink
- Offer them a spotter's fee or commission split for any successful introductions or referrals. Be aware that some professionals may not either for ethical or regulatory reasons be able to accept a spotter's fee or commission split.

Educate exercise

How to generate referrals from a professional networking type of group

Accountants generally find that professional networking groups are a good source of Leads. A professional networking group typically meets weekly, fortnightly or monthly on the same day of the month. Examples of professional networking groups are BNI, Athena, Women in Business. Many of these groups operate a professional lock out system; that is, only one representative from each profession is able to attend. The accountant's seat in these type of groups is always heavily sought after. In fact, BNI discovered that the most profitable seat in any of its networking chapters was the accountant's seat.

Belonging to a professional networking group can be an excellent way of generating regular referrals for your practice. It is one of the most tried and tested channels to market that accountants use to generate Leads. However, it does come with a large time cost. For example, if you are a member of a BNI group, you firstly need to spend two hours every week attending the meeting. Then, to get the most out of your membership of the group, typically spend 2–3 hours a week helping find introductions and referrals for members of your chapter. This is a large time cost for you or any member of your firm. This may not be the best investment of time for your firm!

Tips to help generate referrals from membership of a professional networking type of group:

- Prioritise regular 1:2:1s with members who are highly connected to your firm's Client Personas. But make sure you have put a 1:2:1 in with *every* member of your group within 3 months of joining.
- Set aside 2-3 hours per week to spend getting to know members of your group and helping find them introductions and referrals.
- Don't miss a meeting, the people who get the most referrals show up time and time again.
- Educate all the members of the group about how they can spot a potential Lead for your firm.
- If one of your staff is going to attend a networking group on behalf of the firm, make sure they have enough time to form strong relationships with group members outside of the regular group meetings.

Summary

Generating referrals from existing Clients and well-placed introducers is often the second easiest way to generate new Leads. However, to make sure your firm doesn't waste time networking, be clear about:

- How will your Networking Strategy help your firm achieve its Tactical Marketing Plan?
- Who does your firm want to meet and why you want to meet them?
- Who is the Relationship Lead in your firm for each A- and B-Lister?

Then make sure that every month in your Rhythm Meetings you and your Relationship Leads are updating each other on progress with the Relationship Plans.

To help your firm's network send your firm referrals, you and your staff members will need to :

- Be specific about who you want to meet, i.e. your Client Personas
- Be visible
- Take the initiative
- Collaborate with A-Listers for mutual gain
- Educate your firm's network about how to spot a Lead for the firm.

Action points

- Complete the Network Map exercise with your firm's Relationship Leads and identify three action points to add to new relationships where there are gaps.
- Complete the Deepening A-lister Relationships exercise with your firm's Relationship Leads. Make sure you and your Relationship Leads add in the next steps from your Relationship Plans into your diaries.
- Share the Relationship Lead role out between you and your fee earning members of staff. Develop a handover plan for A- or B-Listers where you have previously been the Relationship Lead. For staff members who are new to relationship management, develop them to be able to manage a relationship.
- Revisit your Content Plan, and revise it based on your work in this chapter.
- Speak to your best Clients who are good examples of your Client Personas and find out where to spend time both physically and online. Go and meet two potential new A-Listers this month.

19

How to generate new clients by running events

Topics covered in this chapter:

- The different types of event available to you, and when to use each event
- The key stages in planning, marketing and running an event
- How to get people to turn up to your firm's event
- How to use a mailing list to make it easier to get people to turn up to your firm's event

One tried and tested route to generate Leads is to run physical or virtual events. Events are good to increase adoption from your existing Clients for a particular piece of software, showcasing your firm's advisory services or showing Prospects how your firm can help them. You may find that software vendors may help fund an event for your firm if their software is promoted to clients. Events give your Prospects the chance to get to know your firm and its credibility in a safe way. This means that events are a great way to help Prospects move from *I may want to work with you* to *Can we talk about how we can work together*? However, running and marketing events are a large investment in time and money. This chapter shows you how your firm can use events intelligently to generate the maximum amount of new business for your money and time.

The different types of events available to you

Technology has moved on so much that you can run an event without your attendees needing to leave their office or home. There are two main types of events that you can run:

Face-to-face event. This is where your attendees come to a venue of your choosing. At the event, you and others from your firm may spend some of the time presenting or facilitating a conversation with the attendees.

Webinar. This is where you try to create the interactivity of a face-to-face event via the web. Typically attendees in a webinar have a suite of tools to help interact with the event, such as polls, asking questions, chatting via text with the presenters and other participants.

Face-to-face event	Webinar
• You can build up trust and credibility with your audience quickly, in a way you can't do if you are not in the same room • You can network one-to-one with Prospects before, during and after the event • It's easy to generate rapport, trust and credibility with your audience • You can piggyback your event onto another more established event, such as a drinks reception after a conference	• Low cost to deliver as technology cost is significantly lower than hiring a venue • Easy to get people to attend as there are no travelling costs normally involved, and less time commitment needed for people to join • You can reach non-local audience • Easier to keep your audience involved and engaged than a teleseminar • Possible to get to a very large audience for your event • You can deliver the webinar at a place of your choosing – even in your pyjamas from home • Cheap to record, share and distribute to people who couldn't attend the event

Table 19.0: Face-to-face event vs. webinar

The key stages in planning, marketing and running an event

Regardless of how and when your firm decides to host its event, to maximise the returns you will need to make an investment in planning and marketing, involving both you and your team.

Planning your event

There are three steps to planning your firm's event:

1. Risk evaluation
2. Identify how the event will help your firm generate new business from Prospects and/or Existing Clients
3. Logistics

Step 1: Risk evaluation

It seems a little pessimistic, but before your firm commits time and resource to this event, do consider what could go wrong, and how you can mitigate this risk.

- What will happen if not enough people turn up?
- What happens if the firm can't get its first-choice venue?

The final part of the risk evaluation is to do a go/no-go analysis. What conditions will your firm need to satisfy to go ahead with the event? This may not be just about getting people signed up, it could also be related to the number and quality of speakers who have committed to contribute to your firm's event.

Step 2: Identify how the event will help your firm generate new business from Prospects and/or Existing Clients

In this step, it's time to put your thinking cap on. What are the things your firm needs to do before, during and after the event to help you generate new business from Prospects and/or Existing Clients? For example:

- How much time should be allocated to the speakers and how much time for networking?
- Who are the right people to have speaking at the event, and in what order?

- How many people does the firm need to attend to make the event a success?
- Considering the available budget, the type of service to be promoted, the proposed audience, what is the best format and medium for the event? Face-to-face event? Webinar?
- What's the hook to help people to sign up for the event?
- Why should attendees give up the time to attend this event?
- What will you need to get attendees to do as a result of the event?
- What will you give (if anything) attendees as a result of attending the event?

Case study: Paul's Growth Story

We typically run an event every month. Most months we are running a free Xero training event for our clients. We have two versions of our Xero-focused events: basic and advanced Xero training. We keep our Xero training events fairly simple and we get a little budget from Xero to help cover the costs of running the events. We run them in our board room, limit numbers to a maximum of ten people and get in some simple catering. Of course, we take photos of the event and share them extensively across our social media channels.

The purpose of our Xero events is to increase our Clients' skill level with Xero. We do this for a multitude of reasons. Firstly, these events generate a huge amount of word-of-mouth business for us from the local business community. We know we win Clients because we run these monthly free Xero training sessions. Secondly, it gives our Clients a valuable service. Just one of the perks of them letting us be their accountant. Thirdly, it gives us the chance to have conversations with Clients about their business; we often pick up bookkeeping work from Clients who attend our Xero events. Fourthly, it cuts down the numbers of queries and the amount of re-work we need to do for our Clients. But finally, it gives me a chance to get my son, Ant, up and in front of our Clients. If I am going to be able to hand over my firm to my son he needs the opportunity to spend time forming a bond with our Clients.

Step 4: Logistics

The final step in planning your firm's event is to draw up a project plan, and decide on the logistics for the event:

- Where (or how) is the event being held?
- What time does the event start and finish?
- Who is responsible for each part of the event?
- How will delegates register or buy tickets for the event? Will your firm use a landing page or ticket/event management software?
- When will the team responsible for running the event meet to discuss progress?
- What physical things need to be produced or done for the event to be a success?

Marketing your event

The hardest part of holding an event is not the running of the event, but actually getting people to commit to attend and then actually attend the event. Combine the fact that the Internet provides most people with information that they require, and people's time fast becoming their scarcest resource, is it any wonder that it is a tough ask to get people to attend events? Even free events with highly respected speakers and delicious canapés. However, events which are well-attended can be a great way of winning new business from Prospects and Existing Clients.

Using your firm's email list and social media community

Having a big list or large community of engaged followers makes marketing an event much easier. If people have taken the time to build up a relationship with you or your firm, and like what your firm talks about, they are more likely to come to an event run by your firm.

Case study:
Kal

Kal runs quarterly Client seminars for his firm. He encourages Clients to come along and bring a friend. As his Clients are normally connected to similar types of business owners, he finds that most of the friends who come along are typically representative of his firm's Client Personas. He finds that 50% of attendees are Clients who sign up as a result of the emails he sends about the event to them. Then 35% of attendees come as a guest of a Client. Finally, about 15% of attendees come as a result of the social media activity surrounding the event. To minimise the dropout rate at the event he calls each booked attendee a week before the event to check they are still coming.

Although Kal runs his seminars primarily to generate more Client Leads, he finds that having existing Clients at the seminar really helps to increase the number of Client Leads his firm generates.

His existing Clients act as great advocates for him and the firm, and often encourage their friends to become a client of the firm. In effect doing the selling on behalf of the firm.

Using direct mail

Before you can use direct mail your firm needs to have a mailing list. If your firm has been diligently collecting your Client's and Prospect's postal addresses then you can use this as your mailing list. There is nothing stopping your firm from finding addresses from the web and directories to create its own mailing list. Or you can rent a mailing list and expect to pay around £100 per 1,000 names. If your firm is creating its own list you must check with the Mailing Preference Service that your contacts have not opted out of receiving direct mail.

The response rate of direct mail is typically about 1–2%. However, if you target the mail shot well and follow up with a phone call after the mail has landed, you can have a much higher response rate, and be more likely to get people to attend your event. If your firm has a large mailing consider using a specialist mailing house to help you print and send out your mail shot. It will save your firm time and money in the long run.

To help increase the success of using direct mail to get people to attend your firm's event:

- Address the envelope and letter to the actual person you want to read it.
- Most businesses respond better to mail shots received midweek.
- Use a headline near to the top of the letter to highlight the key benefit to the reader for reading the letter. This headline must make the reader want to find out more.

- Use the body of your letter to emphasise the key benefits to the reader for attending your event.
- Tell the reader to go to your webpage to secure their place at the event.
- Follow up each letter with a phone call to find out whether the person is coming.
- On the week and day of the event send a reminder to attendees about the event.

Co-marketing and co-running events

Jointly marketing events can be a win-win for both parties. When you are new into a marketplace co-running an event with someone who has a much larger list or more credibility with your target audience, can be the best way to generate leads from events. Before you agree to co-marketing or co-running an event, check carefully the following:

- What you both want to get out of the event
- That the attendees will benefit from the co-operative event
- Who will pay for what?
- Who is responsible for what, and in particular getting people to sign up for the event?
- What activity each of you will commit to do to make the event a success

Case study: Paul's Growth Story

About once a quarter I will co-run an event with one of my A-listers. A very successful event was when we ran a joint mastermind evening. A local financial advisor and I hosted the event and each of us committed to get five Clients along to the event.

Based on my co-hosts ideal Client Persona, I called up ten of my local Clients. Five of them agreed to come along to the event.

The event was a great success, and I picked up three decent Leads as a result of the evening.

Case study: Elinor

Elinor's firm uses webinars to engage with Clients and Prospects. They run one webinar every two months and always start marketing the webinar six weeks before the event. They run the webinar with expert speakers, both from inside and outside of the firm. The firm markets the event by the following methods:

- All members of the firm have a link to the next webinar on their email footer. Her three client managers all have a personal target to get at least five people signed up to the webinar.
- They produce a short 'taster' and 'teaser' video with the expert speaker to generate demand for the webinar

- Each event has three email shots sent out to their list.
- Three weeks before the webinar they personally ring all their Clients and Prospects who have not committed to attend to see whether they are interested in attending.
- 2–3 days before the webinar, they ring each attendee to check they are still coming and find out what they want to get out of the event. They use this information to tailor the event.
- After the event they ring every attendee to find out how they found the webinar, and what worked for them. They use these phone calls to actively get testimonials to use on their marketing materials for future events.
- As a result of this process, they find that they normally get 20+ people on each webinar, and, typically within 12 months generate at least £20k of annual recurring new business from the attendees on each webinar.

Running your event

As your firm's reputation and credibility is on the line with an event, you want it to run without a hitch. As a result, your firm need to focus on both making sure the attendees turn up and that the actual event runs smoothly.

Here is a checklist you may want to use for your firm's event:

Technology:

- Does it work on the day?
- Do all the presenters and participants know how to use it?

- Are all the slides, videos and visual materials pre-loaded in advance and working with the audio-visual set up you are using?
- Do you have a good back-up if the technology doesn't work?

Attendees:

- Has someone in your firm reminded attendees a week before, and on the day before about the event?
- Do all your attendees know where to go and what to do to attend the event?
- Has your firm got an incentive for people listening in or attending a physical event to stay to the end?
- Is the entrance to the venue clearly signposted with the name of the event on the signpost?
- What do you want the attendees to do after the event?

Presenters:

- Do all the presenters know what they are doing and when they are doing it?
- Have the presenters been given the opportunity of a dry run?
- Do the presenters know what will happen if they start to run over time?

Event organisers:

- Have all the people responsible for the smooth running of the event been briefed about their roles and responsibilities?
- Do you have people greeting attendees and briefed to keep them entertained before the event starts properly?
- Have all the name badges, handouts and goody bags been produced and are they where they are meant to be?

Summary

Using events can be a great way of helping potential clients take the step into commitment and sign up as a Client or existing Clients sign up for more services from your firm. However events, regardless of whether they are a face-to-face event or a virtual event such as a webinar or teleseminar, take a large amount of time and resource to do well.

Action points

- Go back and look at your firm's Tactical Marketing Plan, and decide whether you want to add events to your firm's plan.
- Volunteer to be a speaker on someone else's webinar or event.
- Research what events your competitors are hosting or participating in. Identify from your research and your niche market's Pain Points an event your firm could host or co-host.
- Sign up for a free trial of Zoom or GoToWebinar to test out what you can actually do with a webinar.

What now?

It's now time for you to get on with your intention to become a one million pound practice. Reading this book on its own without doing *something* won't help you get there. If you haven't already, go to The Accountants Millionaires' Club – http://www.accountantsmillionaire.club to download your Workbook and the free resources mentioned in the book.

I'd love to know how you are getting on in your journey to grow a one million pound practice. Email me at heather@heathertownsend.co.uk or connect with me on LinkedIn – http://www.linkedin.com/in/heathertownsend or send me a tweet @heathertowns.

And of course, if you are ready to take the commitment to build a one million pound practice come and join like-minded accountancy firm owners in the Accountants Millionaires' Club.

About The Accountants Millionaires' Club

The Accountants Millionaires' Club is not just a book, it's a community, set of tools, regular events and resources for accountancy firm owners. (see http://www.accountantsmillionaire.club)

If you're breaking 6 figures and looking to profitably scale to the magic million pound mark, then The Accountants Millionaires' Club is designed specifically for you.

Members of the club enjoy the following benefits:

- 3 virtual masterclasses a month to help you and your staff grow your practice.
- Fortnightly group accountability calls and weekly accountability emails to keep you accountable to your 3-year Growth Plans.
- Tons of plug and play resources, such as job descriptions for the future accountancy firm structure as featured in this book.
- Access to the club's forums to network virtually with your fellow club members.
- Discounts off complimentary products and services, such as 25% off The Gap 2014 Ltd systems to sell and deliver advisory services to your clients.
- Monthly 1:2:1 coaching calls (GROW and ACCELERATE memberships only)
- Quarterly mastermind days (ACCELERATE memberships only)

If you are ready to make your dream of growing a one million pound practice a reality, get in touch today.

The sooner you get started, the sooner you will get there.

Call Heather on +44 (0) 1234 48 0123 or email heather@heathertownsend.co.uk.

About Heather Townsend

Heather is always up for a challenge. Perhaps this is why she specialises in helping accountants grow a one million pound practice and make it through to partner.

In fact, over the last 12 months Heather has supported her clients to build their profile, differentiate themselves, grow their reputation, and in the process add over £2 million in fees to their client portfolio.

When Heather is not writing, speaking or coaching she can found tearing around the Bedfordshire countryside on her mountain bike, playing or coaching netball and trying to eat as many dairy and gluten free cakes as possible.

Accolades and endorsements include:

1. In 2015 Economia, magazine of the Institute of Chartered Accountants of England and Wales, decided Heather was the top online influencer for accountants.
2. Judging the Practice Excellence Awards three times, and the British Accountancy Awards three times.
3. Publishing 3 books with Financial Times Publishing and Kogan Page, which have collectively been translated into over 7 different languages, sold over 20,000 copies and received over 150 five star reviews on Amazon.

Who Heather works with:

Her work splits into 3 distinctive areas:

1. Helping accountants grow a profitable one million pound practice.
2. Helping high potential accountants, lawyers and consultants build a cast-iron business and personal case to help them make partner in their firm. And when they get there, stay there.
3. Working with owners of small professional practices, often under 4 equity partners, or intact sector teams radically increase their new client leads and wins without resorting to cold calling.

Heather features regularly in the national & trade press, e.g. FT, Guardian, Sunday Times, Managing Partner, Legal Week, Accountancy Age.

To work with Heather

To contact Heather about working together:

Heather can be contacted via email, heather@heathertownsend.co.uk or +44 (0) 1234 48 0123

Other books written by the author

The FT Guide To Business Networking

The book is now in its 2nd edition and has been translated into 5 different languages, been awarded over 110 five star reviews on amazon and sold over 13000 copies globally.

Up to 80 per cent of opportunities come from people who already know you, so the more people you know, the more chance you have of winning the new business or career you want.

The Financial Times Guide to Business Networking is your definitive introduction to a joined-up networking strategy that really works. This award-winning book has now been fully updated to include new chapters on generating referrals and boosting your confidence when networking, as well as the latest advice on social networking sites.

Discover:

- Successfully combine online and offline networking techniques
- Develop the best networking approaches and behaviours
- Make a great first impression, build rapport and generate strong business relationships
- Talk to the right people, have productive conversations and effectively work a room

"A great, practical guide to all aspects of networking – stuffed with lots of quick and easy tips to help you leverage the power of your network."

IVAN MISNER, NY TIMES BESTSELLING AUTHOR AND FOUNDER OF BNI AND REFERRAL INSTITUTE

"This practical and easy-to-read book will quickly get you the results you need from your network."

CHARLIE LAWSON, BNI UK AND IRELAND NATIONAL DIRECTOR

"A "must read" for anyone wanting to use the power of face-to-face AND online networking to generate career and business success."

ANDY LOPATA, AUTHOR OF RECOMMENDED AND AND DEATH CAME THIRD

How to make partner and still have a life

(co-authored with Jo Larbie)

The book is now in its second edition and has now sold over 5000 copies globally.

The burning question on every ambitious fee-earner's lips is: 'how do I make partner at this firm?'

This book is your route map to making it to the top in a professional services firm. It shows you how to stand out, be in the right place at the right time and build your kitbag of skills to overcome the many hurdles and reach the Holy Grail of becoming partner.

This book reveals what it really takes to make it, and what it will involve once you're there. It helps you make an informed decision on whether or not this is the right step for you, and guides you on how to become a partner and still have a life of your own. Heather Townsend and Jo Larbie show you the rules of the game, laying bare exactly what you need to do to take the ultimate step.

"I wish I'd had access to a book like this before I became a partner."

CHARLES H GREEN, AUTHOR OF THE TRUSTED ADVISOR

"If you have aspirations to make Partner and you only purchase one book this year - make this that one. It could quite literally change your life."

DREW MOSS, FORMER HEAD OF LEARNING AND DEVELOPMENT, BDO AUSTRALIA

“Another must-have read from Heather Townsend. A book that looks at the reality of what it is to be a Partner and provides essential practical advice for anyone considering promotion.”

CLAIRE MARTIN, FORMER DIRECTOR TYNDALLWOODS

“The book is an excellent study of the professional services world and the increasingly high demands on partners. Its reach is beyond the practical career roadmap and how-to-do-it guidance which is very helpful. The authors firmly believe that success in business can be achieved without sacrificing the quality of your personal life. It is all about making the right choices and getting all the support along this long journey.

FILIP LYAPOV, SENIOR AUDIT MANAGER GRANT THORNTON

The Go-To Expert

The Go-To Expert has 40+ five star reviews on amazon now sold over 4000 copies globally.

The Go-To Expert provides no-nonsense advice on managing your transition into a well-known and trusted name within your industry. It will help you navigate reputation-building tools with confidence and build a personal brand that wins you business.

Discover:

- Simple steps to raise your profile
- How to market and sell yourself with ease and confidence
- Techniques to make your clients come to you

"If you want to move your career on, shifting from being just another professional advisor to being truly recognised as a go-to expert, this book will show you the way."

RICHARD NEWTON, AWARD-WINNING AUTHOR OF THE MANAGEMENT BOOK

"Differentiating yourself from your peers is the challenge that every professional faces. This book gives you the clarity, process and confidence to make yourself stand out in a crowded market place."

TONI HUNTER, PARTNER, GEORGE HAY CHARTERED ACCOUNTANTS

"The Go-To-Expert is an inspirational guide for accountants, lawyers and consultants who wish to develop their niche specialism. Packed with great ideas and insights, it enables you, the reader, to undertake the journey through a series of exercises, each building on the next, to create your proposition and tactical marketing plan for your target clients. I cannot recommend it highly enough - it will help and inspire you to become the Go-To-Expert."

PHIL MULLIS, PARTNER WILKINS KENNEDY

"Having read the book from cover to cover and now about to reread it my key takeaway was the reinforcement of defining and promoting a niche. Becoming a Go To Expert in a specialist field. I knew I should do it but just not got round to it. It is now a priority of mine, something I shall focus on over the next few months. The book is an education in itself with many practical examples based on real life professionals. It is a must for any one in a professional career that wants to get ahead."

PAUL MILLER, FOUNDER CORNISH ACCOUNTING

"I found this book a really excellent step by step guide for professionals seeking to develop expert status. While it contains very good advice for strategic planning, it also provides very specific useful tactical tips on exactly how to go about things like networking and blogging in a very targeted way.
This book provides a blueprint for practice and personal development for professionals."

FLOR MCCARTHY, AUTHOR OF THE SOLICITOR'S GUIDE TO MARKETING AND GROWING A BUSINESS

Poised for partnership

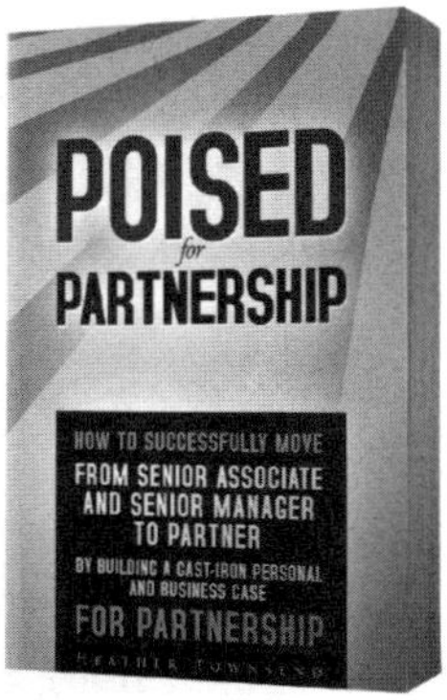

Making the transition from senior employee to partner in a professional services firm is the hardest career move you will ever make.

This book explains how others did it and how you can too.

If you buy this book you'll learn:

- Tried and tested strategies to successfully make it through partner track and the partnership admissions process to partner
- How to create a cast-iron Business Case and Personal Case for partnership, even if you don't have any previous experience of selling services
- How to pace yourself so you don't get burnt out on the gruelling final steps to partnership
- How to find enough time to start to consistently win your own work, even if your billable time targets are sky high

"Having made the somewhat daunting move from in house back to private practice with the primary aim of achieving partner, I am so grateful that I have found Heather Townsend and her books. This easy-to-read book has given me a clear structure upon which I can step up to the challenge, and with greater confidence than I might otherwise have had."

JONATHAN MORE, SENIOR ASSOCIATE

"If making partner feels like a long, winding and challenging journey, this book will be your SatNav, navigating you successfully to your destination. This book is brilliant and I would highly recommend it"

DEV MODI, MANAGING DIRECTOR AT OMEGA ACADEMY

"I've coached a large number of partner potentials (hundreds!) and this action-orientated and practical book brilliantly captures all the things that are crucial to making it to partner. I can't recommend it more highly!"

JOHN MOSS, JA CONSULTING